Becoming African Americans

Becoming African Americans

BLACK PUBLIC LIFE
IN HARLEM, 1919–1939

Clare Corbould

HARVARD UNIVERSITY PRESS

Cambridge, Massachusetts, and London, England · 2009

"The Negro Speaks of Rivers" and "Air Raid Over Harlem" from *The Collected Poems of Langston Hughes* by Langston Hughes, edited by Arnold Rampersad with David Roessel, Associate Editor, copyright © 1994 by The Estate of Langston Hughes. Used by permission of Alfred A. Knopf, a division of Random House, Inc.

Library of Congress Cataloging-in-Publication Data

Corbould, Clare.
    Becoming African Americans: Black public life in Harlem, 1919–1939 / Clare Corbould.
        p. cm.
    Includes bibliographical references and index.
    ISBN 978-0-674-03262-0 (alk. paper)
        1. African Americans—History—1877–1964.   2. African Americans—Race identity.
    3. African Americans—Social conditions—20th century.   4. African diaspora.   I. Title.
    E185.61.C779 2009
    973'.0496073—dc22   2008029259

For Mary Beker, Margarita Beker, and Hal Corbould

Contents

Illustrations

Acknowledgments

It is a great pleasure to acknowledge here the people and institutions who have helped me as I have written this book. Ten years is certainly a goodly length of time in which to accumulate debts, and I have many.

Research for *Becoming African Americans* was made possible by the financial support from the Department of History, School of Philosophical and Historical Inquiry, the Faculty of Arts, and the Research Institute for the Humanities and Social Sciences at the University of Sydney. A senior scholar fellowship from the Gilder Lehrman society supported a much-needed trip to New York in 2005. For these grants I am extremely grateful. In 2003, I met Philip Hosay and Elizabeth Anderson at the Multinational Institute of American Studies at New York University. I am grateful for their continued support, including hosting me as a visiting scholar in 2007.

The reproduction of the wonderful images in the following pages appear thanks to a generous grant from the Australian Academy of the Humanities. Michael Thompson, one of the many terrific students it has been my good fortune to teach at Sydney, undertook with great humor the task of tracking down the copyright holders for those images. My thanks to Michael and to many individuals in archives, libraries, and museums who granted permission for their use.

Research for this book included many months in the incomparable Schomburg Center for Research in Black Culture, where staff in all divisions went above and beyond the call of duty, from my first six-month stint in 1999–2000. Andre Elizée, Steven Fullwood, and Tammi Lawson were especially kind. I would also like to thank the staffs at the Rare Book and Manuscript Library of Columbia University, the Moorland-Spingarn Collection at Howard University, the Amistad Research Center at Tulane

University, and the Harry Ransom Center at the University of Texas, Austin. I won't reprint here an ode a former student of mine wrote, singing the praises of the Inter-library Loan office of the University of Sydney Library. Suffice to say I agree wholeheartedly with its sentiments.

My greatest intellectual debt is to Shane White, whose scholarship on the history of slavery inspired me to pursue my own study of African American history. Shane's unflagging support of this project and his equally unwavering mentorship, to say nothing of coffee and gossip, have been invaluable. A copy of this book, which he has read in so many incarnations, can hardly begin to repay my debt. Shane has, moreover, presided over the creation of a lively environment for the study of US history. Among the core of an expanding Sydney American History Reading Group is Stephen Robertson, who has had boundless enthusiasm for this project and made many incisive suggestions for improving its content, for which I cannot thank him enough. Frances Clarke is a careful and thoughtful reader on whom I depend. She and Michael McDonnell do their best to remind me that United States history does not begin in 1919. I have relied on Michael's counsel regarding every aspect of this book, from the conceptual to the structural, and regarding the big and small processes of publishing. I hardly know where to begin to thank him. Along with more recently arrived colleagues Warwick Anderson and Cassandra Pybus, American history is thriving at Sydney University.

I would also like to thank many other colleagues who make Sydney University such a dynamic and stimulating institution. Along the corridors and over occasionally jammed photocopiers I have enjoyed the good conversation of Robert Aldrich, Emma Christopher, James Curran, Nicholas Eckstein, Charlotte Epstein, Andrew Fitzmaurice, Kate Fullagar, Sarah Gleeson-White, Chris Hilliard, Judith Keene, Iain McCalman, Cindy McCreery, Kirsten McKenzie, Dirk Moses, Lyn Olson, Julie Smith, Martin Thomas, Jonathan Walker, Richard Waterhouse, Graham White, and Richard White. I'd especially like to acknowledge the support and encouragement I have been lucky to receive from Alison Bashford, Julia Horne, Penny Russell, and Glenda Sluga.

A little further afield, Ian Tyrrell at the University of New South Wales has offered guidance, encouragement, and collegiality. Australia is a fair hoof from the United States, but the distance doesn't seem so great thanks to many others around the country engaged in the study of American history. Thanks in particular to Ethan Blue, David Goodman, Marilyn Lake, Amanda Laugesen, Heather Neilson, Michael Ondaatje, and Patrick Wolfe. I have also benefited from presenting several times at the lively and welcoming biennial conferences of the Australia New Zealand American Studies Association, meetings to which I always look forward.

Much further from home, I have been fortunate to present at conferences at King's College, London, the University of California, Irvine, Harvard University, the University of North Carolina, Chapel Hill, and the conference of the Organization of American Historians. Thank you to the organizers and participants of those excellent meetings, and to Alice Fahs, Mitch Kachun, and Patrick Manning for their generous comments that have had purchase far beyond those twenty-minute papers.

On various research trips, I have been welcomed to the United States. In particular my thanks to Jacob Horowitz in New York and Stuart and Glenda Pawsey in Berkeley, who were immensely generous in letting me stay for weeks at a time. When things got a little tight at the end of an early trip (the exchange rate was less favorable then), I put dinners on my credit card and collected Jacob's cash to feed my photocopying habit the following day. It's not a research strategy I recommend but boy was it fun. Much more recently, Steven Hahn and Stephanie McCurry put me up for a fun weekend in Philadelphia. Steve's work has had a huge impact on this book, and I am grateful to him and Stephanie for their encouragement and support. I have also benefited enormously from the expertise and friendship of several other Americans who have read part or all of this book. The late VèVè Clark spent many hours discussing this project when I spent time in Berkeley in 2001. Only when I began working full-time did I grasp fully how kind she was. Fitzhugh Brundage offered invaluable insights into the subject of this book, especially the chapters on making history, and has been very generous in his support for my work. I'm very grateful to him and to Robin Kelley, who shared his vast knowledge and prompted ideas and connections I might never have made. Marcy Sacks is a treasured interlocutor on all things Harlem (and before). Recently, Penny Von Eschen made crucial suggestions regarding the book's substance, and James Campbell helped me to see the longue(ish) durée. I am very grateful to them both.

At Harvard University Press, Joyce Seltzer gave tireless support to this book. I have learned a huge amount from her, for which I am grateful. My thanks, too, to Aria Sloss, a model of patience in the face of my endless questions and requests.

I tend to inflict work on any of my friends who stand still for a moment too long. Ivan Coates, Zoe Couacaud, Cristyn Davies, Nicholas Gebhardt, Catherine Kevin, Sara Knox, Nina Koutts, David Leys, Natalya Lusty, Maggie MacKellar, Stuart Madgwick, Robert Payne, Samuel Solomon, and Genya Sugowdz possibly regret not moving more quickly. A few friends are hopelessly slow; Michael Handler, Megan Dymphna Jones, Sarah Mury, and Zora Simic have each read large portions of this book over the years. I would say that I'm dumbstruck at this point, but as they all know that's never, ever happened before, they'd be skeptical. So, thank you one and all for comments, ideas, and encouragement. Matthew Fishburn and Cam MacKellar in particular heard more than most would bear about the eternal beat of the tom-tom and have been unstintingly generous in discussions of topics related to this book. My thanks.

Other friends have played an important role in the completion of this book, never giving up on me when it seemed I may indeed be glued to the seat in front of my computer. They include Matthew Barnard, Anna Clark, Christina Colegate, Allie Finnegan, Linly Goh, Arlie Loughnan, Olwen Pryke, and Frances Thomas. I owe more to Glenda Guice, the late John Guice, Jen Guice, Dave Lowery, and Jilly Guice than I can possibly express.

This book is dedicated to my parents, Margarita Beker and Hal Corbould, who nurtured in me a love of learning. Their emotional, practical, and financial support has sustained me through the research, writing, and much else besides. My brother, Joe Corbould, has never faltered in his interest in my pursuits, even after it became patently clear that I was wrong each time I estimated when the book would be done. Steve Bywaters, Elizabeth Corbould, the Davidson and Jellie clans, and the Beker movable feast have all been unfailingly supportive. Mary Beker, my grandmother, has inspired me, made me laugh, and always reminded me on the phone how much she's looking forward to reading the finished product. This book is for her, too.

It's a good thing that gratitude has no limits, else I might be running short just when I need it most. So, finally, my thanks to Dugald Jellie, for love and support, for adventures to places far from computers, and for turning my life upside down, in the best way imaginable.

Becoming African Americans

Introduction

The 2000 U.S. census, for the first time, allowed respondents to tick a box marked "African American" in the race category. The new option marked official and bureaucratic recognition of a term that had been gaining currency for some years, particularly since the late 1980s. It also set off a new controversy over just who was eligible to describe themselves as "African American." Many recent immigrants to the United States and their children, including Senator Barack Obama and former Secretary of State Colin Powell, favor the term. Other migrants prefer to include a more specific region in the name they choose to call themselves, such as Nigerian American or Jamaican American. U.S.-born black people are divided. Some embrace the application of the label "African American" to all people of African descent. Others, especially those concerned about access to dwindling affirmative action programs and those who wish to preserve a link to a heritage of struggle within the United States, would prefer to limit the term to those for whom it was originally coined: black people in the United States.[1]

Debate as to nomenclature, and about the identity signaled by one name or another, is not new. African, Colored, Negro, Black, Afro-American, African-American, and African American have all been names of choice at one time or other, usually with some overlap and with fierce debate about capitalization and the use of hyphens. Indeed, on the 2000 census, the check box was marked "Black or African American." The provision of this option reflected the fact that many individuals call themselves by both of these names, while others prefer one over the other.

People often associate the origins of the term African American with Jesse Jackson, the Rainbow Coalition, and the 1980s, but the term's antecedents go back much further. At the end of the eighteenth century and into the first half of the nineteenth century, free people of color sometimes referred to themselves, with pride, as African. They often included the term in the names of their organizations, notably the African Methodist Episcopal and African Methodist Episcopal Zion churches, founded in 1816 and 1821, respectively. Such names reflected a closeness in black society to Africa. Throughout the eighteenth century and into the nineteenth, Americans were exposed periodically to African life and customs, as slaves arrived directly from Africa at various ports along the eastern seaboard. Using "African" to describe themselves also reflected a loss of specific ties to particular places; the slaves who arrived in the New World had a much more regional than continental sense of themselves. To describe oneself as African, then, was to link black culture in the United States to cultures in Africa, and throughout and around the Atlantic Ocean, based on shared experiences of transportation and enslavement.[2]

Names reflecting the African origins of black people in the United States fell out of favor, however, in the second quarter of the nineteenth century. By that point, the slave trade had declined, ending most black Americans' interaction with recently arrived African-born people. Adding to the break in continuity with African origins was the forced migration of some one million enslaved people westward within the United States, which took place in the fifty or so years preceding the 1865 end of slavery. Fragile ties to Africa could not withstand this hardship. Most of all, however, as the lives of free people of color became increasingly precarious, with the slow end of slavery in the North and its cessation within sight in the South, a tie to Africa became a liability. Instead of an origin to be celebrated, it became a destination to be feared, as some white Americans began to plan to "repatriate" freed slaves. Founded in the same year as the African Methodist Episcopal Church, the American Colonization Society aimed to save the United States from the supposed menace of a racially mixed society by sending free black people to a new American colony, Liberia. Some sixteen thousand migrated there, and others tried to make the journey, but the majority remained. To distance themselves from those who would have them exiled, many black Americans stopped using the word "African." At the same time, decreasing direct ties to Africa meant that those enslaved stopped thinking of themselves as African.[3] Many black Americans became simultaneously estranged from and oftentimes ashamed of their African roots.

Scientific ideas that sought to explain differences between groups of people made Africa seem less than attractive. As nations secured their borders in the nineteenth century and demanded of their subjects a sense of belonging to a particular place and people, and as European colonies expanded, the idea that each person was part of a biological race also grew. Notions of race were tied to new theories about the evolution of humankind, a bastardizing of Charles Darwin's analysis in *On the Origin of Species* (1859) and subsequent works. The idea that Africans were inferior beings who had not yet reached the highest, or even the middle, rungs on the ladder of civilization had enormous utility for Anglo-Americans, fearful of the consequences of slavery's abolition. Asserting the inferiority, even inhumanity, of black people meant that former slaves could be mistreated or be regarded as childlike, requiring care. Either way, this model of human development suited landowners and employers seeking ways to maintain a cheap source of labor. Less wealthy white people benefited, too; they collected the "wages of whiteness," the psychological payoff that came from being part of the so-called master race.[4] It was difficult for black Americans to forge connections with Africa, when its people were so thoroughly maligned.

In the popular imagination, Africa became a land of impenetrable jungles and untraceable rivers, there for the conquering by white men. So-called discoverers and explorers such as David Livingstone and Henry Morton Stanley made fortunes selling swashbuckling tales of adventures through Africa. Claiming to have tackled the savage animals and equally wild humans of the "Dark Continent," adventurers gallantly overcame obstacles posed by a hostile climate and rampant disease. Beginning in 1912, Edgar Rice Burroughs published a *Tarzan* novel almost every year until World War II. Several were made into silent films in the 1920s. The advent of sound technology only increased the popularity of *Tarzan*, with Johnny Weismuller starring in a dozen successful movies from 1932. In these tales and films, as in countless others, Africa was exciting—a place where white men could prove themselves brave, strong, and heroic—but also irredeemably backward.

One of the most damning aspects of popular ideas about Africa was that it was a place where time stood still. While America moved forward, defining what it meant to be modern, Africa's culture and people were depicted much as the landscape—either swampy and stagnant, muddled with lianas and giant ferns, bananas, and other tropical flora, or bright and sunny, but not very clever.[5] Images of Africa contrasted dramatically with those of industrial, urban America, with its sleek art deco lines and sharp angles. While America moved relentlessly forward, leading the world's progress, benighted Africa remained unchanged. As the United States moved rapidly away from its past, Africa was ahistorical. Its unchanging people, plants, and animal life were captured under glass transparencies, colored from black-and-white photographs, in the American Museum of Natural History in New York. In the Akeley Hall of African Mammals, which opened in 1936, African life was recreated in spectacular dioramas behind glass.[6] It seemed that in Africa there was nothing of which to be proud; if anything, the continent was a place from which many black Americans wanted to distance themselves, to prove they had left it behind.

Mass consumer culture, brought about by massive changes around urbanization and industrialization in American society, reinforced a sense that black people, including black Americans, lagged far behind. From about 1880 for at least fifty years, American society was awash in stereotyped images of black Americans that depicted them as of a piece with benighted Africans. Picaninnies, mammies, and Uncle Toms stared out at consumers from the packaging around foodstuffs and endless magazine advertisements. As mass media began to develop, first film screens and then radio sets portrayed and broadcast black people as foolish, stupid, and occasionally cunning, but never as noble or even competent. Most nonblack Americans understood such images to represent a race of people inferior in every way to white Americans and linked very closely to backward Africans.

From the end of Reconstruction in the 1870s through to 1930 or so, many black American activists aimed to prove that racial inferiority was unfounded and that America's black citizens were the equal of white Americans. One way to achieve this was through a strategy of "uplift," whereby the leaders of the race would prove they were equal to whites. At the nineteenth century's end, uplift ideology dominated the influential National Association of Colored Women, which coordinated the mass of black women's club activities across the country and whose motto was "Lifting as We Climb." Black elites used as evidence of their racial equality achievements in oratory, poetry, literature, education, visual arts, and music. "No race that produced a great literature," James Weldon Johnson, secretary of the National Association for the Advancement of Colored People (NAACP), proclaimed in 1918, "has ever been looked upon by the world as distinctly inferior." According to Johnson, great art, too, could persuade racists of black equality, a belief he maintained until the end of his life.[7] Such a strategy to improve American race relations had little place in it for an identification with Africans or Africa itself. Rather, these activists drew distinctions between various classes of black Americans and attempted to solidify black elites' identification with their class peers in other races.[8] Uplifters' clamor neither celebrated African culture nor held Africans as kin. On the contrary, uplift politics based around the attainment of middle-class respectability implicitly disavowed Africa as primitive and somewhere from which black Americans had evolved.

Elites' claims to equality did not stifle a continuing interest among most black Americans in things African during the nineteenth century, even as most black Americans strove to make the United States a viable home. Early black historians, marginalized from the growing profession of historical scholarship, made Africa a key focus of their studies.[9] Folk culture remained suffused with tales and songs that had roots in Africa.[10] The very style of black life, as observed by white diarists, journalists, travel writers, and visual artists, revealed a desire to take culture from Africa and combine it with that of the New World to create something altogether new.[11]

In popular culture, too, black Americans at the beginning of the twentieth century represented Africa in ways that challenged stereotypes about the continent's retrograde nature. From 1902 to 1905, on regional American stages, on Broadway, and in London, vaudeville stars George Williams and Bert Walker delighted audiences with *In Dahomey*. In a series of scenes and songs, the performers parodied racist stereotypes and explored the recent history of black Americans' engagement with Africa, primarily through a treatment of emigration schemes. *In Dahomey* ran for over one thousand performances.[12] W. E. B. Du Bois, a doctor of philosophy who specialized in history and sociology and edited *Crisis*, the journal of the NAACP, argued long and hard for care to be taken in public representations of black people and black history. His pageant, *The Star of Ethiopia*, had scenes set in ancient Africa through to the present day. It aimed to rectify erroneous accounts of history in which black people contributed nothing to the progress of the world, and to instill pride in black Americans at how far they had come since the dark days of enslavement. *The Star of Ethiopia* had just four productions, starting in New York in 1913 and ending in Los Angeles in 1925; but with between 350 and 1,000 people in its cast, the pageant reached tens of thousands of audience members.[13] These two plays heralded developments in culture that would play a major role in the expansion of black public life after World War I.

A connection between black Americans and Africans remained especially strong in the late nineteenth and early twentieth centuries in one vital area of black life: religion. Preachers and songs referred frequently to Old Testament stories involving exodus from Egypt and, from the book of Psalms, the future redemption of Ethiopia.[14] Sometimes they mobilized such tales in service of a secular vision of the United States, delivered to peace and unity from its current racial fractures.[15] Other times, these accounts were used to make sense of yet more movement, as freed slaves searched for estranged family members or escaped from stultifying conditions. Some preachers reworked biblical accounts to inspire congregations to look forward to a day when blackness, and black masculinity especially, would be "restored," once black Americans returned to Africa. Such ideas, centered on Ethiopia, Egypt, and sometimes Liberia, were linked closely to religious, emigrationist, and missionary movements. They were given voice and word by various thinkers, writers, and churchmen, whose views spanned a wide spectrum, from David Walker to Reverend Henry Highland Garnet in the first half of the nineteenth century, to Martin Delany, preachers Alexander Crummell and Edward Blyden, and Bishop Henry Turner in the century's later decades. Africa was always present in black American religious life, and there were always those who wished to emigrate, either as temporary missionaries or for good.[16]

The enduring question of what bearing Africa ought to have in black American consciousness expanded into various new forms of debate and public expression after 1919. At this time, a confluence of events and novel ideas made possible an explosion of black public culture. Black Americans' distinguished involvement in World War I surely demonstrated their fitness for genuine citizenship, as they pointed out over and again, and yet race relations remained unchanged.

Black public life transformed partly because of a steady movement of black Americans to towns and ever bigger cities. This Great Migration, as it has come to be known, brought to life black metropolises that gave new feelings of militancy a permanent address. Where just under twenty percent of black Americans lived in urban areas in 1890, by 1920 the figure was thirty-four percent, and a decade later it reached nearly forty-four percent.[17] Migrants contributed to new political organizations that gave voice to black Americans' growing discontent. Though these groups were often at odds with one another, all were concerned in some way with Africa, with black Americans' relationship to the continent and its people.

Also contributing to the expansion of black public life were new ideas emerging from social science disciplines, which were beginning to change Americans' ideas about race. When they went out into the field, anthropologists began to think that accepted truths about racial hierarchies and the evolution of human species were not quite right. They argued instead that human difference was best explained by culture and history. Franz Boas, a German-born Jewish social scientist who led the first academic department of anthropology in the United States at Columbia University, did much to champion these new ideas. Black newspapers and journals often featured Boas's work and ideas during the interwar years. A second generation of professional anthropologists, including black Americans whom Boas had helped train, continued the assault on nineteenth-century racial science.[18]

Theories in the discipline of psychology likewise affected predominant notions of race, though these new ideas did less than those in anthropology to disrupt racial hierarchies. Physicians and psychologists had for some time been diagnosing Americans, particularly women, with a condition called neurasthenia. Its symptoms were fatigue and ennui; its cause was civilization itself. The cure, or the preventative medicine, many fashionable white Americans (and Europeans) decided in the 1920s, was exposure to less civilized people. When white New Yorkers headed uptown to Harlem after dark, therefore, they were not going just for the speakeasy booze and the fun to be had in a moderately taboo environment. Rather, there were medical benefits to be had from shaking one's stuff among more primitive folk. These new ideas led to a veneration of supposedly primitive people, which contributed to making Harlem, in particular, a center for black public life.

Helped along by the spread of these ideas and by the support of New York publishers, within a few short years, visual arts, literature, music, and stage shows coalesced into a self-conscious movement, dubbed by those involved as a New Negro Renaissance and a cultural "awakening." This flowering of black culture, as its names suggest, sought to revive the glories of ancient Africa. New culture, fresh intellectual currents, demographic change, and political agitation following hot on the heels of black Americans' service in World War I all combined to ensure that "Africa" moved away from the imaginative preserve of nineteenth-century religious discourse and black folklore and squarely into black public life.

At the very beginning of 1919, on January 6, James Weldon Johnson, composer, author, editorialist, and former diplomat, now representing the premier organization in the struggle for civil rights, the NAACP, took the stage at New York's Carnegie Hall. The occasion was a mass meeting to discuss "Africa in the World Democracy."[19] Tickets were free, the hall packed. Johnson shared the spotlight with four other speakers. Entertainment came from the celebrated Fisk Jubilee Singers and the band of the black 369th Infantry Regiment, recently returned from Paris, where the entire regiment received the Croix de Guerre. That such an event took place, and that news of it could spread around the country via black print media, was testament to the expansion of black public life in the United States. It was also typical of the symbiotic relationship between the growing black public sphere and questions to do with Africa and the black world in general. Membership in the NAACP increased tenfold from the beginning of 1918 to the end of 1919, and the number of branches tripled, with about one hundred in the South.[20] It was just one of a host of organizations and other avenues of public expression that came into their own after the war.

Looking out at the vast pit and glancing up frequently to those in the four tiers above, Johnson confronted criticism of the NAACP's decision to send his colleague, the indefatigable W. E. B. Du Bois, to Paris for the second Pan-African Congress. Convened at the same time as the Paris Peace Conference following World War I, fifty-seven black delegates from around the world came together to discuss matters of importance to all and, in particular, to advocate on behalf of former German colonies in Africa. The first Pan-African conference, in London in 1900, had failed to make a lasting impact. In its second incarnation in 1919, the congress was plagued with problems but was succeeded nonetheless by another three meetings, in Europe and the United States, by 1927. In 1919, however, NAACP members demanded to know why their hard-earned contributions were being spent on issues external to the United States.

Members had no small cause for concern; there was plenty to do at home. The year 1919 was one of exceptional violence in the United States, even for black Americans, whose lives had long been subject to turmoil if a white man lost his temper or a white woman made an accusation—founded, misguided, or scurrilous—against them. In that year, the disgraceful treatment of returning black soldiers reached its zenith, with lynchings of men in uniform frequent in the South. Brewing, too, at the time of the NAACP meeting was tension that would explode in a season of race riots as the weather warmed up. During the so-called Red Summer of 1919, blood flowed in the streets and ditches of cities, towns, and rural areas, south and north, east and west.

Wariness among NAACP members about Du Bois's Paris trip stemmed not simply from a desire to focus on domestic affairs but from a more general antipathy toward Africa. "There has been some slight criticism of the Advancement Association," Johnson announced, "for the steps it has taken to bring Africa to the attention of the Peace Conference and the civilized world. There are those who profess to see in such a move a danger to the cause of the American Negro." Johnson argued that, to the contrary, Du Bois's presence at the congress and the fact that "the question of Africa is an international question" would enable the NAACP to "pursue the very wisest and best means of focusing the attention of the peace delegates and the entire civilized world on the question of the just claims of the Negro everywhere." Claiming Africans as "blood brothers," he rebuked American parochialism on the basis that Africans worldwide were kin. Moreover, as Johnson admonished his audience not to forget, there were people everywhere in pain and suffering, with whom black Americans had much in common.[21]

Not everyone was convinced; it was hard to conceive of the struggle for better conditions in international terms, let alone as a transnational campaign. Despite Johnson's assertions that the fortunes and interests of Africans and black Americans were inextricably linked, as he moved into the second half of his speech, he assured his audience that "the main interest of the Advancement Association, notwithstanding its broad sympathies for all oppressed peoples, is not in Africa and Africans, but in America and colored

Americans."[22] War and peace may have transformed antiracist activism in the United States, but its members forced the NAACP executive to keep the organization's primary focus within national boundaries. Therefore, the theme of the NAACP's annual conference in June 1919 was "To Make America Safe for Americans."[23] President Woodrow Wilson had famously pleaded with Americans to support the World War I effort in order to "make the world safe for democracy." Wilson's claim that the world ought to be remade in America's image seemed both ironic to black Americans, given the state of United States race relations, and hypocritical, given Wilson's own very negative views about black people. Yet, while NAACP executives accepted the limits placed on them at this time by their members, they also sought to redefine in international terms the struggle in which they were engaged. The desire among black Americans for "national self-determination," another concept Wilson had championed worldwide, was something they shared with oppressed people everywhere.

The NAACP was only one organization among many whose members were questioning what Africa meant to them. "Africa"—as it was depicted in newspapers, journals, political speeches, visual arts, fiction, poetry, music, and stage shows from Broadway to small-town pageants—was a constitutive element of the new black public sphere. It was not that black Americans all began to call themselves Africans or to think of themselves as Africans' blood brothers, as Johnson urged, though some certainly did so. Rather, it was that in striving to find new and dynamic ways to represent themselves both individually and collectively, in increasingly open and mobile urban environments, Africa was vital.

Harlem, the black diaspora's capital city, made it all possible. In the words of Howard University philosopher Alain Locke, the northern Manhattan neighborhood was "the Mecca of the New Negro."[24] Following a crash in real estate prices that gave entrepreneur Phillip Payton Jr. the opportunity to usher black residents into Harlem, tens of thousands traded away the known quantities of their lives in the South, the West Indies, and elsewhere to relocate, looking for better lives. By 1930, almost a quarter of Harlem's population was Caribbean-born.[25] Even if they never traveled to Harlem, black Americans nationwide, and worldwide for that matter, turned their attention toward it and derived pleasure from the simple fact that it was there. The cultures and politics that made Harlem distinctive—from

Marcus Garvey's plan to repatriate American blacks to Africa, to the allegedly African medicine men who, turban-clad, hawked their wares on the streets and storefronts, to the literature and arts of the New Negro Renaissance—revolved around Africa.

In this volatile black cauldron of aspiration and expectation, a black public sphere flourished during the two decades following World War I. It comprised political and cultural organizations of all stripes, the best known of which were the NAACP, the Universal Negro Improvement Association (UNIA), and the Urban League. Lesser-known organizations included countless history and literature reading groups, communities that gathered around public and private libraries, with lecture series and reading groups of their own. Churches, though battling waning attendance, continued to play an important role in black life. Black newspapers had existed for some time, but the urban weeklies, including the *New York Age* and *New York Amsterdam News,* expanded and were now joined by pamphlets and journals across the political spectrum. Magazines published articles on all manner of topics, both American and international, as well as fiction, poetry, plays, photographs, and illustrations. Some sponsored annual writing contests, kick-starting the careers of many authors who went on to prominence in black circles and beyond. Journals were not the only outlet for writers and visual artists; newly established publishing houses, mostly in New York, were not only willing but keen to take on black authors and illustrators. The development of this extensive written culture helped to create a modern black identity that looked outward to the world beyond the United States, especially to Africa.

Black public life extended well beyond the printed word, as inhabitants of Harlem and other places of concentrated black populations quite literally made city spaces their own. The style, as well as the content, of black life was intended to mark it off as separate and different from America's mainstream public sphere, ideally a scene of refined debate composed of all citizens, but in reality based on the exclusion of all but a few.[26] Whereas the white public sphere relied on the written word, black public life also embraced music (live, recorded, and increasingly on radio), performance, and a vibrant street culture.[27] Harlem had the most well-developed black public presence, but urban areas such as Beale Street, Memphis, and Chicago's South Side were also physical embodiments of the burgeoning black public sphere. Their inhabitants brought out into the open all of those vernacular strategies developed under more straitened circumstances, which had allowed enslaved or oppressed working people to communicate with one another away from the ears of white people.[28] Citizens of black public places used style to distinguish themselves from white Americans and to link black America to Africa, a continent where oral cultures dominated. Making noise, in particular, whether through music or other sorts of sound, was considered to be an African trait, distinct from the visually oriented mainstream American public.

Though the black public sphere was not defined wholly by race relations in the United States, it was shaped by its members' central concern that conditions in which black Americans lived be improved. Debate as to the best means of achieving change was itself a major component of black public life. Some were eager to reform the United States and to make the nation live up to its stated ideals—that all men were created equal and all were similarly entitled to life, liberty, and the pursuit of happiness. During the interwar years, most came to believe that reform needed to be worldwide, that American racism was but a local strain of a global disease that needed curing. Still others could see no place in America for the descendants of African slaves and turned to the UNIA. One of the most-loved aspects of the association's political platform was a "Back to Africa" movement. Under the stewardship of a charismatic immigrant from Jamaica, Marcus Garvey, the organization gathered enough funds from black Americans to incorporate two shipping lines. Garvey's explosion onto the American scene, at just the time after the war when black Americans were most frustrated with America's lack of change, rapidly focused attention on the question of where black Americans belonged. Was it the United States, or was it Africa? Garvey's challenge to domestic black politics forced Africa into a prominent role in black public life.

No matter where black Americans thought they might best locate themselves, everyone agreed on the imperative to refute widespread assumptions about black racial inferiority. To this end, many black Americans expended an enormous amount of energy to demonstrate in the widest variety of forums possible that black people, past and present, had contributed to, and indeed begun, the world's civilization. This collection of voices was far louder than that of those who tried to suggest that biological race was no more than a scientific rumor, an absurdity, though such opinions were also expressed, aiming to undercut the very idea of racial evolution. Righting misapprehensions about Africa by drawing attention to its glorious history became a regular tactic for activists of all political persuasions. The pursuit of the study of black history became one of the central planks of black public life. Africa's status as the cradle of civilization served as the basis for black claims to a rightful place as citizens in the American polity as well as providing Afrocentrists the best reason possible for swearing allegiance to a mighty black nation.

Rehabilitating Africa's reputation required a massive effort at reeducation. A Western colonialist approach to history, geography, and politics needed overturning. Building a black community was linked to the distribution of knowledge, through elementary and secondary schools, colleges and other tertiary institutions, and through political and civic organizations, churches, libraries, and all sorts of informal networks. Activists in education aimed especially to ensure that black children matured with a healthy sense of themselves, which would come from a pride in their recent and long-gone ancestral past. Black adults, too, participated in various forums to overcome what they described as a deep-seated sense that they—like Africans—were less worthwhile people than their white neighbors.

A growing pride in an African heritage meant embracing Africa as the place of black Americans' origins. This in turn enabled clearer recognition that black Americans shared their history with African-descended people dispersed worldwide. "Negroes" thus began to imagine themselves much more self-consciously as members of a modern black diaspora. The effort to forge links with others was rooted not only in shared history, but also in the recognition of differences and the process of translation between disparate diaspora groups.[29] Diaspora, after all, was not singular or total. Different people moved to various places over time; diasporas overlapped.[30] Diaspora politics, as they developed in the expanding black public sphere in the interwar years, looked not only to the past but also offered alternative models for the present and future.[31] Whereas black nationalists tended to emphasize a model of diaspora that envisioned a reunification of the black family in Africa, others articulated a version of diaspora whose future remained scattered worldwide. In the latter case, racial affiliations became a precursor to more broad-based coalitions premised on antiracist and anticolonial politics.[32]

Debates over the future of black Americans included significant discussion about the roles to be played by men and women. Popular histories of Africa emphasized the achievements of great men. They rested on a model of relations between men and women in which women were relegated to the domestic realm of child raising and housekeeping. In the idealized future envisioned by many who remade the past, women would stay home to concentrate on educating the next generation of proud African Americans. In short, men would create and write history, while women would pass on to their children a pride in their past.

Women's role in public life was limited further by a popular way of understanding Africa: as a motherland. Activists in all political camps spoke and wrote of Africa as though she were a doting mother grieving for the loss of her sons. By using language that idealized women as mothers of the race, they left little room for real women in the imagined future. Black politics in the interwar years, especially the 1920s, have often been seen as divided into two main camps: the integrationist "civil rights" campaigners and the black nationalists, with communists and others on the left hovering somewhere in the background, poised to come to the fore the 1930s. Paying more attention to how gender divisions shaped politics makes it clear that integrationists and nationalists shared as much as divided them. Diaspora narratives, whether advocating for the return of black Americans to Africa or for their continued residence in the New World, were about connections between men who lived in and moved between lands imagined and described as female. Asserting and maintaining a link to Africa and to others in the black diaspora was therefore more difficult for women than for men.

Further limits to black diaspora identity came, too, from the dominant image of Africa in Westerners' minds. Most Americans, when they thought of Africa at all, imagined a place of unrelenting savagery, where heat and disease hampered all forward movement. Whenever black Americans endeavored to connect themselves to their place of origin, these predominant images formed a large obstacle that had to be overcome. It was not all calumny, however, when white Americans spoke or thought of Africa. Many in the interwar years found in its so-called primitivism a value missing in

Western life. For trendy New Yorkers, like their counterparts in fashionable districts of Western European cities, blackness was desirable. It had the power to cure them of what they called, in the thrall of a watered-down Freudian theory of individual psychology, overcivilization. A trip to Africa—or Harlem—could provide a means to access their overly repressed inner selves. Such approbation proved as damaging as negative views of Africa; these were, after all, notions occupying two sides of the same coin. Any black American effort to portray Africa in a way that conflicted with the dominant image of it as primitive, whether a playground or place of forbidding menace, pushed up against these imposing ideas, which were in turn propped up by the support of white cultural patrons and their institutions. The process of becoming African American was always shaped in some way by white Americans' assumption that black Americans and Africans were intrinsically the same, and that all were inferior to white people.

Clashes between black Americans' interrogation of their relationship to Africa and white Americans' expectation that black people everywhere were alike became obvious in public representations of Haiti. The neighboring republic was regarded as something of a stepping-stone between West Africa and the United States. Haiti was also of signal importance to black Americans because of its heritage as the only black nation founded in the revolutionary overthrow of white colonial and enslaving masters. White Americans were aware, too, of the small nation, because an occupation by United States Marines, beginning in 1915 and lasting until 1934, had propelled Haiti into the unlikely situation of being the setting for much popular culture produced in the interwar years.[33] From lurid best-selling books reporting on tourists' experiences on the island, to zombie films in the 1930s, Haiti became a kind of New World proxy for Africa as well as a site for desires and fantasies of all sorts. White Americans found their ideas about racial evolution confirmed by voodoo and other Haitian customs. Black Americans, by contrast, regarded Haitian culture as evidence of the syncretism and adaptability that characterized black life throughout the diaspora, and which formed the basis of black political struggle.

The marriage of a vigorous black public sphere and debate about Africa came to a climax in 1935 as fascist Italy prepared to invade Ethiopia. Ethiopia was long the jewel in the crown of an imagined black world, having retained a special place in black religious thought throughout the nineteenth

century and into the twentieth. With the coronation of Emperor Haile Selassie I in 1930, Ethiopia's status as an independent and apparently func-
tional black nation (as opposed to Liberia, about which allegations of slavery
and misrule had sullied its reputation, and distinct from Haiti, occupied by
U.S. Marines), free from colonial rule, secured its place in black Americans'
hearts. The months during which Italian forces under Mussolini sat with a
powerful air fleet, waiting until the weather was good enough to ensure victory, saw one of the high points of black Americans' identification with Africans. But almost as soon as the initial heat of the 1935–1936 conflict
passed, and the Italians settled into an occupation that would last until
1941, events in Europe impelled black Americans to make explicit their
commitment to people everywhere under the thumb of colonial or violent
rule. Becoming African American was never a simple process; identifying
with those on the ancestral continent was for many only a first step to an
antiracist and anticolonial global consciousness.

Black American activism was shaped decisively by the failure of the United
States and its nonblack citizens to recognize the equal claim on the nation
of their black brethren. Though black Americans already had citizenship by
name, they hoped that the sacrifice of black soldiers on the battlefields of
World War I, as in previous wars, would demonstrate once and for all their
fitness for true equality. Instead, the "Negro" remained a problem, and the
barriers to integration into the body politic remained in place.

In this, black Americans were set apart from recent immigrants who had
arrived in the United States in the hundreds of thousands in the last decades
of the nineteenth century and up to 1924. American nativism, more viru-
lent during and after World War I, led to an insistence that such immigrants
whiten up, become "100 percent American." Immigrants were regarded as
assimilable, in varying degrees and at differing speeds, but ultimately able
to be transformed into Americans without substantially altering the whole.
In the 1930s, groups from Europe began to develop what was newly named
as "ethnicity," or variations on whiteness. By contrast, black Americans remained "raced," always on the outside.[34]

Such ethnic variations would eventually become the "hyphenated" or
dual identities that are commonplace in contemporary America, but not

until after the horrors of World War II lay bare the possible results of racism in an industrial economy. When the children, grandchildren, and great-grandchildren of migrants from Europe began to look to their places of origin and to fashion themselves as, for example, Italian-Americans or German-Americans, they drew on an example set by black Americans in the interwar years. It was never possible for black Americans to feel completely "at home" in the United States in these decades. They therefore made a virtue of a necessity, developed a rich culture in new urban environments, and mapped out a way of being—with at least one eye focused on the world beyond the borders of the United States—that became the model for generations to come.

But, finally, although black Americans' politics and culture were shaped by the mainstream attitudes of their white compatriots, racism was not the beginning and end of black life. Culture, in particular, as writer Ralph Ellison so elegantly observed, cannot be made by simply reacting. Discrimination, prejudice, and violence—America itself—were not the only factors shaping black lives; rather, black Americans, in Ellison's words, "made a life upon the horns of the white man's dilemma."[35] That life consisted in part of a conscious effort to draw on what was widely regarded as a lost culture, in Africa, and to identify with people beyond the borders of the United States. Such connections extended, in varying degrees throughout the 1920s and 1930s, not only to Africa but around the diaspora and to disenfranchised people everywhere. Making such alliances—whether concrete or imagined in the pages of newspapers and books and the performances of stages and streets—was a radical act at a time when the state demanded fealty, as captured in the slogan "100 percent American." In doing so, black Americans in the interwar years pioneered the sort of acceptable hyphenated identity that has become widespread. They became African Americans.

1

Africa the Motherland

Africa, said Marcus Garvey, was "the noble black man's home and Motherland."[1] In 1919, a year of tumultuous change in the United States and worldwide, Garvey began to make his mark. Garvey had migrated from Jamaica in 1916, bringing with him a self-improvement league known as the Universal Negro Improvement Association (UNIA). He preached the message that black Americans were not and would never be accepted in the United States and that they should embrace their true identity as Africans. The second plank in his organization's program followed on from the first: as Africans, they were in the wrong place and ought to go home. A vanguard group of talented and useful people, such as carpenters and teachers, would pave the way for all to go back to Africa. There, they would join with Africans in remaking the continent, ejecting European colonizers, and creating a federated United States of Africa, of which black people worldwide would be citizens. In the meantime, Garvey declared himself the provisional president, designed a flag, chose an anthem, decreed August 1 a public holiday, gathered together a group on whom he bestowed titles and honors, and planned for the future.

Garvey's rise in the United States was possible only because of the particular circumstances that followed World War I. Having served in vast numbers and contributed to the war effort, black Americans expected better conditions and improved race relations after the war. They felt cheated when, instead, lynchings, massacres, and other less spectacular forms of violence, which had declined in the years leading up to the war, spiked in 1919 once again. In the summer, race riots ripped through cities and towns nationwide. Having endured decades of racism in various forms since slavery ended, black Americans' disaffection with the United States was at an all-time high. Their citizenship seemed to be in name only. When Garvey took to podiums or wrote blistering editorials about race relations on the front page of the UNIA newspaper, the *Negro World,* he both echoed and magnified the sentiments of those listening and reading. His proposed solution, to return to Africa, tapped into an idea that had existed in black life since the first slaves arrived, though by 1919 calls for exodus were few and far between. Garvey combined his promotion of emigration with rhetoric of national self-determination, which dominated the Paris Peace Conference of that year. In this new era of nationalism, he told listeners forcefully, if they did not belong in the United States, then they ought to find an alternative home for themselves. That place was Africa.

Whether or not black Americans agreed with Garvey that they ought to go to Africa, he galvanized black politics and culture by insisting that Africa was their natural home and motherland. Black Americans did not have the luxury of feeling "at home" in the United States. They were subject in the South to the daily violence and indignities of Jim Crow segregation and in the North to discrimination, including the psychological impact of incessantly anticipating unpredictable slights. All over the country, the difficulty of finding decent work while living in the so-called land of plenty left them feeling they were strangers in the land. A nation where one felt at home, after all, was commonly thought to nurture its inhabitants, not to ask them repeatedly how it felt to be a problem.[2]

Garvey's programs resonated loudly in an era when most Americans thought of the United States as a Protestant Anglo-European nation. Increasing numbers of Americans believed the nation to be under threat from vast numbers of the wrong types of immigrants from Europe and from the continuing scourge of descendants of slaves. Best-selling screeds with titles such as *The Passing of the Great Race* warned ominously against the mongrelization of the national family.[3] Immense anxiety about national identity resulted in calls for recent arrivals to become "100 percent American." They were to be immersed in the great "melting pot," from which all newcomers emerged the same.[4] When it no longer seemed possible that immigrants could be grafted seamlessly onto the American nation, in 1924 Congress finally passed laws it had been debating for a decade, to restrict the entry of immigrants. This legislation lessened the anxiety somewhat, so that state policies and people's ideas began to transform to enable ever larger number

of European immigrants to be assimilated into an imagined family of
Americans. Blackness, however, remained a problem, a dilemma.[5]

In the late 1910s and 1920s, then, most Americans changed their ideas
about national identity away from a model in which citizenship could be
acquired through naturalization, to an idea that true Americans were already part of a family.[6] According to prevailing views of national belonging,
those who were genuine members of the American family had both inherited their citizenship and could prove their relation to other living Americans. True allegiance was therefore made up of vertical and horizontal com-
ponents, both of which excluded black Americans.[7]

If the nation were a family, then the production of citizens was linked
closely to their reproduction. Most people believed that "legitimate" Americans were all descended from common ancestors, who were also, obviously,
white. In a nation where publicly, at least, the idea of interracial relationships was anathema, with marriage between white and black citizens banned
in thirty states in 1919, there was official denial that black and white people
could really be related. Add to that a pervasive sense that black people were
of a lower order on the evolutionary scale, and then even their claim to humanity, let alone relation to white folk, was questionable. Moreover, because
black people had not been considered citizens in the past, their claim on
citizenship in the present was also tenuous. Until 1915, many black male
Southerners were prevented from voting by the notorious "grandfather
clause," which determined that only those whose grandfathers had the fran-
chise could exercise the privilege. Even after the clause was deemed illegal, a
black person's citizenship, if his or her grandfather had been denied it, was
dubious by extension.

The legal fiction that "one drop" of black blood made a child black served
to erase from white Americans' consciousness the presence of white ancestors or parents to black men and women, and upheld political and economic
divisions between black and white. It was clear, however, given the history
and continuing problem of sexual violence in the United States, that this
was absolutely not the case. As one of the characters in a Langston Hughes
play noted, racial purity was a fiction, for the "ways o' de South" had produced "mixtries, mixtries."[8] Ignoring the history of white sexual violence
against black women, white Americans tended to maintain that black men
had uncontrollable sexual urges toward white women. The purity of white

women therefore required protection by morally upstanding white men. Black American women, according to these codes, were so morally loose that their children could never be sure of their paternity, and thus their legitimacy and their citizenship were always questionable. Similarly, by erasing from historical accounts the devastating effects of enslavement on kinship, whereby familial ties could be disrupted at any moment by violence or by the sale of slaves, white Americans dismissed as pathological the inability of black Americans to trace back their family histories in reasonably straight lines. Unable to prove descent, black Americans' citizenship became uncertain.[9]

Marcus Garvey's broad and deep impact on postwar black life stemmed in part from a powerful evocation of an alternative black family and black nation, on which his movement rested. In Garvey's hands, the return to Africa was not merely an escape from adverse, and sometimes terrifying, circumstances in the United States and other places in the black diaspora, but was also a reunification of an unnaturally severed family. Garvey referred again and again to Africa as a motherland from which her children had been tragically torn. For many of Garvey's followers, the fact that Africa was their motherland meant it was only natural that they ought to return home. Garvey's conjuring of Africa as a motherland was in marked contrast to nineteenth-century black political thought, in which Africa figured usually as a fatherland.[10] To call Africa a motherland implied a place of birth, like those homes that more recent immigrants had left behind. It therefore became easier to imagine a return home to Africa, now a warm and welcoming motherland rather than a remote and distant fatherland. A good part of Garvey's appeal lay in his imagery of Africa as an inviting motherland, quite distinct from the cold and uncaring United States.

Historians have argued that Garvey appealed to black Americans in spite of his campaign for repatriation. In this analysis, Garvey's popularity rested on his brilliant oratory that demanded racial pride; on his strong message of economic independence, which tapped into a long tradition of self-help in black communities; and on his ability to hammer home his message in a religious mode that appealed to black Americans.[11] Though all of this is true, the tendency among Americans to regard the United States as a "nation of immigrants," combined with a lingering sense of Africa's backwardness and unattractiveness, has eclipsed from view the very real possibility that people in the past wanted to leave the so-called promised land. History up to the 1920s demonstrates black Americans' willingness to move whenever possible to improve their circumstances. They had, too, a longstanding devotion to biblical tales of exodus, in which the weak triumph over the strong by fleeing to better places. Having said that, whether or not they wanted to go, leaving for the African motherland was just about impossible for almost all black Americans.

The idea that Africa was the black man's motherland, which Garvey did so much to promote, had traction well beyond the UNIA and its members. Even those who opposed Garvey, envisioning their future in the United States, were affected by his powerful rhetoric. The image of children ripped prematurely from their mother's milk was echoed in every aspect of black public life: in politics; in new histories of Africa and enslavement; on stage; in fiction; and in the visual arts. Garvey's ideas offered to activists of all political stripes an imagined lineage in which all people were descended from African mothers. Given that all Americans could trace familial lines back to Africa, there was thus no "white" American nation. Members of the National Association for the Advancement of Colored People (NAACP) and other activists used Garvey's language to criticize the United States as an inadequate mother who had neglected her black children. Their aim was not to create a black nation instead, but to transform America into a nation that recognized all of its citizens as members of the family.

Whether they saw their future in Africa or in the United States, activists shared a common language of sexual difference that tended to remove women from black public life, instead linking women to a feminized African continent. Most black men accepted Garvey's contention that Africa was their motherland. In doing so, they rejected stereotypes that they were either lazy Sambos or aggressive and animal-like, styling themselves instead as chivalrous and courageous protectors, both of Africa and of black American women. The impact of such rhetoric on gender relations in the United States and on imagined roles for men and women in the future, whether in Africa or in the United States, was most obvious during a heated public contest over how to remember Southern slavery. That debate, in 1923, centered on the figure of the mythical black "mammy."

Becoming African American was quite a different process for women than for men. The prevailing symbolism in black public life linked women to land and cast them in roles as nurturers of men and boys. Many women, most obviously those who joined the UNIA, found it liberating to contemplate a future in which they were free from the drudgery and danger of low-paid work in white people's homes or on factory floors. Other women, particularly the female writers associated with the cultural movement known as the New Negro Renaissance, were less taken with an imagined future in which women became helpmates to men, and in which public and private spheres were divided along gender lines. They alone resisted the characterization of Africa as a motherland, recognizing its potential to elide women's voices from the public sphere altogether.

When twenty-eight year-old Marcus Garvey arrived in the United States in 1916, he was excited at the prospect of visiting the Tuskegee Institute in Alabama, an industrial and agricultural school begun by the famed Southern educator, Booker T. Washington. Garvey hoped to establish a similar institution in his Jamaican home. Washington's death put an end to those plans, however, so instead Garvey settled in New York City. After a disastrous first appearance as a public speaker, Garvey quickly developed a reputation for his streetside oratory and embarked on a speaking tour of thirty-eight states. He was politically aware, not only from his experiences in Jamaica, where he had trained and worked as a printer, but also from years of travel and activism in Costa Rica, Panama, and London. Conversations with activists, including his one-time employer, Duse Mohamed Ali, editor of the London *African Times and Orient Review,* inspired Garvey. Returning in 1917 to the black metropolis of Harlem, Garvey set about reviving an organization he had founded three years earlier in Jamaica, the UNIA. By 1919, the joint was jumping, with chapters nationwide, a growing international component, and headquarters in Harlem's "Liberty Hall." A weekly newspaper, the *Negro World,* spread the word, with pages in French and Spanish added later. Meanwhile, Garvey turned entrepreneur, incorporating a brand-new, all-black shipping enterprise designed to close the gaps between black people of the world, the Black Star Line. The following year saw the first UNIA annual convention, with delegates from around the world, including Africa and as far away as Australia.[12] Its climax was a show-stopping parade through Harlem and downtown, which ceased only when marchers reached Madison Square Garden, where Garvey and others addressed an adoring crowd of 25,000 people.[13]

Estimates of the numbers of black Americans, and indeed black people worldwide, who joined the UNIA vary wildly, but the impact of Garvey's ideas and rhetoric on black public life in the United States is unmistakable.[14] Proclaiming "Africa for the Africans," Garvey looked to unite the black world through black-run and supported enterprises, such as the Black Star Line, and a migration scheme that would eventually pave the way for the formation of a single nation on the African continent, under his leadership. In 1920–1921 and again in 1924, Garvey made concerted overtures to convince officials in Liberia to accept the first of a convoy of black migrants from the United States.[15] A small republic in West Africa, Liberia was ruled by a handful of Americo-Liberian elite, descended from free black settlers who began moving there in 1820. None of these efforts of Garvey's resulted in the mass migration for which he hoped, but these failures were not for a lack of enthusiasm among his supporters.

Garvey attacked stridently the idea that the United States could be reformed into a suitable home for black Americans. As far as he was concerned, no self-respecting black person should even want to stay. The real home of black Americans was with their brothers in the land of their fathers: Africa the motherland. This firmly held belief provided the impetus for his campaign to convince black Americans to go back to Africa. Garvey and his followers drew great strength from Psalm 68, verse 31: "Princes shall come out of Egypt; Ethiopia shall stretch forth her hands unto God." In their speeches and writings, Garvey and those he influenced repeated the verse as a prophesy that lent weight to their hope that Africa might be, in their words, redeemed. Restoring Africa to its rightful place in the world required, they argued, the bringing together of disparate, displaced Africans. They understood black nationalism to be the reunification of a severed family. In Garvey's words, "Africa still has her hands outstretched beckoning to her children scattered the world over to come to succor her, and to be the fellow citizens of the scattered sons and daughters of Africa. The disunited units everywhere must . . . come together."[16] With American citizenship cast as something shared by those related to one another by blood, and with a prevailing mythology that those of black and white blood were not, and could not be, related to one another, black people did not belong in the

United States. Garvey did not challenge these views; rather, he insisted that all black people together belonged in Africa, a welcoming motherland.

In Garvey's view, the unnaturalness of the United States as a home for black people was evident in the poor material circumstances of black people's lives and in violence, prejudice, and discrimination. But, for him, it was nowhere more obvious than in the disarray of black families. It is well known that Garvey derided mulattoes. His frequent epithets for mixed-race people were derived partly from his theory of racial purity, but also from his fury at the abuse of black women at the hands of white men.[17] Why, he wondered, would anyone want to stay in a country where black men were tortured and murdered for alleged transgressions of a hypocritical moral order that preached the sanctity and separation of races, while at the same time the rape of black American women by white men went ignored? In his epic poem, "The Tragedy of White Injustice" (1927), Garvey railed against the rape of black women and the "shameful" result, mixed-race children, in both colonies and nations such as the United States:

> Black women are raped by the lordly white,
> In colonies, the shame ne'er reaching light:
> In other countries abuses are given,
> Shocking to morality and God's Heaven.
> Hybrids and mongrels are the open result,
> Which the whites give us as shameful insult:
> How can they justify this? None can tell;
> Yet, crimes of the blacks are rung with a bell.[18]

Highlighting the hypocrisy of white Americans who argued for racial purity and fondly castigated black misdeeds while ignoring their own, Garvey called for an end to miscegenation and for the foundation of genuinely racially pure families and racially pure nations.

Garvey hoped to return these "hybrids and mongrels" to a state of blackness, both by instating the nuclear family and also by ending the dispersal of black people. Racial unification could take place only in Africa, where it would also prompt the rise of the continent from its present depths to its former glory, when Egypt and Ethiopia led the development of world civilization. In another poem, Garvey predicted: "Once more we shall, *in*

Africa, fight and conquer for you, / Restoring the pearly crown that proud Queen Sheba did wear."[19] The diasporic family—the scattered sons and daughters—were to return to the mother at the site of the motherland; the family was to reconvene within a single boundary, that is, on the continent of Africa. Garvey's model of the African nation was based on an idealized family whose boundaries were secure, defended by an unchallenged male head of household: "The privilege of men to protect home / Was established before the days of Rome."[20] In these restored and historically natural families, there would be no leakage in the form of illegitimate, mixed-race children. Secure families, Garvey believed, would enable ancient African civilization to rise again, and the black nation to prosper. The UNIA's repatriation campaign was a return to a home arranged around a "stable" family in which paternal privilege was inherited through the male line. Garvey's message was that women should focus on their role as keepers of men and reproducers of men's children, who would in turn emulate their parents' existence in separate spheres.[21]

The organization of the UNIA paralleled and reinforced its ideology of separate spheres. It was modeled on fraternal lodges, which had long been a mainstay of black communities both North and South. UNIA members adopted formal modes of masculinity drawn from Victorian-era culture to demonstrate their distance from stereotypes about the way black men behaved.[22] Men assumed most of the leadership roles in the UNIA, and those women with prominent roles in the organization derived much of their power from their relationships with Garvey himself.[23] While male UNIA members comprised the militaristic African Legion, women belonged to auxiliary units, the Black Cross Nurses and the Universal African Motor Corps.[24] Men and women marched separately in the annual parades.[25]

Manhood was expressed prominently in the Black Star Line, the shipping venture begun to transport scattered Africans all over the diaspora, including back to Africa. The Line's stock certificates illustrated the hope that African repatriation could restore putatively natural gender roles. A strong man and a steamship each flank a globe of the world. The man gestures with pride at a map of the world that has Africa at its center, bearing the inscription, "Africa: The Land of Opportunity." This slogan reflected Garvey's belief that the black man could just as easily benefit from Africa's riches as the white, but the image conveyed another message. Its scale

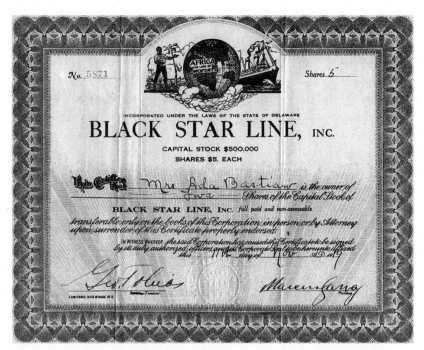

Stockholders in the UNIA's Black Star Line shared Marcus Garvey's dream of linking black people around the globe. Africa would be the center of the black world, just as it dominated the globe in this image. (The Marcus Garvey and UNIA Papers, UCLA.)

rendered visually Garvey's aim to "restore" manhood to the scattered children of the diaspora. Moreover, there was no slave ship to be sighted on this journey. Instead, the Black Star Line would allow the journey across the Atlantic to be made, and imagined, in a new way. The ocean itself was barely visible in the image, suggesting that the Black Star Line could erase the memory of the Middle Passage and replace it with an overwhelming sense of Africa at the center of the world and the black man's rightful home. These men would return not as they had come, in chains, huddled in the hold, but upright, towering over the world and overcoming past oppressions. Africa and its descendants, now scattered, would be reunited. An elderly woman recalled that these certificates had pride of place in her childhood home. They sat on her father's dresser, and as she reached for them he told her "'Touch them and feel the power that the black man will someday know.'"[26]

Garvey's plan to restore black manhood to its "African" state found expression in UNIA theology. In it, the black Father, black Virgin Mary, and black Son together comprised a simple family unit that paralleled the nuclear black family with which Garvey hoped to populate a renewed Africa. In an important speech at Carnegie Hall, Garvey reminded his listeners that "God tells us to worship a God in our own image. We are black, and to be in our image God must be black." He continued on: "Our people have been lynched and burned in the South because we have been worship[p]ing a false God. But what can you expect when we have adopted the idolism of another race? We must create a God of our own and give this new religion to the Negroes of the world." His words explained his claim that "we are not preaching race hatred, but the fatherhood of God and the brotherhood of man."[27] By replacing the ultimate father, usually conceived of as white, with a black God, Garvey rebuked a history of rape and illegitimacy. By claiming descent from a black God, black Americans could bypass the question of their mixed-race heritage in the United States.

While Garvey sometimes argued that God's color might be white, black, or red, depending on the worshipper, others were defiant in their ascriptions of blackness to Christ.[28] The UNIA's Bishop Barber delivered a genealogy that made the Virgin Mary black. Fellow Garveyite Bishop McGuire predicted forcefully that if the Second Coming were to happen in New York, Christ "would be forced to dwell in Harlem, because He certainly was not white."[29] McGuire dubbed Jesus Christ "The Black Man of Sorrows." He "exhibited pictures of a mulatto Christ crowned with thorns and of a Black Madonna. 'If God is your Father, He must be the same color as you are!'"[30] This insistence on physical resemblances and racial bloodlines in families was defiantly contrary to the American experience. It was born of a politics elaborated around anxiety and anger at white paternity, which was often forced by rape, and then denied by a culture that held that black women were lascivious. These powerful messages tapped right into the political, social, and cultural currents in black America and inspired many to want to leave for Africa.[31]

Garvey's followers included many from the West Indies, who, like him, had emigrated to the United States hoping for better lives and were disappointed. In general, these supporters have left a more extensive record of their ideas and hopes than have his American-born followers, being on the whole better educated and more literate. New York resident Ernest Mair, who hailed, as did Garvey, from St. Ann Parish, Jamaica, viewed emigration as the only reasonable vision of black people's future. Mair was shocked that any black American could believe that oppression in the United States would ever end.[32] Excited letter writers, eagerly anticipating the return to the motherland, were published frequently in the *Negro World*'s pages. A founding member in 1920 of the Dominican branch of the rapidly expanding UNIA, Ralph Casimir, wrote to the treasurer in New York: "I hope when Headquarters have been removed to AFRICA that the Corporation will be able to establish a regular steamship communication between Africa & the West Indies (Dominica included) and trust that we West Indians, especially we in Dominica, will give the Corporation all the necessary support."[33]

Many U.S.-born black Americans similarly imagined themselves making the voyage "back" to Africa. Reminiscing in 1925, former *Negro World* editor William Ferris stated that although West Indian immigrants made up most of Garvey's initial followers, "now the greater majority of the membership consist of native Americans."[34] Reflecting on his visits to the UNIA's New York headquarters at Liberty Hall, writer Arthur Davis recalled that "Garvey's followers took his program seriously, almost religiously. Their faith in the Back-to-Africa promise was a thing that transcended everyday logic and it *was* a real faith, something that gave meaning to otherwise drab and oppressed lives."[35] This was true of followers in the small-town South, who were known as "Black Star Liners," as well as in the urban North.[36] Signed-up UNIA members and fellow travelers bought up enough five-dollar shares to support the purchase of three overpriced ships.

Many of Garvey's speeches, and much of the symbolism of the Black Star Line, stressed the role the Line could play in bridging the gap between people in the Americas and Africa.[37] Without a doubt, the Line was also a gutsy effort at entrepreneurship that tapped into existing traditions among black Americans of black self-help and dreams of economic independence.[38] Nobody reading through the collected papers of the UNIA could fail to notice Garvey's emphasis on the viability of the Line. But that insistence was made necessary by the fact that from the moment the idea of a shipping line became public, Garvey's critics, including government officials who watched his every move, assumed that there was never going to be any genuine business and that the whole venture was fraudulent.[39] Who ever heard of a black man running a shipping line? As well as forecasting a viable black business, however, Garvey's public utterances appealed to those who wanted to leave the United States and who wished to make connections with black people elsewhere. In a speech predicting that within a couple of years the UNIA would be the body in charge of issuing African passports, Garvey exhorted his listeners to buy shares in the Black Star Line. At present, he fumed, the authorities had issued him a passport only on the basis that he not go to Africa. This, he argued, was the very reason to support the black shipping line: "later on," he said, "we can sail from anywhere and reach Africa; and that is just why I am appealing to you tonight to give us sufficient money to buy ships that we can sail from anywhere and everywhere."[40] In "The Tragedy of White Injustice," he made the point that the Black Star Line was more than a straightforward commercial enterprise:

> The white man controls cable and wireless,
> Connections by ships with force and duress:
> He keeps black races of the world apart,
> So to his schemes they may not be smart:
> "There shall be no Black Star Line ships," he says,
> "For that will interfere with our crooked ways:
> "I'll disrupt their business and all their plans,
> "So they might not connect with foreign lands."[41]

Enterprise was the means, in the stanza quoted here, by which black people could connect to one another. It was not the cargo—whiskey, coconuts— that was important in Black Star Line voyages; rather, it was the transporting of people that was significant.

The sheer number of people who contributed funds to the Black Star Line cannot be explained by followers' interest in economic self-help alone. Although contributors were also enthusiastic about the commercial possibilities the Line's ships represented, it was the ability to ferry black people to and from Africa, and to all nodes in the diaspora between, that really excited Garvey's followers. Thousands of them gathered at the dock at West Twenty-fourth Street to view a ship after it was purchased; the lucky ones paid half a dollar to tour the ship before it sailed.[42] Thousands gathered again some months later to see it off on its maiden voyage; this time the price to tour onboard was a full dollar.[43] Similar crowds greeted the Line's ships up and down the eastern seaboard and through Central America and the Caribbean. When composer Shirley Graham dramatized the Garvey movement in 1932, she recognized that investors wanted a shipping line that would link people, not just merchant shipping lanes. In *Tom-Tom*, an opera performed for two nights in Cleveland Municipal Stadium, Graham took the Black Star Line's history one step further than Garvey had managed. She portrayed ships that were preparing to transport black American emigrants to Africa. Very close to the opera's conclusion, enthusiastic supporters swarmed a docked ship, until it sank under the weight of the movement's success.[44]

In fact, the Black Star Line failed as a result of incompetent and corrupt management. Garvey's ability to raise funds among even cash-strapped black Americans far outstripped by his skills as a shipping line director. Inexperience and corruption among his staff resulted in the purchase at grossly inflated prices of three ships that were only just seaworthy. Repairs and the loss of cargo eroded quickly the capital raised so effectively. In 1921, needing funds to keep the Line afloat, Garvey sent out brochures featuring a ship bearing the name SS *Phyllis Wheatley,* named for an enslaved African woman who had become a celebrated Boston poet. As the company did not yet own such a ship, the mailed brochures presented government officials with an opportunity to prosecute Garvey for mail fraud, thereby attempting to discredit him, the Black Star Line, and the UNIA. Garvey had been under the surveillance of the Bureau of Investigation and other intelligence organizations worldwide for some time. His ability to fire the imaginations of not only black people in the United States, but of colonized people worldwide, and to encourage them to think of themselves as connected in a global struggle, made him a threat to powerful people everywhere. Charged in January 1922, Garvey was convicted mid-1923, imprisoned for three months, released on bail pending an appeal, and then incarcerated once again in the Atlanta Federal Penitentiary at the beginning of 1925. His five-year sentence was commuted by President Coolidge, and he was deported in December 1927, never again to set foot in the United States.

Black Americans continued to contribute their hard-won earnings to schemes for their passage to Africa, even after the Black Star Line's collapse, Garvey's 1922 arrest, and his imprisonments in 1923 and 1925. The faith many UNIA members had in Garvey never wavered. Convinced he was the victim of a conspiracy because he was a black man brave enough to stand up for the race, the Black Star Line itself was, in the words of one observer in 1924, "still something of which they dream."[45] In the fourteen months or so between his stints in prison, Garvey incorporated a second shipping venture, the Black Cross Navigation and Trading Company, and sold enough shares to buy a fourth ship, which he renamed the SS *Booker T. Washington*.[46] Supporters hoped that their money would contribute to the transportation of pilgrims to west Africa.[47] In 1924, Garvey was once again in negotiation with Liberian officials and hoped to establish there the initial seat of a black African government. "I long to trod on the soil of our motherland Africa," wrote one North Carolina correspondent. "May God help us ever to press on and on until we reach a better land and see a brighter day."[48] The UNIA and Garvey Clubs kept the dream alive long after Garvey sailed from the United States.[49]

Other organizations bent on returning black Americans to Africa emerged. In Florida, a Ghanaian immigrant, Laura Kofey, broke with the UNIA and enticed followers to join the African Universal Church with promises that members would soon emigrate to West Africa.[50] One hundred or so black Americans in another group emigrated to Ethiopia following the 1930 coronation of Ras Tafari Makonnen as Emperor Haile Selassie.[51] Many of them were followers of Rabbi Arnold Josiah Ford, a Garvey follower who struck out on his own to lead Beth B'nai Abraham, a congregation of black Jews.[52] In 1933, the president and secretary of the Nationalist-Negro Movement and African Colonization Society wrote from New York to the League of Nations, requesting that in recognition of 250 "years of unrequited services we rendered without recompense," the League turn over to them control of the Cameroons, a former Germany colony.[53] Nearly a decade later, a woman named Mittie Gordon led some 300 people from Chicago to Washington to offer support to a notoriously racist Southern senator, Theodore Bilbo (D-Miss), who was introducing a bill for government aid to send blacks to Africa. Gordon and her followers were active into the mid-1940s.[54]

Garvey's followers hoped, too, to join him in unifying the African continent into a single nation. This aspect of Garvey's program was much ridiculed at the time. A. Philip Randolph, founder of the influential union the

Brotherhood of Sleeping Car Porters, pointed out pithily and a little angrily that "Africa is a continent, not a nation."[55] A play lampooning the Black Star Line's inefficiencies mocked in particular Garvey's view of Africa as an undifferentiated continent. Jeremiah, the title character who closely resembled Garvey, adorned his office wall with a large map of Africa, undivided and colored all in black.[56] Such scorn ignored the point that in the early 1920s a unified Africa, or a United States of Africa in Garvey's words, that followed the model of nineteenth-century Italian or German unification, was not completely outside the realm of possibility and certainly not impossible to imagine. Garvey thought of himself as an Otto von Bismarck of Africa, with an admittedly more difficult task given the scattered locations of those of African descent and the effects of colonization within Africa.[57] His plan made sense given the prevailing idea of national self-determination in which the race or ethnicity of inhabitants was supposed to be uniform, and in which national citizenship was shared as if between members of one family. To this end, he introduced an anthem and flag and planned on issuing passports in the future.[58] Though the president's residence, the "Black House," would be on the African mainland, the federated black nation would encompass noncontiguous states, much as did the United States of America.[59] A manuscript written by a young John Henrik Clarke demonstrates that some of Garvey's followers believed unification was possible. Clarke described "the relation of Ethiopia to the world" using this equation:

Ethiopia: Africa = Sardinia: Italy
or
Ethiopia: Africa = Prussia: Germany
In other words Ethiopia is to African liberation and unity
as Sardinia was to Italian liberation and unity.[60]

Others' derision notwithstanding, Garvey's view of Africa as a continent ripe for national unification had powerful appeal. Insofar as Africa was regarded as a place of related people that had been "carved up" by European powers in the 1880s, then a unification based on the popular ideology of national self-determination and on the expulsion of those colonizers was both imaginable and desirable.

The Black Star Line was by far the most criticized aspect of UNIA activism. W. E. B. Du Bois stifled his distaste for Garvey until, he said, he was moved by the faltering fortunes of the shipping company to come out swinging in a pair of scathing articles in *Crisis*, the journal of the NAACP, a civil rights organization he helped found.[61] The *Chicago Defender*, the nation's premier black newspaper, ran several unflattering cartoons of Garvey. In one he was depicted as a clown whose suit was covered in dollar signs, towing a toy ship labeled "The Black Star Line." In another, Garvey appeared as Sisyphus, pushing a large rock up an incline marked with a sign reading "Back to Africa." A third depicted Garvey being carried away by a hot air balloon labeled "'Back to Africa' Movement," only to have the bottom fall out of the basket before it was much off the ground, and a fourth depicted him butting his head against a brick wall.[62] Such critiques of the Black Star Line and Garvey's emigrationism in general drowned out the voices of the followers themselves. That is no wonder, as critics included most of the black political and literary establishment. Repetitions of such criticism began as early as the 1930s: two full-length plays and a film portrayed Garvey as vainglorious and the Black Star Line as singularly ill-conceived. Followers interested in going to Africa came in for the worst drubbing of all, depicted as unthinking and moronic.[63] Even Amy Jacques Garvey, Garvey's second wife and an important figure in the UNIA, said in the 1960s that "Back to Africa" was not intended as a serious mass migration campaign but rather as a spiritual movement.[64] Garvey must have turned in his grave. To be sure, many of Garvey's supporters and UNIA members did not wish to go to Africa, but to be equally sure, many did.

The image of Africa as a motherland fell on the fertile ground of a society saturated with new ideas about individual psychology, particularly the theory that a rupture in the process of a child differentiating itself from its mother could result in long-term trauma. Slave trading was violent—an unnatural severing of the relationship between mother and child. In Garvey's view, neither side was coping particularly well in the aftermath. Others agreed, representing Africa time and again as a mother cauterized with unending grief for her missing children, especially her lost sons. Proponents of this view drew, implicitly, on Sigmund Freud's argument that "aggressiveness . . .

forms the basis of every relation of affection and love among people" with only one exception: "the mother's relation to her male child."[65] Just as a mother's love was incorruptible, so, too, was the devotion of the African motherland to her scattered children. Black people of the diaspora would always be welcomed home.

When contemporary historians came to treat the slave trade as a subject of study, they generally ignored the involvement of Africans in the buying and selling of human beings, instead mobilizing the metaphor Garvey had done so much to popularize. Benjamin Brawley, one of the foremost and widely read black historians of the day, described the effect of slave trading upon Africa using the figure of "an old woman sadly typical of the great African mother." Brawley wrote that "she better than any one else perceived the meaning of it all. The men with the hard faces who came to buy and sell might deceive others, but not her. In a great vague way she felt that something wrong had attacked the very heart of her people." She stood on the shores of the continent and, paraphrasing Matthew 2:18, "wept for her children and would not be comforted because they were not."[66] Du Bois was another accomplished historian although when he became the first black American to be awarded a PhD from Harvard, his field was sociology. Like Brawley, Du Bois imagined that at the west African shoreline, "a black women is weeping and waiting."[67] According to historians, her life was in abeyance—time in Africa was at a standstill—as she awaited the return of her children.

Africa-as-motherland found its most striking portrayal on stage, with women and girls bringing the metaphor to life. Theater was still an enormously popular cultural form among Americans in the 1920s and into the 1930s, challenged but not superseded by film. Black activists and educators harnessed the resources of local and school stages for the rewriting of black history; time and again, the curtain rose on dramatic productions in which Africa was depicted as a woman weeping, grieving endlessly for her lost children. The prologue for Dorothy Guinn's 1924 pageant, "Out of the Dark," was titled "The Rape of a Continent." Directors were instructed to create a tableau centered upon "the figure of the sorrowing mother helplessly watching her children carried away. As she looks and weeps, we recognize in her bereaved figure the spirit of Africa, no longer joyful, but grief-stricken at the terrible outrage of the slave trader."[68] As the play progressed and

slaves were taken from Africa, the action stayed focused on those left behind, so the audience could see "back on the shore the aged mother, so symbolic of Africa, [who] wept and is still weeping for the loss of her strongest
children."[69]

Quite often in stage productions, Africa was personified specifically as
Ethiopia. That nation held a special place in black Americans' imaginations,
for its exalted place in the Bible and, more recently, for its success in 1896 at
fending off Italian forces at the Battle of Adowa and remaining independent
of colonial control. When Africa became Ethiopia, she was a young mother,
innocent and even virginal, somewhat like Mary, whose child went into exile when first born. Like the older versions of Mother Africa, Ethiopia, too,
was always marked by grief and endurance. A pageant created for a 1921
New York City exposition on the contribution of various groups to "America's Making" opened on "Ethiopia," a tall female character whose "dark face
shines forth from the mass drapery of a white Sudanese bernouse which
flows down in folds to the ground and has perhaps a single splash of crim-
son color." As in other productions, "the face has closed eyes and on the
cheek a slight trace of tears."[70] In yet another pageant, Frances Gunner's
1924 "The Light of the Women," Ethiopia was the first character introduced
onstage. The narrator heralded her as the perfect mother, whose love—and
grief—for her children was perpetual: "This dusky queen, to whom has
been so great a portion of earth's care and sorrow, answers always to my
call," the narrator assured audiences. "Often her eyes are wet with tears, and
her ears heavy with the sorrows of dark mothers and the oppressions of her
people, yet faith and courage never leave her, and of all the earth's queens
there is none braver."[71]

Accounts of the African motherland in both black public culture and
politics were suffused with descriptions of her selfless generosity, an element sorely lacking in America's character. In these portrayals, Africa had
sacrificed herself by giving to the world her many gifts. Among these gifts
were her children—those slaves transported north and across the
Atlantic—but also such technologies as iron smelting and writing; arts including music, dance, and oratory; and, in general, the gift of civilization.
Du Bois suggested that Africa's greatest gift to the world was motherhood
itself, both as ideology and in fact, being the location of the world's first
human beings. "The great black race," he wrote, "gave the world, not only

the Iron Age, the cultivation of the soil, and the domestication of animals, but also, in peculiar emphasis, the mother-idea." It was in Africa that motherhood, which Du Bois thought the noblest of pursuits and which he associated with peace, civilization, and justice, began.[72]

In portraying Africa as a helpless mother to whom violence had been done, black Americans set themselves up as her savior, and it was on this issue that Garvey had one of his greatest successes. Again it was a case of him tapping into an existing trend and extending it. Idealized manhood had long included the ability to provide for and protect women and children. Garvey envisioned a redeemed continent made up of nuclear families with male heads of households supported by virtuous women who would focus on raising children industrious and independent enough to facilitate the business of nation-building.

But first the continent itself had to be rescued from imperialism. If the land of Africa were female, then European colonial domination was rape. A poem published in the UNIA's *Negro World* opened: "Imperial mother of great nations! Thou / Whom envious lands have wickedly despoiled."[73] An editorial in the same newspaper asked readers: "Africa, the land of our fathers, beckons us home, if not in person, in sympathy, in sentiment and in moral and financial help, so why shouldn't we help Mother Africa to redeem herself? Why shouldn't we help her to throw off the shackles placed upon her by an alien civilization and alien races?" It continued in the questioning vein: "Why shouldn't we help her put to flight the enemy within her doors who seeks her very vitals?"[74] It was hard to miss the metaphor of rape. The author evoked a familiar image of Africa as a known coastline surrounding a big gaping hole, a heart of darkness, but unlike in most accounts, that dark interior was not the essence of Africa; rather, it was the damage done by violent colonial exploitation. It was crucial that Africa's sons return in order to nurse their motherland back to health and to protect her from further harm.

Garvey's message about a vulnerable motherland being despoiled became ubiquitous in 1920s black culture. Lewis Alexander's sonnet "Africa" (1924), appeared in *Opportunity,* the journal of the Urban League, an organization devoted to change within the United States. The poem is worth reprinting in full because it exemplifies so many of the ways Africa was imagined:

Thou art not dead, although the spoiler's hand
Lies heavy as death upon thee; though the wrath
Of its accursed might is in thy path
And has usurped thy children of their land;
Though yet the scourges of a monstrous band
Roam on thy ruined fields, thy trampled lanes,
Thy ravaged homes and desolated fanes;
Thou art not dead, but sleeping,—Motherland.
A mighty country, valorous and free,
Thou shalt outlive this terror and this pain;
Shall call thy scattered children back to thee,
Strong with the memory of their brothers slain;
And rise from out thy charnel house to be
Thine own immortal, brilliant self again![75]

With her ruined fields and trampled lanes, Africa was a woman violated. She was also a slumbering mother of sons in Africa and scattered elsewhere and of those "brothers slain." It was the duty of these sons to reunite and repair the damage done to the motherland.

Well into the 1930s, similar imagery continued to appear in essays as well as in poetry and on stage. Arthur Schomburg, a New Yorker originally from Puerto Rico whose extraordinary collection of books and other materials formed the basis of the collection of the Harlem branch of the New York Public Library (now the Schomburg Center), wrote a piece for Paris-based Nancy Cunard's transnational collection, *Negro: An Anthology* (1934). In it, he, too, personified Africa as female and vulnerable: "From the bosom of black Africa, we are to see other, greater deeds that will be called marvellous, when Ethiopia stretches out her hands unto God. From Africa's great lakes and waterfalls mighty rivers flow in many directions." Embarking on an extended metaphor, Schomburg continued: "These rivers afforded the Portuguese, Spaniards, Dutch and English splendid opportunities to ascend their navigable waters and streams to view the panoramic landscape of the vast interior as a worthy place to grab, a prelude to plunder, loot, rapine and murder. These were the watery highways that had made it easier for travellers and explorers to ascend and penetrate within her unknown interior."[76] Ascending mountains and penetrating the interior, Europe's rapacious colonizers knew no mercy. Schomburg looked forward to their replacement by more sympathetic travelers who could help the mother nation undertake the "greater deeds" he predicted for her future. Africa's helplessness against the ravages of colonization meant she desired the return "home" of her scattered children every bit as much as those children pined for the reunification of the black family and nation.

It was not unusual that land should be regarded as female. European colonizers often feminized the land they seized, both to make the unknown territory less terrifying and to make its penetration and conquering seem a reflection of the natural social order.[77] Black American men used European colonial language, but by altering the language of feminization from the general to the particular—from woman to mother—they protested vehemently the grip of those colonizers. They achieved this by emphasizing Africa's virtuous maternal qualities, which they likened to untouched nature.

In rescuing the African motherland from the ravages of colonization, black American men hoped to bring to life the biblical prophecy that when Ethiopia stretched forth her hands unto God, so, too, would princes come out of Egypt. They updated the prophecy, though: both Lewis Alexander and the UNIA editor wrote that Africa would "call" or "beckon" her children home, so it was more a case of Ethiopia stretching a hand out to her long-lost children in order that those princes might return to Egypt. It was as if the slave trade had perverted the future predicted in the Bible. A return "home" by America's black people was required in order to right this great wrong and to fulfill the verse's vision.

However much the symbolism of Garvey's rendering of Africa as a motherland resonated throughout black culture and with activists of all political persuasions, his campaign to repatriate black Americans to Africa forced a contest between those who saw Africa as the future home of black Americans and those who hoped that the United States could be made to uphold the democratic principles upon which it was founded. This was a contest over identity: Garvey regarded black people of the diaspora as displaced Africans; Du Bois had proclaimed in 1903 that black Americans regarded the world with a "double-consciousness" that came from being both black and American, and he continued to adhere to that belief; others saw the answer in worldwide socialist reform and urged black Americans to identify with their working class brethren rather than those of the same race.[78] There were many, however, who stressed the Americanness of black identity, even if the nation's institutions and most of its people excluded and denigrated black Americans. Responding to dominant ideas within the United States that the people who truly belonged to the American nation were all white and all related to one another, and to Garvey's forceful message that black people were a nation and family, this group likewise framed its politics in terms of kinship. While they were happy to accept a heritage in the African motherland, their future lay in the nation for which their fathers and mothers had given so much: the United States.

Among the group who saw an American future for black Americans were many of the executives and members of the NAACP. Founded in 1909 by both black and white Americans, the NAACP's primary aim was the integration of black Americans into the nation's polity. These people expressed their fidelity to the United States and opposition to Garvey's ideas by insisting that black Americans belonged to the United States just as much as did white Americans. A certain obtuseness in Garvey's character meant that he failed completely to appreciate the depth of many black Americans' attachment to the land of their birth and their desire to be recognized as full members of the nation fast becoming a world superpower. Forthright William Pickens, NAACP field secretary, wrote to Garvey that "We will give up all our homes, our lives, our rights, our past and future in our native land, providing you give us a free and undisputed title to the *moon!*"[79] In specifically denouncing Garvey's repatriation scheme, such activists did not reject an affiliation with black people outside the United States. In Pickens's words, "by being good citizens here we can help the African negro best."[80] It was not that Pickens felt no affinity with Africans, just that he refused to forfeit his right to life in the United States, the land of his birth and citizenship, and the home, too, of his more immediate ancestors.

In order to campaign effectively for their full citizenship rights in the United States, these activists could not simultaneously claim a home elsewhere. Garvey's opponents felt, at a time when the doctrines of "100 percent American" and national self-determination were in fashion, that their agitation was best served by being framed as a narrow sort of patriotism.[81] Thus, Walter White, at the time the NAACP's executive secretary, replied to a member who called for government assistance to repatriate "two or three hundred thousand" blacks to Africa:

> Of the twelve million or thirteen million Negroes in the United States practically all of them and their ancestors have been here in the United States for many generations. Most of them have been here much longer than many of the white people in this country. The Negro has contributed of his strength to the building of America and . . . his roots are so deeply imbedded in American soil that he is more thoroughly American than a great many white Americans.[82]

More often than not, the claim that America was the black man's homeland was based on the labor that black ancestors had long ago contributed to the nation. Rewriting the genealogy of the American family, activists regarded their own ancestors as among the "founding fathers" of the land. They even predated the nation's existence: "We antedated the Pilgrim Fathers by one year," wrote J. A. Rogers in *From "Superman" to Man* (1917), a much-reprinted fictional dialogue between a lively Pullman porter and a bigoted Southern senator.[83] These paternal figures, unlike those in such UNIA hymns as "Freedom's Noble Cause" and "Centenary's Day," were tied explicitly to the project of American nation-building. In James Weldon Johnson's "Lift Every Voice and Sing," he asked, "Have not our weary feet / Come to the place for which our fathers sighed?" This song came to be known as the "Negro National Anthem" and was sung on formal occasions throughout the twentieth century. As Johnson himself recalled in his autobiography, the original poem was forty-one stanzas long, but after much agonizing, he cut the final fifteen in order to change the tone from one of despair to one of hope. "This land is ours by right of birth," began the eleventh stanza:

> This land is ours by right of toil;
> We helped to turn its virgin earth,
> Our sweat is in its fruitful soil.[84]

Citizenship here was something passed down; as long-standing inhabitants of the nation, black Americans deserved recognition of that status. The hopefulness of those who sang was based, too, on a faith in history making, that in retelling the past to include the contributions of their "fathers," their inherited place in the present nation would be recognized.

The blood black men shed in battle for the nation was just more evidence that the United States was their natural home. By giving their lives alongside whites, black men delivered the United States into existence. This idea of the birth of the nation was dramatized frequently in pageants, which often began their accounts of national history with the death of Crispus Attucks, a black man, the first to die in the Boston Massacre. Since then, black Americans had contributed to every war, both civil and international; had demonstrated their devotion to the American nation; and had proven that they deserved the full rights and responsibilities of citizenship. They were as much members of the American family as any white person who could trace his or her roots to the Puritans, and perhaps more so than more recently arrived immigrants.

As well as stressing the role played by their black forefathers in the making of the nation, many black American activists also adopted celebrated figures in American history in order to write themselves into the prevailing familial tropes of American identity. Two prominent black Americans wrote pageants to commemorate the 1932 bicentenary of George Washington's birth. Both took as their starting point Washington's response to a poem that Phillis Wheatley, an African-born enslaved woman and poet, wrote in his honor. Educator Mary Church Terrell intended that black children could "revere" George Washington as other children did, knowing that even though he "was a slave-holder, in accordance with the deplorable custom of his time, nevertheless, he was broad-minded, generous-hearted and just enough to make written acknowledgment of the talent of an African girl and to pay homage to her, while she was still being held as a slave."[85] Like many of her contemporaries, Terrell rewrote American histories to include interaction between black and white people and, insofar as the classic American narrative was a genealogical one, to re-pot the family tree to include black roots.

Though he emphasized male achievement, Du Bois went even further in challenging the idea that the national family derived from white founding fathers. He suggested in his 1932 pageant that Crispus Attucks "was the original father of the country: 'The Fourth of July displaces the Fifth of

March. Washington succeeds Crispus Attucks.'"[86] What he meant was that prior to 1784, Attucks's death was commemorated annually in Boston until July 4 displaced it as the national holiday. Du Bois redesigned the American family by making Washington, long regarded as the father of the nation, secondary to Attucks. Americans had mixed origins. There was no racial purity, and therefore the exclusion of black Americans from the putative national family had its basis in faulty history.

Far from following Garvey back to Africa, NAACP activists and others emphasized the contributions black Americans had made to the United States in order to force white Americans to expand the definition of the national "family" to include black brethren. The makeup of the national family was the subject of a playscript titled "The Balance," contained in the papers of the NAACP. The title referred to the Scales of Justice, which, according to a female character called Democracy, needed to be in harmony for her to survive. This would be achieved only when the nation's family had fair representation of children from "the Orient and . . . the dark continent" as well as from Europe. The pageant's climax came when America, another female character, declared, "Democracy, you must not die here." In order to forestall this tragedy, America had to rescind her statement to Ethiopia, played by a girl, that "you seem so different—your color. How can you become a part of this country? You can't." Finally, the children all joined America on stage, in the national dress of their forebears, and sang together "The Star Spangled Banner" in front of the national flag.[87] The spotlight shifted from America to Democracy. "The Balance" was one of several pageants that explicitly rejected the famous "melting pot" of earlier stage productions.[88] Instead, America became just one character among the many children, representing many backgrounds, who all together comprised the diverse nation.

Stressing their allegiance to the United States, many black Americans rejected Garvey's model of a black family, connected through time and space to an African motherland. Instead they relied on a horizontal kinship with their white American brothers. Equality demanded fraternity. Thus, whereas in 1919 James Weldon Johnson had labeled American Negroes and African Negroes as "blood brothers," the success of Garvey's "Back to Africa" campaign meant that by 1922 Johnson was stressing the view that "a common origin and even color do not make American Negroes

Africans."[89] Johnson's view of a United States brotherhood was shared by a woman who criticized Garvey's repatriation project in a letter she wrote to the UNIA newspaper, the *Negro World*. Maria Milam defiantly asserted her Americanness to the point where she declared that it would be God, not Garvey, who "will handle the African proposition through a black and white Americanite. . . . If God wants us to go back to Africa, He will send us an American leader and we will follow." Although it is likely that Milam's mistrust of Garvey rested on the more general antagonism between locally born black people and West Indian immigrants, it is still the case that she tacitly claimed a brotherhood with American men from a viewpoint that resembled Johnson's. "The black and white Americanite we know him," she wrote. "We have been here with him for over 300 years. We have worked for him, we have fought for him and we fought him, and we love him; and we will follow no one else but black and white Americans."[90]

Completing this effort to rewrite the national family to include black Americans, activists and others who opposed Garvey's repatriation scheme heralded publicly the contributions made to the making of America by their black foremothers. At no time was debate over the role of women more heated than in 1923, when the United Daughters of the Confederacy (UDC) petitioned the United States Senate to erect a monument in Washington, D.C. in memory of the "Faithful Colored Mammies of the South." A bill in favor of the motion passed the Senate, though it never made it to a vote in the House of Representatives.[91] According to the *New York Amsterdam News,* Hungarian-born George Zolnay's statue, which was to form the centerpiece of the mammy monument, depicted "a Negro Mammy holding a white child in her arms while her own colored child [stands] at her side crying for attention."[92] Black Americans in the North responded swiftly and vociferously. "Practically all colored people are opposed to the move," declared the *Amsterdam News*.[93] The *Norfolk Journal and Guide*'s editor publicly supported the monument and was quickly denounced as an Uncle Tom for his trouble.[94] The UNIA's *Negro World* suggested that a better monument would memorialize Joe Pullen, a black tenant farmer in Mississippi who, having been hounded for a debt he said was fabricated, shot and killed nine white men and injured nine others before being killed himself.[95] The mammy monument, noted a furious left-wing editor, would be "a memorial of the Southern white's good times gone."[96]

Opponents of the sculpture adopted language used by those who wished to save the motherland from rape and pillage. In these activists' hands, women became victims needing to be rescued. Black writers were moved to remind readers of the true history of Southern slavery, in which women who nannied and nursed white children were likely to have been young and vulnerable to the stalking of predatory slave owners and other white men.[97] In an editorial, the *Amsterdam News* exclaimed in outrage: "A monument to 'black mammies' is a mockery, a farce, and a disgrace to the intelligence of the United States Senate. Likewise," it continued, "it is an affront to every American citizen that descends from those saintly women who were sacrificed to the avaricious beastly natures of Southern gentlemen."[98] Picking up on the same theme about the rape of black women by white men, a cartoonist in the *Chicago Defender* portrayed "A White Daddy," tall and menacing above a black woman whose hair and clothes were in disarray from his attack.[99] Its title read "Since Statues Seem to be All the Rage, Suppose We Erect One." Chandler Owen, editor of the left-wing *Messenger*, proclaimed that should any statue be erected to honor black women, "let its white shaft point like a lofty mountain peak to *a New Negro mother*, no longer a '*white man's woman*,' no longer the sex-enslaved '*black mammy*' of Dixie—but the apotheosis of triumphant Negro womanhood!"[100]

The mammy's preference for white children was taken in Old South mythology as simply more evidence of white superiority, but black activists used it to demonstrate how virtuous black women were and to show the depth of their contribution to the nation's development. Just as Africa had given civilization to the world, so, too, did black women in the United States sacrifice themselves for the good of the nation. Mammies were morally superior, saintly martyrs who selflessly (though not willingly) forfeited the care of their own children for that of their white charges. In the pageant *The Light of the Women*, Frances Gunner paid tribute to the mammy. "In the dark days of bondage," said the narrator, "she trod the humble paths of service and gave herself in unstinted fidelity to the families of the nation. She it was who mothered all the children of the Southland."[101] Far from demonstrating white superiority, black mammies in Gunner's estimation retained an innate maternity lacking in white women. If the nation's so-called founding fathers were white, then its mother, like Africa, where life itself began, was a black woman.

Black activists at the NAACP, their members, and others insisted that the United States was home and that they had every right to full citizenship, and yet they never could bring themselves to call America a motherland. They had no intention of joining Garvey in any expatriation to Africa, but they nevertheless more often than not followed him in identifying themselves as the sons and daughters of Africa. To attribute the natural and sacrosanct relationship between mother and child to a foreign country was in some way to disavow one's ties to the United States, or at the very least to point out the deficiencies of America's nurture of her own black citizens. The United States was inevitably contrasted to the natural and endlessly giving, selfless, maternal land of origin, Africa. Consider Virginia Jackson's 1919 poem "Africa," published in the *Crisis*, in which America, neither motherland nor fatherland, was imagined as a second-rate foster mother:

> Often now I hear a voice a-calling
>   Calling me across the mighty sea,
> And responsively my heart is swelling,
>   Native land, I long to answer thee.
> Long to leave the hate of foster mother,
>   To be nurtured by thy kindly hand,
> Sitting at thy feet with my black brother,
>   Africa! to know thy sunny land.[102]

America, the white foster mother, could not compete with the naturally caring and generous African motherland. Her wards, Virginia Jackson suggested, were biding their time before returning to where they belonged, with their natural family: their brothers in the motherland, Africa.

At the same time as responding to American racism by insisting on their place in the national family, NAACP activists used kinship metaphors to denounce the United States as inadequate and thoroughly unexceptional. In Du Bois's view, "instead of standing as a great example of the success of democracy and the possibility of human brotherhood America has taken her place as an awful example of its pitfalls and failures, so far as black and brown and yellow peoples are concerned."[103] Du Bois cast America as an unfeeling and dictatorial female. "She stands today," he wrote, "shoulder to shoulder with Europe in Europe's worst sin against civilization." His personification of the United States as too tough to be womanly meant that in fact the nation had no place in the great human family: "The father and his worship is Asia; Europe is the precocious, self-centered, forward-striving child; but the land of the mother is and was Africa."[104] America really was a foster mother, and not a very good one at that.

America's failures as a mother extended beyond her citizen-children to wards she had voluntarily adopted: Liberians. According to the black newspaper the *New York Age,* America was incapable of mothering even in the colonial sense of being a "mother country"; rather, she was more of a neglectful, aloof stepmother. Liberia was never the child of the United States but "has been known to the world as America's step-child."[105] The *Age* called Liberia "America's Responsibility" and chided the United States for letting the League of Nations assume its "guardianship."[106] In George Schuyler's stinging critique, "America fathered Liberia, but has failed to mother her."[107] For most commentators, the American treatment of Liberia was not exactly startling given the state of race relations within its own borders. Those at the *Norfolk Journal and Guide* seemed unsurprised: "That is America for you! Especially the imperialistic America, falsely professing to wear a halo of justice and to being the protector of the weak and champion of right against might." The image of the haloed woman, embodied most obviously in the Statue of Liberty, was being used in vain according to the Norfolk newspaper. Really the United States was an exploitative, imperialist monster in bad drag, whose treatment of Liberians and Haitians matched exactly the "Hoover attitude" to black people within its own borders.[108]

In those instances where the United States was personified as female, it was not imagined as motherly. In civil rights activist Archibald Grimké's bitter post–World War I poem, "Her Thirteen Black Soldiers," a passage toward the end of the poem delineated the conditions in the United States, imagined as female:

She, who put her uniform on them, heard their enemy.
She flew at its call and hanged her brave black soldiers.

She hanged them for doing for themselves what she ought to have done
   for them,
She hanged them for resenting insult to her uniform,
She hanged them for defending from violence her brave black soldiers.[109]

Grimké rendered the United States as unfeeling and harsh, not only by the
actions described but also through the repeated use of the pronoun "she."
She was female, but she was not feminine. Her characteristics were the very
antithesis of maternal traits. This depiction was in stark opposition to the
more familiar portrayal of Africa as a sorrowful old woman weeping over
the loss of her children, or as a beautiful young woman, often called Ethiopia, dressed in white, stretching forth her hands unto God and to her scattered children worldwide. If the "she" of Grimké's poem, who offered her
soldiers no sympathy but demanded only their attention, loyalty, and obedi-
ence, resembled any woman, it was the classic Spartan mother, but even
then her unjust treatment and lack of respect for black soldiers rendered this
analogy void. A motherland was somewhere its inhabitants felt at home. No
matter where black Americans saw their future home, in the present, America was no motherland.

In both the political and cultural realms, then, the idea of Africa as both
female and a motherland had significant purchase. An ideology of sexual
difference underlay public representations of black Americans' imagined
connection to the African motherland, whether or not people saw their future on the African continent. This ideology cast men in the role of women's
protectors and implicitly silenced women in the public realm. It would be
men, not women, who would make statements against sexual violence,
whether those attacks were metaphorical ones on Africa, historical in the
case of American slavery, or present-day, including the abuse suffered by
black women, especially domestics and factory workers.

   It was difficult enough for men to protest against sexual violence, which
explains in part why they were so vociferous in their denunciations of the
UDC's proposed mammy statue. That controversy allowed them to draw
attention to the issue of sexual abuse, but more safely in the past than in
the present. Even for men such as Du Bois and for poets such as Langston

Hughes, it was sometimes hard to speak directly to the point, so they often talked about sexual violence during slavery and made indirect comments about ongoing sexual abuse of black women.[110] Of the many crimes of slavery and racism, there was just one wrongdoing that Du Bois said he could never forgive, not even in "the world to come": the white South's "wanton and continued and persistent insulting of the black womanhood which it sought and seeks to prostitute to its lust."[111] The language men used tended both to idealize and to silence women, just as Garvey and others did when they described Africa as a weeping motherland.[112] For a woman to speak up would be to buck against the gender ideologies that both propelled black nationalism and animated civil rights activism. It was in any case very difficult for women to make public any abuse they had suffered. Sexual assaults were nearly impossible to report, both in the North and South; arrests of white men for rapes of black women were rare, convictions in court almost nonexistent.[113] Such quietening of women in the public sphere was not unique to black activist politics.

The most extreme instances of this ideology of sexual difference working in practice were in the South, where UNIA members were either involved in, or approved of, the physical punishment of black women who engaged in consensual sexual relations with white men.[114] Certainly, the emphasis Garvey placed on "race purity" circumscribed both men's and women's choices in relationships, but a special burden fell on women, as reproducers of the race. Nowhere in the pages of the UNIA newspaper, which ran reports of retribution meted out to black women who crossed the color line voluntarily, was there any suggestion that black men be so treated should they engage in relations with white women.[115] Although this was an extreme case, the elision of women from the public sphere was typical of diaspora politics, regardless of whether those involved envisioned their future in Africa, or in the United States. By accepting that nations and families were connected, and therefore that citizenship was linked to reproduction, women's role in future polities was limited to motherhood.

Many women nevertheless found the UNIA program extremely attractive because becoming a homemaker, wife, and mother would be liberating. It would free them from the drudgery of poorly paid and menial work as maids, nannies, cooks, and factory workers. What was more, it would give them a means to escape the constant slights and worse—sexual violence included—that came with their jobs. Thousands of women joined the UNIA, sometimes becoming active in the women's auxiliary organizations, such as the Black Cross Nurses.

Other women, however, saw no promise in this future. For them, Garvey's Africa was a motherland, populated by fathers in the past and brothers in the present, with daughters seldom mentioned and with no active role to play. They denounced the general trend to regard Africa with a nostalgic simplicity, because it belied the real difficulty in relationships between family members, especially when those families were put under the strains of racism, violence, and poverty. These women, mostly writers, some artists, saw how the ideology that linked mother and home made it impossible for them to speak truthfully about the conditions in which black American women lived, trying to hold together families in mostly adverse circumstances. By linking femininity and maternity to African land and history, moreover, women were elided from public debate. These associations left women little room to talk about their ambivalence about becoming mothers in a country where their children would suffer from the effects of racism. In the words of one *Negro World* writer, if "you find any woman—especially a black woman—who does not want to be a mother, you may rest assured she is not a true woman."[116]

Garvey's vision of a redeemed African world in which women would play out their supposedly natural role as helpmates resonated in domestic black politics, where male activists imagined a future in which women were partners to successful New Negro men. One of the fullest expressions of these beliefs came in the radical left magazine the *Messenger*. An editorial claimed a special role ahead for the New Negro Woman:

> Upon her shoulders rests the big task to create and keep alive, in the breast of black men, a holy and consuming passion to break with the slave traditions of the past; to spurn and overcome the fatal, insidious inferiority complex of the present, which, like Banquo's Ghost, bobs up ever and anon, to arrest the progress of the New Negro Manhood Movement; and to fight with increasing vigor, with dauntless courage, unrelenting zeal and intelligent vision for the attainment of the stature of a *full man,* a free race and a new world.[117]

Iconography of the Harlem Renaissance made women heroic but also monumental and unreal. (Aaron Douglas, "The Burden of Black Womanhood." By permission of the Crisis Publishing Co., Inc., the publisher of the magazine of the NAACP; image first published in the September 1927 issue of *The Crisis*.)

In much protest politics, women were accorded a secondary role, which consisted mainly of assisting black men in shucking off the remnants of a supposed slave consciousness to become complete men. Women supposedly did not need to exorcise internalized feelings of inferiority, because they were supposed to accept a position inferior to men. The tendency to frame black activism in this particular gendered way was not unique; it dated backwards in time and would continue well into the postwar civil rights and black power movements.[118]

The pervasiveness of Garvey's extensively articulated vision of the future is evident in the repetition of his ideas in the journals edited by some of his most fervent critics. Aaron Douglas, the New Negro Renaissance's premier artist, gave visual form to the sentiments contained in the *Messenger* editorial a few years later on the cover of the *Crisis*. Flanked by art deco–style pyramids on one side and skyscrapers on the other—images that over the past few years had come to represent in a sort of visual shorthand Africa and the United States, respectively—the statuesque woman holds aloft the world. Her disproportionate size relative to the globe indicates her largely symbolic function; though with the weight of the world in her hands she might seem powerful, the title of this cover was "The Burden of Black Womanhood."

In black politics' utopian future, black manhood would stride ahead, buoyed by the support of black womanhood. Special education issues of both the *Messenger* and *Crisis* made that clear and demonstrate that ideas Garvey did so much to popularize had spread far and wide. The *Messenger* went on sale in mid-1923 with a cover illustration that transformed the subject of Rodin's celebrated sculpture, *The Thinker,* into a black American man. A. Philip Randolph, editor in 1920, had said in the same magazine that the New Negro's "social methods are: education and physical action in self defense. That education must constitute the basis of all action, is beyond the realm of question. And to fight back in self defense, should be accepted as a matter of course. No one who will not fight to protect his life is fit to live."[119] The robust muscularity of the image on the cover gave Randolph's statement a militancy appropriate to the character of the "New Negro," a putatively male subject. On *Crisis*'s cover, a man achieves academic honors following a path lit for him by a woman. The woman is not real or at least does not exist in the present day: her sandals, flowing garb, Egyptian headdress, monumental posture, and ancient torch mark her as mere symbol. Standing in the foreground with the urn, she is the conduit through which the man has acquired an education rooted in the classics. There's a touch of Lady Liberty about her, too. The young black man has inherited ancient civilization, and now he is a citizen of the American nation, whose universities' architecture also echoes that of ancient Greece. She lights the way, but he walks alone.

Other reform groups saw the future panning out the same way. On a cover of the journal of the Urban League, whose motto was "Not alms but

The New Negro was strong and thoughtful. He was also male. (*The Messenger,* May 1923.)

opportunity," the woman pictured was no more real. In this case, the improved conditions were most definitely within the United States. What could be more American than a man and woman coming together to share, and give thanks for, the spoils of the land at Thanksgiving? On closer inspection, it was again a man of the contemporary era alongside a monumental woman, a stately black Columbia in classical robes. Whereas he can be proud of the fruits of his labor, grown in the ground, she is the land, the nation. Once again, in the imagined future, whether in the United States or Africa, men stood tall, but women—real women—were nowhere to be found.[120]

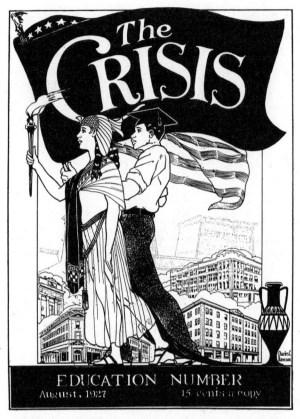

Both those who wanted to go back to Africa and those who wished to remain in the United States tended to see men as history's actors and the agents of change. In the imagined future, it would be men who would take the lead, while women would play supportive roles. (Charles C. Dawson, "Drawing with Five Great Negro Buildings." By permission of the Crisis Publishing Co., Inc., the publisher of the magazine of the NAACP; image first published in the August 1927 issue of *The Crisis*.)

Women writers, in particular, challenged the ideology of sexual differ-ence that underlay prominent ideas about Africa and about black Ameri-cans' future, whether in Africa or in the United States. Unlike male writers of the Harlem Renaissance, female authors very rarely treated directly the subject of Africa, a significant absence. Instead, they focused on the strains to which black mothers and black families were subjected, topics difficult to broach in black civic culture, where women by and large were idealized as perfect mothers. In countless plays, short stories, novels, and poetry, as well as nonfiction, women writers dealt with such subjects as violence, including lynching and rape; racism in general; poverty; self-loathing; and color hierarchies within black families and society.[121] For various reasons beyond their control, women in these works decide not to have children, murder their children, or mistreat them in some way. Set usually in the home, women's writing, especially their novels, was dismissed by male contemporaries (and many critics since) as the bourgeois dabblings of apolitical women.[122] On the contrary, such works provided a collective riposte to the silencing of women in the public sphere. Taken together, they undermined the idealization of women as mothers and the relegation of women to private duties, as prescribed by the dominant visions of black Americans' future, whether that future lay in Africa or in the United States.

Nostalgic renderings of Africa as motherland seemed to women writers both sentimental and unrealistic. Black Americans could never really know where they came from, argued Jessie Fauset, one-time literary editor at *Crisis* magazine and, with four novels published, among the most prolific of the Harlem Renaissance writers. Unlike, say, Greek or Italian migrants, she wrote, black Americans had nothing to which to go back. Even the children and grandchildren of European immigrants had more legitimacy in being nostalgic for their homelands, Fauset claimed, having had a memory of the place passed down to them from parents and grandparents. For blacks, on the contrary, "the past is too far past for him to have memories. Very, very rarely does he have a backward reaching bond."[123] Fauset diverged sharply from the usual sentimentalizing of Africa as a motherland, rewriting it into "that mysterious fatherland" for which they could have only "spiritual nostalgia." She resisted the temptation to cast Africa as an ever-welcoming woman, well aware of the limiting effect such rhetoric was having on women's opportunity to participate in the American political sphere. Moreover, in referring to Africa as a fatherland, she implied that black Americans could never be certain of their relationship to it, as children can always be about mothers.[124]

Notwithstanding the powerful critique offered by women writers, Garvey's idea that Africa was the black man's motherland and home had rapid and widespread penetration. His popularity cannot be accounted for as simply a "politics of revitalization"—"Back to Africa" was more than a catchy slo-gan. It captured his followers' utter discontent with their lives in the United States, where a complicated set of ideas about their inferiority, based on a bogus racial science, served to reinforce the fact that their citizenship was not worth the paper on which the Fourteenth Amendment was written. No matter what they did, short of "passing" over into white society if they were light-skinned enough, they were never white enough to be considered by most Americans to be a genuine part of the American family. Conditions were so tough that many wanted to leave.

For those who did not want to follow Garvey back to Africa, his politics nevertheless gave them ideas and language to respond to their exclusion from America's body politic. Just like more recent immigrants, black Amer-icans had an original home elsewhere, and what was more, Africa had a long and proud history before the slave trade. Having Africa as their motherland, they argued, gave them more legitimacy as American citizens, not less. Since everyone was from somewhere else, Americans would do well to em-brace heterogeneity at the same time that they recognized the longevity of black Americans' presence and contribution to the United States. As the bi-ological basis for racial connection that underpinned much of Garvey's program came under sustained and increasing scrutiny, his successors in the black public sphere found other means, cultural means, to forge an alli-ance with Africans, black people of the diaspora, and, ultimately, colonized peoples everywhere.

2

Discovering a Usable African Past

Newspapers worldwide ran the story with banner headlines: English archaeologist Howard Carter had had the find of his life. By candlelight, he peered into an Egyptian tomb in the Valley of the Kings, trailed by his financier, Lord Carnarvon, who asked if he saw anything. "Yes," replied Carter, "wonderful things."[1] Inside was a treasure of riches, including the gold mask and the mummy of a young pharaoh, Tutankhamen. The 1922 discovery turned Westerners' fascination with ancient Egypt into a mania that percolated through all forms of popular culture. In fashion, literature, architecture, and film, jeweled Egyptian motifs, pyramidal forms, and mummies swathed in bandages enraptured and spooked a generation of consumers. But just eight months after the tomb was cracked open, an unnamed contributor to a Harlem weekly newspaper noted something amiss. The print media, the writer observed, having closely followed the story, dropped it cold after the tomb's secrets were revealed. Why? The author asserted it was because whites could not afford to let the truth out: Tutankhamen was as black as "unbleached coal," and so was almost everybody around him.[2]

Debate about the race of the ancient Egyptians was heated then, as now, because many believed that the roots of modern civilization lay in the banks of the river Nile.[3] Even if modern forms of social organization, such as democracy, came through the polis of ancient Greece, their origins were thought to date from pharaonic Egypt. Discoveries such as Carter's were a boon to black Americans, who took at face value, as it were, depictions of the ancient Egyptians as dark-skinned and haired and claimed them as ancestors. Doing so enabled them to refute common perceptions that they were a people with no history. White supremacist ideology held that Africa was a land where nothing ever changed, and whose inhabitants were benighted until they were brought into the New World. Egypt's rising reputation helped to make a mockery of such beliefs, transforming them from science into racist superstition. If it could be proved that the supposed inferiority of black people in the past had at its base erroneous history, then the science of present-day racial hierarchy was also suspect.[4] A struggle over the meaning of the past therefore became central to interwar black politics and public culture.

Mainstream history in the 1920s served a growing public culture of memorialization that emerged as a result of a feeling that the nation was under siege from an influx of immigrants. The nationalist memory was homogenous, as though by agreeing on a set of shared traditions, Americans could smooth over the differences and disagreements provoked by the diversity of the populace. Following the Great War, too, a shared history could solidify American identity against the perceived decadence and ruin of Europeans. With the difficulties of the Depression, such tendencies only increased.[5] It is no coincidence that the phrase "a usable past" was coined in this era.[6] Replacing narratives of conflict in America's history with consensus, dominant accounts of the past either ignored, sidelined, or misrepresented black Americans' experiences. Slavery became a relatively benign institution, there for the benefit of underdeveloped "darkies," who were grateful for having been rescued from a godless land of swamps and disease: Africa.

Black activist historians took exception to such accounts of the past, posing a counternarrative that emphasized their contributions to the making of the United States and to world civilization. To be sure, a small clutch of black activist historians and bibliophiles had for some time been busy advancing challenges to accepted wisdom about Africa's eternal stagnation.[7] Likewise, certain groups had been at odds for decades over the history of slavery (especially Southern slavery) and the role of blacks in America's past.[8] But in the 1920s and 1930s, these efforts became central to black public life as activists countered dominant interpretations of history. Just about all black Americans, regardless of region, gender, class, and political affiliation, participated in the promulgation of these alternative historical accounts. Africa's past splendor was something of which to be proud, not ashamed, just as Americans were proud of the republican democracy they had built and defended.

The extensive focus on African history in black public life raised questions about the nature of the relationship between black Americans and Africans in the present day. For many activists, Africa's apparent decline since the majestic days of Tutankhamen's rule was evidence that Africans needed help to restore the continent to its former glory. A strain of neocolonial thought emerged in black nationalism and pan-Africanism. Black men and women in the United States, sometimes with colleagues in Europe, planned to assist Africa in progressing into the modern age. They met with fierce resistance from government officials in nations with African colonies and from American government departments, not least those in the Bureau of Investigation, who began investigating Marcus Garvey and others who advocated overthrow of white colonizers in Africa. Black neocolonialists in the United States also came in for criticism from left-wing activists, both black and white, and from some Africans themselves, who were no more interested in being under black control than under white rule.[9]

A more common approach than black neocolonialism when it came to imagining Africans in the here and now was to ignore them. History as popularly understood was a movement forward, a consistent march of progress, and Africans, suffering under colonial oppression, had no place in such accounts of time and change. Unlike the neocolonialists, who believed time moved in cycles, so that Africa would rise again, many black historian activists moved in their narratives straight from ancient Africa to the contributions enslaved Africans and their descendants had made to the building of the United States. American slavery was difficult, but slaves had survived it triumphantly and subsequent generations were continuing to rise up and up. In these historical accounts, the three hundred years since the 1619 arrival of the first African slaves at Jamestown became a middle passage of sorts, linking a glorious African past to an equally bright African American future.

Africa had no role to play in a version of history in which Americans trumpeted their success as the first truly democratic republic, as heirs to principles derived from ancient Greece. White Americans held themselves up—along with the British and their descendants in the empire and Commonwealth—as the creators of the world's most advanced civilization.

The progress of the United States contrasted sharply with the perceived stagnation of the African continent. In German philosopher G. W. F. Hegel's 1830 maxim, America was "the land of the future," while Africa was an ahistorical place, where time stood still and had no meaning.[10] Westerners' Hegelian ideas about African history remained unchanged into the next century. The *Encyclopedia Britannica* in print between 1911 and 1933 held that "Africa, with the exception of the lower Nile valley and what is known as Roman Africa, is as far as its native inhabitants are concerned a continent practically without a history and possessing no records from which such a history might be reconstructed."[11]

Two groups of white Americans who challenged the theory that Africa never changed were liberals and big game hunters. Concerned by the rapid transformations wrought by colonization, they hoped to preserve Africa's animal kingdom and for that matter, its people, going so far as to exhibit them in American natural history museums, zoos, and, increasingly, on film. Although the period of such exhibitions had passed by 1919, it was not that many years since Congolese Ota Benga was taken from Africa to be put on display at the St. Louis World's Fair in 1904, and subsequently exhibited in the Bronx Zoo in the same cage as a monkey. Benga could escape the constraints of white Americans' ideas about race only by committing suicide in 1916.[12] As late as the mid-1910s, gorillas and apes were dressed in costumes and provided with props in tableaux arranged to remind viewers of black minstrel shows, P. T. Barnum's circuses, and other popular entertainment.[13] Whether regarded as stagnant or as the victim of colonial intrusion, as far as most Westerners were concerned, Africa was a benighted land with an unknowable heart of darkness. Its people were backward, to be disdained or rescued, depending on one's politics, but not to be respected, let alone revered as having contributed anything to the world's development.

Africa's perceived torpidity was extended to black Americans. Just as Africans supposedly had nothing but their rich natural resources to offer the world, black Americans were good for nothing but hewing wood, drawing water, and, more recently, offering entertainment to their white fellow citizens. Africans had no place in world history, nor did black Americans hold a place of any significance in American history. It was this whitewashed account of the advance of civilization that Carter's discovery challenged and that black Americans aimed to overthrow. For some, doing so would prove their place in a nation whose citizens prided themselves on their role in the world's progress. These black Americans continued a tradition of messianic assimilationism that dated back to the nineteenth century.[14] As the years passed, however, more and more activists saw their illustrious African heritage as something akin to that of the imagined pasts of European immigrants and their children. As the "melting pot" slowly fell out of favor as a model for integrating immigrants into American society, and diversity gradually became something to celebrate, black Americans insisted that they, too, had a collective past of which they could be proud and that defined them as a group at once separate from others, but also a part of the American whole.

The first step in righting the wrongs of history was to show the role Africa had played in world development. For black Americans, the dark color of the Egyptians' skin was proof positive that the first civilization in the world was a black one. After Tutankhamen's tomb was uncovered, images of dark-skinned pharaohs abounded. A drawing of Tutankhamen by Aaron Douglas, one of the foremost artists of a cultural movement known as the New Negro Renaissance, adorned a 1926 cover of *Crisis,* published by the National Association for the Advancement of Colored People (NAACP). The following year, *Crisis* published a photograph of a 1450 B.C. bust of an unidentified Egyptian king.[15] Visual representations were the best way to ascertain someone's race; thus, the North Harlem Community Forum invited locals to learn the "truth" about the Egyptians at two illustrated lectures that Harlem residents could "not afford to miss." Tutankhamen's grandmother's race would be self-evident to those who attended because they would see "pictures of the black grandmother of the much-talked-about Egyptian Pharaoh."[16]

Denial in the white press that the king had dark skin confirmed a long-suspected conspiracy to conceal that modern civilization originated in black Africa. The *Negro World,* a Harlem newspaper published weekly by the Universal Negro Improvement Association (UNIA), penned an editorial on the matter. The world may never know the "truth" of the great king's race, it concluded, because "the excavation of his tomb is in the hands of British Europeans, like the white Americans who call nothing creditable Negroid if they can possibly find another name for it."[17] Here was a rare point on which black Americans of all political stripes could agree. A 1925

After Howard Carter's electrifying discovery of Tutankhamen's tomb, black Americans were quick to seize the pharaoh's dark visage as proof that their history was long and distinguished. (Aaron Douglas, "Mask of Tut-Ankh-Amen." By permission of the Crisis Publishing Co., Inc., the publisher of the magazine of the NAACP; image first published in the September 1926 issue of *The Crisis*.)

Crisis editorial exclaimed hyperbolically, "one of these days we are going to die of apoplexy superinduced by reading the latest explanations of the origin of the Egyptians." The editorial catalogued recent efforts of a white commentator to explain the pharaoh's dark skin as neither "Negro" nor "Negroid." The Egyptians' race, the *Crisis* concluded incredulously, was "*very* mysterious!" Similar claims were made, according to the editorial, about Ethiopians' racial identity, with readers invited to adjudicate for themselves by looking at the photos of Abyssinians published elsewhere in the issue.[18]

It is unsurprising that the paper of the nationalist UNIA claimed these dark-colored ancients as members of the "Negro race," and therefore as predecessors of present-day black Americans. In *Crisis,* however, it was more unexpected. Its editor, W. E. B. Du Bois, was a great champion of the work of anthropologist Franz Boas, who was busy discrediting the biological basis of race. Boas, a German Jew who had migrated to the United States in 1887, had more success than anyone before him in arguing that differences between human beings could be explained better by culture than by biology. Boas and Du Bois both promoted the idea that race was a category created by culture and historical circumstance. *Crisis* published articles on the ways race was defined and worked in other places, such as Brazil, in order to demonstrate the arbitrariness of racial designation.[19] Whereas the United States had a legal "one-drop rule" that decreed that anyone with any "black blood" was indeed a Negro, in other places different rules applied. Such inconsistency allowed Du Bois and others to criticize the science used to define a person's "race." Despite these earlier critiques of the biological nature of race, Du Bois sidelined this research in order to claim Tutankhamen as an ancestor, as if blackness in ancient Egypt meant the same as blackness in contemporary America. His decision to do so demonstrates how vital in the 1920s a history of glory and contribution to civilization was to black Americans. While recognizing that racial classification was contingent upon historical circumstances, black Americans were indignant at white America's willingness to disregard the "one-drop rule," which upheld segregation in the United States, when assessing this ancient civilization. Carter G. Woodson, founder of the Association for the Study of Negro Life and History (ASNLH), reminded readers sarcastically that if a "small percentage of Caucasian blood" made the Egyptians "white" in the opinion of biased Europeans, "then, there are no Negroes in the United States."[20]

Tutankhamen's tomb enabled black Americans to transform a heritage of which they had been ashamed into something quite the opposite. The archaeological discoveries in Egypt were reported widely in the presses of both black and white America, with black Americans across the land identifying

Mae Walker was the adopted daughter of A'Lelia Walker, heir to the fortune of hair-product entrepreneur Madam C. J. Walker. Her headdress was inspired by Egyptian treasures buried with Tutankhamen. (By permission of the Crisis Publishing Co., Inc., the publisher of the magazine of the NAACP; image first published in the January 1924 issue of *The Crisis*. Photograph courtesy of A'Lelia Bundles/Walker Family Collection/madamcjwalker.com.)

with the legacy and adopting their newly legitimized history in creative ways. A fraternal organization in Cleveland, Ohio, chose the moniker King Tut Lodge.[21] In New York, a wealthy socialite opted for a bejeweled bridal headdress of lustrous sea pearls inspired by treasures entombed with Tutankhamen.[22] Her bridesmaids each received a bracelet charm of a miniature enameled mummy inside a small sarcophagus that could open and close.[23] The eagerness with which black Americans grabbed hold of their newly unearthed African heritage reveals much about their marginalization from mainstream American life and their willingness to look beyond national borders for a collective identity of which they could be proud.

All took heart from the fact that while African civilization was in the ascendance, those in the West had been little more than barbarians. While one civilization was up, historians assured readers and listeners, another was down. "The black man, like the Aztec," said one popular history, "was civilized when the dominant branches of the Caucasian variety were savages."[24] According to NAACP executive secretary James Weldon Johnson, Africans reveled in a glorious civilization "while the progenitors of present-day Anglo-Saxons and Teutons and Slavs were hairy savages living in dark caves and crunching on raw bones; savages that had not yet the faintest glimmer of a knowledge either of religion or letters or government."[25] Just as African civilization had moved out of the sun and into the shade, so, too, would Western civilization eventually "fall," and Africa would rise again.

The idea that civilizations come and go, rise and fall, was popular among black Americans because it meant that they could rewrite not only the past but also imagine and hope for a better future, one different from that bound to emerge from dominant histories of the day. This future would be the denouement of their time in the wilderness, a time of deliverance from the trials of the New World. Those who heard the message hoped to live to witness the fulfillment of the biblical prophecy in Psalm 68:31: "Princes shall come out of Egypt; Ethiopia will stretch forth her hands unto God." Drawing heavily on Oswald Spengler's popular *The Decline of the West,* the first volume of which was translated into English in 1918, black historians foretold an end to Western civilization. A 1923 edition of the *New York Amsterdam News* reported on the work of an English professor who likened the downward trajectory of white civilization to that of the Roman Empire and, inevitably, to that of all civilizations. On this occasion, humility was in short supply; the editors' delight palpable in the article's headline: "White Civilization in Death Throes."[26]

If it were the way of the world for civilizations to rise and fall, it followed that there was no ignominy in the present-day eclipse of Africa's once-mighty society and culture. Johnson aimed to demonstrate that "the fact that dark ages fell upon Africa and her people is no more of a discredit than the fact that dark ages fell upon the buried empires of Asia Minor, of Asia, and of ancient Greece."[27] Woodson declared, "the fact [is] that there is nothing in the past of the Negro more shameful than what is found in the past of other races. . . . The Negro, like others, has been up at times; and at times he has been down."[28] With a frank tone striving for the impartiality the discipline of history demanded, these observers predicted, as did many modernists around them, the decline of the West. Racial inferiority could not account for Europe's domination of Africa; rather, the seesawing of civilizations up and down was just "the whirl of God's great wheel."[29]

Even artists and writers, who often probed their sense of individual disengagement from Africa, claimed proudly their collective inheritance as the world's founders of civilization. Harlem-based painter Malvin Gray Johnson, for instance, displayed in his work an ambivalence about the relationship between African Americans and their putative ancestors. He nevertheless painted *Negro Pharaoh—Eighteenth Dynasty* (1934), a study that was to form part of a series planned with colleague Earle Richardson entitled "Negro Achievement."[30] The painting's title alone indicated Johnson's belief about the race of ancient Egyptians and their relationship to modern-day black Americans. If centuries had lapsed since Johnson's forebears were forced from the African continent, and he no longer felt any innate connection to his African ancestors, at the very least he thought they, like him, were black and that they therefore shared something. Hoping to have the painting displayed in public as part of a large mural commissioned by the federally funded Works Progress Administration, Johnson made a clear statement about all black Americans' African heritage.

Visual artists were particularly interested in the creative legacy ancient Egypt left them. In a six-panel painting, Richardson, or possibly Johnson, traced the development of "Art, Music, Literature" each from ancient Egypt to present-day America.[31] Fellow artist Loïs Mailou Jones, in her 1932 painting *The Ascent of Ethiopia*, suggested that pharaohs and pyramids—metonyms for ancient African culture—undergirded the artistic achievements of contemporary black Americans in art, music, and drama. Her painting argued further that American life in general had grown out of the soil of those earlier achievements. At the top of a hill, representing time's forward movement, perched two skyscrapers, icons of modernity. The building closer to the foreground, with its near-triangular shape, rising from a point underground, echoed the shape of the pyramids at the foot of

Black American life, and American life in general, here represented by the skyscrapers, owed much to its foundation in black Africa. (Loïs Mailou Jones, *The Ascent of Ethiopia*, 1932. Courtesy Milwaukee Art Museum and Loïs Mailou Jones Pierre-Noël Trust.)

the rise. Jones depicted visually the assertion that modern Western civilization had its roots in ancient, black, Egypt. By implication, the United States owed a debt to black people of the past, which could be paid by righting the country's treatment of its own black citizens, the descendants of those mighty Egyptians.

Tutankhamen's reign was only the most spectacular of manifold achievements of the ancient black races. A list of other "firsts" became something of a litany in black activism of the era. In a 1923 speech, James Weldon Johnson outlined these firsts: "in the misty ages of the past, pure black men in Africa were observing the stars, were turning human speech into song, were discovering religious truths and laying the foundations of government, were utilizing the metals, developing agriculture and inventing the primitive tools; in fact, giving the impulse which started man on his upward climb."[32] Iron smelting, sculpture, oratory, regal systems of government, and the great library at Timbuktu were the most commonly cited examples of ancient Africans' pioneering spirit and aptitude for invention. These achievements were not the political preserve of black nationalists; on the contrary, they were a staple of interwar black activism. The white educational director of the Commission on Interracial Cooperation, Robert Eleazer, used just such a list to rewrite American history (not just black history). "Did these slaves come to America empty-handed, or did they bring some heritage of native endowment and skill, and even of civilization?" he asked. "For answer we must look to their African background and to their early record in America." There Eleazer found an inventory of attainments: ironwork and blacksmithing; artisan crafts, such as weaving, pottery, and carpentry; and "a fund of folklore and a distinct gift for music." The intellectual legacy was evident in the eighteenth-century poetry of African-born enslaved woman Phillis Wheatley.[33] Clearly, Americans owed much to their black citizens, from whose ancestors these treasures derived.

Righting the account of Africa's past was a clear refutation of the assertion that black people were worthless and savage until brought into the light by the slave trade. As Johnson said in his 1923 speech: "Makers of history have taught the world that from the beginning of time the Negro has never been anything but a race of savages and slaves." By contrast, he asserted, anyone "willing to dig out the truth can learn that civilization was born in the upper valley of the River Nile."[34] According to dominant historical accounts among whites, black Americans' history began with the seventeenth-century landing of slaves in Virginia. Without a deep-rooted history, black Americans owed their existence—insofar as individual and collective identity was dependent on understandings of ancestry and the past—to their captors and enslavers in the New World. Yet the achievements of Africans revealed that black Americans were not inferior to other races. Rather, they were descended from a proud and royal line. By undermining the pseudo-historical basis for their unequal treatment in the United States, they argued further that it was about time their status as American citizens be recognized.

Americans of African descent enjoyed learning that not only did they have a vast and rich heritage to celebrate, but also that white Americans' grip on the past was dubious. Many black Americans were pleased to find that long before Columbus sailed to the New World, West Africans had "discovered" North America. They celebrated the publication of Leo Wiener's three-volume *Africa and the Discovery of America* (1920–1922), which claimed African precedence in the discovery of the Americas on the basis of etymological research and histories of agriculture and consumption, especially of tobacco.[35] The book was reviewed widely and mentioned repeatedly in the black press, magazines, and subsequent histories. Wiener, a Harvard professor of Slavic languages and literature, was invited to speak at the twenty-fifth annual meeting of the American Negro Academy alongside Alain Locke and Arthur Schomburg, two black intellectuals devoted to the study of African history, and Duse Mohamed Ali, an Egyptian-born writer and activist visiting from London, who lectured on "the Necessity of a Chair in Negro History in Our Colleges."[36] Wiener's research had a long-lasting impact on black Americans' creation of a usable past.

Subverting the myth of America's national origins required black Americans to hijack for themselves the esteem in which the English pilgrims were held. Like black Americans, immigrant groups insisted that they were the first founders of the United States. A medal sold as a souvenir at a four-day celebration of one hundred years of Norwegian American life featured a picture of a Viking immigrant flanked by the dates 1825 and 1925. The medal's reverse side featured a Viking ship and the date A.D. 1000, the year that Lief Erikson allegedly discovered America. At the same time that the medal commemorated one hundred years of Norwegian immigrant life, it challenged dominant accounts of American history by suggesting that Columbus's discovery of the New World was preempted by Norwegians by some five hundred years. In the words of one participant, this history demonstrated "'that men of Norse blood have those qualities that make for desirable American citizenship and that the earlier Norse immigrants not only conformed to American standards and ideals but were among the very people who created them."[37] Both Norwegian Americans and black Americans used similar evidence in their quest to define themselves as members of distinguished groups, whose earlier members displayed the kind of ingenuity and courage Americans had come to value as national characteristics.

Wiener's findings appealed particularly because of the way he portrayed black men. Although ancient Africa itself was often personified by black historians as a woman, sometimes named Ethiopia, "her" inhabitants were most often thought to be male. Men's achievements were celebrated, as were their characteristics, especially ingenuity, courage, strength, and commitment to family and tribe. Such attributes were quite the opposite of those commonly attached to black American men. Stereotypes portrayed them as lazy and shiftless, comic and harmless, cunning and untrustworthy. Wiener's history was especially welcome because the Harvard professor—who could not be accused of racial bias as was often the case for black historians—gave black Americans an alternative history of the ocean-crossing from Africa to America. Africans in Wiener's history were bold seafaring discoverers, as fearless and brave as any celebrated European adventurers. Moreover, they predated the European "discoverers" of America and influenced markedly the culture of the native inhabitants. Lorenzo Greene, for example, "took issue with the current theory that the Negro has always lacked pioneering spirit, by pointing out that recent investigation has shown that Negroes actually visited America long before Columbus."[38] This heroic history provided a pleasing antidote to the emasculating, shackled horror of the slave ship voyage.

There could be no more better demonstration of strength, courage, and determination than in traveling and conquering peoples and unknown territories, in crossing oceans and penetrating lost interiors. Black imperial conquerors were now heroes. Under the headline "Color No Handicap"—a pointed comment on American race relations—a weekly Harlem newspaper printed a series of excerpts from *World's Greatest Men of African Descent* (1931) by J. A. Rogers. Born in Jamaica, Rogers migrated to the United States in 1906, worked as a Pullman train porter, became a journalist in the 1920s and a foreign and war correspondent in the 1930s. All the while, he wrote histories bringing to light black heroes of the past. Continuing the Egyptian theme, one excerpt profiled Thotmes III, who "built the first real empire and is thus the first character possessed of universal aspects, the first world hero."[39] Around the same time, in another journal, Rogers recalled with pleasure the martial successes of other black warriors such as Hannibal; Massinissa, king of Numidia; and "Metinus, the mulatto."[40] By rewriting the past to focus on black heroes, black men in the present day were, in the words of the usually satirical writer George Schuyler, rendering "history not only closer to their hearts' desire but also closer to the facts."[41]

Powerful men of history—black conquerors, emperors, explorers, servicemen—discredited the damaging stereotype that black American men were physically weak, pathetic, and/or comedic. According to some, black American men's present weakness was a result of enslavement and emasculation. "The black man," reported one newspaper article, "judged by four thousand years of recorded history, is the greatest fighting machine on earth. The pitiful weakness of the few American Negroes here, after two hundred and fifty years, has fooled white observers into thinking they know the blacks. Just as they are heedless of the past greatness of our race," the story warned, "so they do not know our fighting strain."[42] Virility and physical strength were the hallmarks of black masculinity, and the weakness of modern black American men was evidence only of the corrupting influence of slavery and subsequent race relations. A 1920 cover of *Crusader,* a radical black magazine, featured a spear-clutching African warrior flanked by crests bearing images of the pyramids and the sphinx. The warrior provided the connection between the journal's content—radical and modern—and the classical African (Egyptian) civilization.[43] With the emergence of the New Negro, a North American equivalent of a martial African persona was born, creating a link between past and present.

Black Americans took heart from this revised history, especially when it was given the kind of legitimacy that someone of Wiener's stature in the profession could offer. Members of the Boston branch of the UNIA met on Sunday afternoons at their local Liberty Hall (the name, too, of the UNIA headquarters in Harlem) to distribute, read, and discuss the *Negro World* and *Journal of Negro History.* With membership swelling, George Weston, who would in 1926 lead the New York division that broke with Garvey, recalled:

> One Sunday we read, in the *Boston Sunday Globe*, that Prof. Leo Weiner, an archeologist and anthropol[o]gist of Harvard University, wrote a featured article after his return from Mexico where he did excavation and research and said that American History had to be re-written in order to [be] correct. . . . He stated that the Africans had crossed the bulge of South America and entered in what is known as the United States of America today, 10,000 years before Columbus was born and that they brought the potato, the peanut plant and tobacco from Africa and taught the Indians the use of these things. Rev. Scott wrote a letter commending him upon his audacity for bringing the truth to light, at a time when the [Ku] Klux Klan and the 100% American were riding high in intimidating, lynching and heaping all kinds of insults and harassments upon the black people of America. The following Sunday he read a short letter from Prof. Weiner thanking him for his appreciation. He said in addition that true science knows no question of race and bigotry. True science deals with truth and truth alone.[44]

For Weston and his contemporaries, there was a direct link between, on the one hand, the violence of the Ku Klux Klan and the abeyance of civil rights and, on the other, the denigration of black Americans as part of an inferior black race. Between these lay the chasm that black Americans hoped to bridge by proving their inferiority was unfounded. Wiener's research enabled black Americans to entwine two strands of histories: the contributions made to world culture by their African forebears and those made by Africans and black Americans to the building of the United States. If only all Americans could be made to appreciate the role played by black people in world civilization and national development, then they would see that the whitewashing of American history (and citizenship) was not only grossly unfair but also counterproductive. Only by recognizing the diversity of the origins and experiences of its inhabitants could the American nation live up to its potential, enshrined in its founding documents.

Black activists did not just challenge whites' conception of the past; they actively challenged contemporary historical practices. Just as the Egyptian pharaoh's tomb had to be unearthed, so would black activists dig for the truth, long buried by whites in the West. Some regarded the erasure of blacks' contributions in the past as a tacit process. Carter Woodson argued that in omitting the African influence in the "Mediterranean Melting Pot" of ancient Greece, teachers were guided by their unconscious; they were guilty of "making desire father to the thought."[45] Garvey extended Woodson's argument about the unconscious to the collective, arguing that races do naturally that which benefits them most. History making was no exception; the stories told about the past were for Garvey a product of a collective unconscious will to power.[46] It was entirely natural, in his view, that individuals writing their own history would be influenced by their race and, depending on where they were from, by their national affiliation. Most black Americans, however, saw the erasure of their ancient ancestry as a deliberate process, part of the institutionalized racism of enslavement and the segregation that followed. Bishop Reverdy Ransom of the African Methodist Episcopal Church was appalled by efforts to advance the theory that the ancient Egyptians were white. "The white man has tried in every way to rob us of Egypt," he wrote, "because she is the mother of his modern civilization."[47] Lorenzo Greene, assistant to Woodson at the ASNLH, accused whites of deliberately tampering with the evidence, suppressing willfully the history of black civilization. Their aim, he surmised, was to undermine the significance of Africa's past, to psychologically weaken black men and women. This history, he said, was "calculated to demean and to debase the Negro not only in the eyes of the world, but of the Negro himself." In a rallying call, he concluded that this "made the study and circulation of the real facts of Negro history imperative."[48]

Still others made an explicit critique of the relatively new academic discipline of history, which they regarded as steeped in bogus racial science. They went back to the evidence of the ancients, citing frequently Herodotus's mention of the Egyptians as "black and curly-haired," thereby laying claim to a prior, more correct version of history before scientific racism "colored" the lens.[49] As the protagonist in J.A. Rogers's perennially popular *From "Superman" to Man* said to an unbelieving senator, Herodotus was "an eye-witness" to Egyptian physiognomy.[50] (Rogers's short book was published in 1917, serialized by the *New York Amsterdam News* in 1923, and released in its fourth edition by 1924, its fifth edition in 1941, and in several editions since then, thus demonstrating the commitment of black Americans to new accounts of the past.) The "young" version of history, a nineteenth-century academic invention, was naive enough to be duped by contemporary prejudices, whereas the "old" version was a venerable tradition, based on visual evidence, that was being ill-served by contemporary research.

In one of an engagingly blithe series of articles published in the *Amsterdam News* by an anonymous member of the Hamitic League, an Afrocentric organization, the author told the story of "Old King Toot," whose tomb was opened earlier that year. The writer wanted history retold, this time frankly:

> Toot was the color of unbleached coal. . . . Let the truth come out. It won't hurt anybody. It may give a gentle jolt to history but the old girl can stand it. She has stood worse than that in her sweet young life. In fact, things may seem a little more homelike—maybe. She knows that when it comes to claiming a place in the sun, old Africa staked the first home-site.

The author suggested that history could cope with being rewritten, concluding that it was no longer possible to ignore the wonders of the African past: "the time is here. Africa is holding a royal flush." Tutankhamen's tomb busted open, according to this author, the fiction perpetuated by the "Kliques and Klans . . . that the Negro never was anything, isn't anything now and never will be anything."[51] By disproving the first of these negatives, it followed that the present and future could no longer be shaped by false racial hierarchies.

Black Americans' experience of having their historical record warped by those who sought to oppress them was just one of a number of similarities they bore to those colonized in other parts of the world, including Africa. Colonialism, as Martinican psychiatrist Frantz Fanon observed in 1961, "is not satisfied merely with holding a people in its grip and emptying the native's brain of all form and content. By a kind of perverted logic, it turns to the past of the oppressed people, and distorts, disfigures, and destroys it." But the colonized resisted attempts to dominate them mentally. According to Fanon, rebellious efforts were concentrated on the rehabilitation of a collective culture, which would provide "hope of a future national culture."[52] Fanon's analysis, drawn from Martinique and Algeria in the 1950s and 1960s, could well have been about interwar black American history making. Black Americans refashioned the past in order to change the present and to reimagine the future.

For those subjugated in colonized Africa and in the United States, remaking black history required the imposition of a coherent "black" identity onto people in the past to whom such a category would have made no sense. In the colonial context, "national" rehabilitation referred to the entire continent of Africa, because redefined tribal and ethnic boundaries made more specific remembrance either impossible or politically unhelpful.[53] In the United States, dislocation resulting from the slave trade meant that very few black Americans could trace their origins to a specific place. While slaveholders, and of course slaves themselves, may have maintained some differentiation, such distinctions were lost by the third and fourth decades of the twentieth century. Despite this homogenizing of past differences, by identifying with Africa, black Americans rebutted the usual designation "Negro." This "Negro," as political scientist Cedric Robinson pointed out, "was both a negation of African and a unity of opposition to white. . . . [The term] suggested no situatedness in time, that is history, or space, that is ethno- or politico-geography. The Negro had no civilization, no cultures, no religions, no history, no place, and finally no humanity that might command consideration."[54] In terms of nomenclature, "black" was slowly gaining precedence over "Negro." More importantly, a sense of connection to Africans, and, increasingly, to black and colonized people worldwide, enabled black Americans to reorient their consciousness away from something defined by the American experience of enslavement and its aftermath, to something that both insisted America was their home as well as acknowledging with pride that their roots were elsewhere. Furthermore, the shared experience of displacement meant that while they were American, they felt an affinity with people beyond the borders of the United States.

Insisting with such force and consistency that they had inherited a marvelous history from ancient black Africa raised an implicit question about black Americans' relationship to Africans in the present day. While a sense of kinship with other colonized people was slowly taking shape, nevertheless much of the history making of the immediate postwar years focused on African wonders and took little note of the experiences of colonized Africans. Contemporary Africans rarely appeared in new histories acknowledging African origins because colonized peoples were assumed to have little to offer to a celebration of black achievement. The effect of paying scant attention to Africans in the here and now was to imagine an Africa locked in the past and needing assistance to be dragged up into the present.

Black nationalists in particular took it upon themselves to rescue Africa from the slumber in which she seemed to languish. Marcus Garvey agreed with Johnson and others that civilizations proceed in cycles, that Africa's time would come again—"bottom rail top this time" to use an expression slaves favored in their visions of the future—but he suggested that Africa would need a nudge along.[55] In speeches and writing, Garvey developed memorable images of white men living in forests and caves, their faces painted blue, as civilization flourished in Africa. He reversed the usual signifiers of race to claim that Africans had enjoyed a wondrous civilization by the waters of the Nile, while whites engaged in cannibalism.[56] As early as 1913, he asked, "would Caesar have believed that the country that he was invading in 55 B.C. would be the seat of the greatest Empire of the World?" He reckoned that the fortune of subjected peoples would change "as surely as there is evolution in the natural growth of man and nation."[57] Though the model of cycles of civilization did not follow directly from Darwin's ideas of evolution, Garvey nonetheless hitched his view of change to the wagon of these dominant ideas, in order to assert that Africa's rise was as certain, and as determined, as the processes of natural selection and progress. All Africa required, according to Garvey, was help in being awakened to her destiny. Black Americans had to provide the alarm clock.

Rhetoric regarding the restoration of Africa's greatness had implications best described as neocolonial. Garvey regarded slavery as providential, that is, God's intention was to provoke former slaves to return to Africa to spread the Christian gospel. Assuming black Americans were the inheritors of the rich African past, Garvey proclaimed that they, rather than Africans themselves, should be the leaders of a rescued civilization. Three

hundred years of slavery was a reasonable price, he said in 1924, for a marvelous eternity beginning with the "return to Africa and [the restoration
of] the ancient glories of Alexandria and Timbuctoo."[58] Combined with his
general doctrine of self-help, he argued that black men could help themselves to a preordained fate only if they acted now. From 1913 until his
death, he exhorted his readers to remember that "continents are yours, nations are yours, all civilization will be yours when you make up your mind to
possess them."[59] Although many black Americans disagreed with Garvey
that it was their destiny to return to Africa and lead the world from there,
the combination of his voice with so many others with whom he had such
public disagreements made a convincing case for the revision of African
history. All black Americans would at least take great pleasure in the continent's redemption, not least because it would mean defeating Africa's white
overlords.

Many black Americans did share Garvey's assumption that Africa would
need assistance to renew "her" greatness. Aiming to reverse Africa's decline,
their statements were so imbued with presumptions about the helplessness
of Africans that they sometimes sounded like Africa's colonial masters.
These activists believed that the role currently played by white Westerners
in Africa would be better occupied by black people returning from the New
World. One *New York Age* contributor encouraged exploration of the African continent by black men from the New World, who would then enlighten
the world as to Africa's true delights.[60] Another writer in the same newspaper, John Haughton, similarly overlooked Africans themselves as he mapped
out the continent's future. He suggested that "a commission composed of
black men . . . be appointed to see that fifty per cent of the annual yield of
Africa be spent to develop, civilize, educate, and to provide better conditions for the people of Africa. We must take hold of this task ourselves if
Africa is to be brought to a recognized standard of civilization, and if we
desire that the resources of Africa should be spent for the actual uplift of the
people." In imagining black Americans as nurturers and administrators in
Africa, Haughton envisioned a future in which, under the guidance of its
New World descendants, Africa's past glories would be reignited. He concluded: "It is our duty to occupy Africa. The time has come: if we are looking forward to a great and prosperous future for ourselves. I invite your attention across the Atlantic ocean. Africa must be considered! The future is

both dark and bright for us."[61] Haughton's proposal radically redistributed the wealth produced by Africa's natural resources, but even still, foreigners were to oversee the continent, and only fifty percent of those revenues were to be reinvested there.

The future emerging from steadfast efforts to reimagine Africa's past had at its helm African-descended black men from the New World; in the early interwar years, such sentiments were not confined to black nationalists. A 1919 meeting of black Americans and black colonial subjects from around the world, called the Pan-African Congress, came to similar conclusions. Fifty-seven delegates convened in France to lobby on Africa's behalf at the Paris Peace Conference. Only twelve of the representatives came from nine African colonies. Du Bois was the most vocal of the English-speaking participants. His counterparts included Blaise Diagne, a Senegalese representative with a significant position in the French government. Garvey and others hoped to attend but were refused passports by the United States government.[62] Those denied exit included Madam C. J. Walker, a hair-product millionaire and president of the short-lived International League of Darker Peoples. She hoped to establish a college of vocational training in Africa, modeled on Alabama's Tuskegee Institute.[63] At the meeting, as at the peace conference, national self-determination was the hottest topic. In the final resolutions, however, the Pan-African Congress called for a period of trusteeship for the former African colonies, under the guardianship of diaspora Africans.[64] On the face of it, the statement was neocolonial, echoing the language of childishness and development that was used to justify European colonization of Africa and elsewhere. Thus such activists both confirmed and subverted the ideas that dominated the peace conference. Neocolonial attitudes concurred with the prevailing sense that the races of Africa and Asia could not fend for themselves, and yet rejected the assertion that black Americans, whom Woodrow Wilson had deemed irrelevant to the discussions of the official conference, could not perform the duties of nationhood. These duties included the burden of caring for the underdeveloped.[65]

In the very early postwar period, the only sustained criticism of black neocolonialism within the United States came from those on the left, both black and white. The socialist magazine the *Messenger*, edited by Chandler Owen and A. Philip Randolph, reprinted a 1920 article from the *New York*

Call denouncing the recent flurry of calls to recolonize Africa with black men. The article declared: "Capitalism dominated by Negroes is the same as capitalism dominated by whites."[66] *Crusader* magazine condemned the resolutions of the Pan-African Congress, writing that the "entire continent of Africa is seething with dissatisfaction of alien rule."[67] Such critics rejected also the romantic racialism of the act of looking to the past in order to remake the present and future. A 1919 *Messenger* article entitled "The New Philosophy of the New Negro" catalogued the fields of study in which "he" was interested. The list was extensive, including almost all fields other than history, a pointed omission for the time.[68] In a review of Du Bois's *Darkwater*, William Colson, a *Messenger* contributing editor, stated categorically that "we care little about where the Negro came from or what he brought. What we want to know is where he is going, and by what way."[69] By disavowing the study of history, the *Messenger* rejected prevailing models of black historiography, which exhibited an implicit faith in progress.[70] It was not that the contributors to the *Messenger* did not hope for a better future. Rather, their utopian vision was one in which workers, together and irrespective of race, revolted against capitalist exploitation and thereby established a fair and just society. The twentieth century's problem, according to Colson, was not the color line, as Du Bois had memorably said at the beginning of the century, but rather "the distribution of wealth and knowledge."[71] The "New Negro" that the *Messenger* championed was not a warrior so much as a worker, or perhaps even a union organizer, who was certain that class difference was fundamental and that racial pride was false consciousness. He believed the last thing Africa needed was a black empire and recognized that a despot was a despot, whether black or white.[72]

Not unexpectedly, 1920s black neocolonialism was criticized by European colonial powers who were intent on guarding their African territories.[73] It also sparked the interest of the Bureau of Investigation, and intelligence organizations in other countries, which kept close tabs on Garvey and took special note of any attempt by black Americans to connect to Africans.[74] Further critique of this imagined African future came from Africans themselves. Garvey's message, according to one report, had been spread by drum communication the length and breadth of the continent, and yet, Africans had no interest in replacing one colonial regime with another.[75] In various places on the continent, Africans heard of Garvey and bent his message to their own ends. They did not foresee him becoming the president of a United States of Africa. Instead, they adapted him as befitted their local dreams of freedom. For instance, in South Africa, Garvey's "Back to Africa" campaign cohered well with long-held local beliefs that the residents' ancestors would one day return to claim the land. It coincided, too, with more recent hopes that technically advanced black Americans would return to help liberate Africa from colonialism.[76] In the layers of black Americans' imagined future, Africans found for themselves spaces to resist their own colonial masters.

As time went on, many black people in the United States distanced themselves from earlier efforts to establish a means to lift up Africans to be on par with the rest of the world. The socialist critique offered by the *Messenger* and others came to the fore in activist circles, especially in the 1930s as black Americans forged links with oppressed people around the diaspora, and beyond, more on the basis of a shared experience of subjugation in general, rather than of racism specifically. Du Bois, for one, published *Black Reconstruction* (1935), one of many books whose authors made up a group of left-thinking intellectuals on both sides of the Atlantic. Their coupling of a pan-African vision with a rejection of capitalism was more egalitarian than the romantic histories of a heroic African past, which tended to ignore the experiences of ordinary African people, past and present, who were assumed to have little to offer to a celebration of black achievement.[77] In the 1930s, histories focusing on the glories of Africa's past began to fall away, to be replaced by histories of Africa in more recent times and by social science studies of contemporary Africa and Africans.

Many black Americans rejoiced in the knowledge of their forgotten history because it provided them with potent ammunition in the fight for better conditions in the United States. Even those who would have liked to leave for Africa had little chance of emigrating, so in the meantime, they used black history to prove they were as eligible as the next American for the full rights and responsibilities of citizenship. The Fourteenth Amendment had secured nominal citizenship for black Americans in 1868, but as activist historian Carter Woodson averred in 1921: "the citizenship of the Negro in this country is a fiction."[78] Du Bois agreed. In his words, black Americans were "a nation without a polity, nationals without citizenship."[79] Yet because black Americans were direct descendants of people who built the world's first civilization and of those whose sacrifice—in labor, war, and other fields—contributed to the nation's well-being, then clearly they were excellent candidates for inclusion in the American body politic.

Aiming to retool the conditions of entry to the category "American," black activists remade American history as well as African history. As the bibliophile and writer Arthur Schomburg said, there were. ample "materials not only for the first true writing of Negro history, but for the rewriting of many important paragraphs of our common American history."[80] Leo Wiener's research argued that the nation's founding moment was its discovery not by Columbus but by ocean-crossing Africans. Commonly held assumptions as to the very origins of the United States, the question of its native inhabitants left aside, were suspect. Black people's efforts had likewise made the nation what it was by the 1920s and 1930s. Their contributions were evident in a 1923 pageant, which, as the *New York Amsterdam News* reported, "artistically depict[ed] the progress of the race: first, exhibiting ancestral idol worship in Africa and proceeding to American citizenship and participation in the World War."[81] It was no coincidence that these two events bookended the pageant's action; many black Americans argued that one led to the other. The contribution made to civilization by ancient Africans paved the way for those made by their descendants in the United States. It was from a sophisticated civilization in Africa, whose members invented religion, language, science, and all the basics of modern societies, that black Americans had been unjustly ripped. Despite hardship, they similarly contributed to their new environment, making of it something with the potential to be equally grand. All that was left before the United States could reach the heights of ancient African civilization was for all Americans to be allowed to enjoy the privileges, rights, and responsibilities of citizenship.

Gifts given to America by its enslaved African and free black populations became a dominant theme of black history and culture in the interwar years. For many, the generosity of black Americans giving so much to a country that gave them so little in return was itself inherited from the selfless motherland, Africa.[82] This was a theme Du Bois worked on often. In a

short story, published in a 1925 special "Harlem" issue of *Survey Graphic,*
"The Black Man Brings His Gifts," Du Bois none too gently poked fun at
Americans' ignorance about the origins of their national life. In the tale,
members of a Southern committee who convened to organize an "America's
Making" pageant in their town were shocked to discover that all the achievements they would like to celebrate had roots in black culture.[83] Gift giving
became one of the themes of the most well-known publications of the cultural movement now known as the Harlem Renaissance. Titled *The New
Negro* (1925) and growing out of the Harlem number of *Survey Graphic,* it
suggested that not only music and dance, but labor, defense, and techno-
logical innovation were among the major contributions black people had
made to America's development.[84]

Given the disappointment most black Americans felt at the poor treatment meted out to soldiers returning from the war in Europe, it is not surprising that activists focused a great deal of attention on the "gift" of military
service. In modern nations as in ancient polities, men's sacrifices in battle
demonstrated their fitness for citizenship, in ways that women, whatever
their wartime roles, simply could never prove. Therefore, those black Americans who had committed themselves to a future in the United States not
only commemorated African military heroes but also paid special attention
to their descendants. Countless short histories, newspaper editorials, and
cultural products of all types memorialized the achievements of Toussaint
Louverture and his Haitian contemporaries, who overthrew European colonizers at the dawn of the nineteenth century to create the second republic in
the Western Hemisphere. Black American descendants continued the tradition of fighting for what was right, performing gallantly in all wars dating
back to the Revolution. Black men could be formidable warrior soldiers.
This topic enticed even black author and newspaper columnist George
Schuyler, who normally enjoyed skewering any statement that smacked of
racial romanticism. Schuyler wrote that when a black man "is told that he
submitted supinely to chattel slavery, he but points to the more than thirty
insurrections and conspiracies of slaves up to the Civil War and the perilous
flight of thousands of his ancestors to freedom in Canada, Spanish Florida,
the wild West, the Caribbean islands, and Suriname." Schuyler listed seven
historical military leaders by name, concluding with the "deeds of Negro
soldiers and sailors in every American war from colonial days to the World

War."[85] Such commemoration served two purposes, both to prove beyond doubt the eligibility of black Americans for full citizenship in the United States and to show their allegiance to a black world beyond the borders of their country.

An excellent opportunity to demonstrate the contributions made to both world and American civilization arose when in 1921 the NAACP got wind of a forthcoming two-week "America's Making" festival to be held in New York. Executive members campaigned hard to ensure that black Americans were represented alongside more recent immigrant groups. Organized under the auspices of the state and city education boards, the festival aimed:

> To show in popular form, by means of exhibits and pageantry, the most important historical, economic and cultural contributions that Americans of various descent, from the original Colonists down to the present, have made to the American nation. Thereby to give each group a fuller sense of appreciation of its own share in the nation's up-building, promote still closer American union, and point the way by which we may further enrich our national life.[86]

Typical in interwar public historical culture, the exhibits and pageants minimized conflict, past and present, between the various groups who made up the American populace. At the same time, organizers wished to show the role of various immigrant groups in developing the nation. Even this was not without its threat to those who, like one N. Devereau Putnam, "believe[d] in the maintenance of our fundamentally Anglo-Saxon civilization." He called for particular attention to be paid in the pageant to the English heritage of the United States, lest the "predominating part that England had in shaping our destinies" be inadequately portrayed.[87] Members of the Negro Committee were determined to ensure that the contributions made by black folk were given due recognition. A document they prepared noted that "we have been so overfed with publicity on 'Americanization' that we have almost forgotten how this America whose ideals the immigrant is to grasp came into being. To many, it seems that like Topsy [America] just grew and then set up the standards by which all the citizens of the world should be measured."[88] The festival aimed to right this misconception.

The very basis of the set for the Negro section of the exhibit and pageant demonstrated the extent to which black Americans were now embracing their African heritage. An Egyptian pyramid was divided horizontally into seven areas of differing widths. On two sides were images of the Sphinx. Upon the pyramid were inscriptions of the major categories of achievements and contributions black people had made to colonial America and the United States. Intended to portray "The Seven Gifts of Ethiopia to America," the bands of the pyramid represented, from bottom up: exploration, labor, self-supporting womanhood, the emancipation of democracy, defense, literature, and music. Labor and music were the two largest, while literature, exploration, and self-supporting womanhood occupied small spaces.

Music, especially jazz, was often held up by activists as the only original art form given to the world by Americans, and activists proudly pointed to the fact that jazz was a black cultural form, with roots in Africa.[89] Each of the seven "gifts" was scripted with reference to accompanying music, starting with "The African tom-tom" for exploration, then the "War Dance" to be played during the section about labor. The third band of the pyramid was enacted to the strains of "Primitive Slave Song"; next came the "Triumphant Negro Melody" and the "Developed Folk Song." Finally, "The New Negro Music," represented by Nathaniel Dett's "Listen to the Lambs" (sung by the children), accompanied literature. The choices implied an evolution of music from Africa through to the 1920s in America, and yet Samuel Coleridge-Taylor's "Bamboula" accompanied the war dance. This choice demonstrated an acknowledgment that Coleridge-Taylor, a celebrated black British composer, had folded back into his own compositions those which he thought were African musical themes. And in the pageant's final scene, Coleridge-Taylor's "Onaway" was played while the American children were joined on stage by the Ethiopians and Egyptians (black American children) from earlier scenes, who emerged from the pyramid as it was lit. While the choice of music seemed "developmental"—from African to American—the pageant simultaneously confounded any simple notion of black American heritage that drew a straight line from Africa to America. Rather than mixing into a single, homogenous melting pot, the children retained some of their African origins, and continued to mix their culture with people in the diaspora, in this case, from England. Joining hands with those black children representing America, together the pageant's actors confounded any simple idea that the United States was monocultural.

The inclusion of girls as well as boys in the America's Making pageant was also more typical of the histories of contribution that extended into the United States, as opposed to those more squarely focused on Africa. Men took the starring roles in histories of Africa, excepting mothers and queens, but when it came to cataloguing the contributions made to the budding United States, women, too, took to the stage. Carter Woodson's *Journal of Negro History*, begun in 1916, featured history writing by and about women far more often than any other history publication of the era.[90] The most sustained account of the various achievements of women came in a pageant published by Woodson's publishing house and written by Kentucky-born Frances Gunner, who worked at the Brooklyn YWCA in the 1920s. In "The Light of the Women," Queen Ethiopia and the Spirit of Service were joined on stage by a Slave Mother and seven named historical figures, including Sojourner Truth, Harriet Tubman, and Phillis Wheatley. Contemporary figures included the Mother, the Teacher, the Minister, the Doctor, the Nurse, the Student, and War Workers.[91] If it was difficult for black men to find characters in mainstream history whose achievements they could celebrate, Gunner argued that it was harder for women still. She wrote the pageant because "Negro women know nothing of those of their sex who have achieved so much as heroines."[92] Women, too, were becoming African American through the rewriting of history, but finding female heroes of the same gender in the African past was a little more difficult for them.

Black counterhistory challenged profoundly the discipline of history—and the past as most Americans understood it—by relocating its supposed origin to Africa.[93] As Harlem writer J. A. Rogers in 1930 attested bluntly, "Grecian civilization was almost a direct fruit of Egyptian culture, which was Negroid."[94] Not only did modern civilization start in Africa, these activists argued, but the beginning of life itself was located there. New scientific theories about evolution meant that polygenesis—the belief that humans were descended from several, racially distinct, individuals—was on the wane. Even liberal monogenists, however, were alarmed to learn that they, too, were descended from the first human being in Africa.[95] Histories of black contribution to civilization unsettled and decentered Western historical narratives.

It was a substantial feat, given the era and circumstances, to insist on the inclusion of an African dimension within black American identity and, in turn, within American identity. This was a time of tightening strictures on the way people were supposed to feel about themselves as Americans. Heavy immigration inspired the hope that all newcomers could be made to resemble a mythical and idealized "American," a process represented by their metaphorical immersion into the "melting pot." Nativist agitation for a homogenous population resulted, in 1924, in the end of relatively unmonitored immigration. In the same year, following the lead of other states, Virginia formalized the "one-drop rule," determining that anyone with black "blood" was Negro. The dictates of race and racism by this time rendered European émigrés as white and assimilable, but black Americans remained apart. Where others developed an "ethnic" identity based on their place of origin, slowly being absorbed into the ever expanding category of "white American," "the Negro" remained a racial subject.[96] Despite rhetoric insisting that immigrants become "100 percent American," the idea that people could be white Americans and have a heritage elsewhere was becoming increasingly acceptable, as Norwegian Americans, Irish Americans, German Americans, and Italian Americans flourished. Black Americans sought their roots elsewhere as well. They resisted a homogenized American identity based on a limited historical memory and began to seek the very richness of their ancestral origins and their past in the same way that their fellow Americans did.

The quest in which all these groups engaged was fundamental to the modern era. Nostalgia for an idealized past was typical at a time most believed was moving faster than any other before it. Black Americans' engagement with American and world history, however, was central to activist politics, because the assumptions about the torpidity of black people, past and present, in Africa and America, had the effect of stultifying expectations that they were capable of amounting to very much. The African and diasporic past that black Americans looked to reflected their needs in the present. Warriors and god-kings such as Tutankhamen demonstrated a simple point that black men once held positions of power and could again.

Whether black Americans envisioned their future in the United States or in Africa, all were moved by the discovery that they came from a place where the very highest human traits were achieved and celebrated. Taking on a new past—an African past—was fundamental to the process of altering their sense of themselves from Negro to African American.

3

Institutionalizing Africa, Past and Present

Black Americans in the interwar years took it as axiomatic that having a past of which one could be proud was essential to psychological health. History, properly taught, could provide children with a protective coating that would help to deflect the scoring of American racism. Becoming African American was therefore a collective and institutional enterprise as well as an individual one, as various organizations sprang up around the country to pursue knowledge about the black past, in Africa, in colonial America, throughout the diaspora, and in the United States. To a remarkable degree, black civic life was devoted to this part of the process of becoming African American.

Adults organized and took part in both informal and formal groups and clubs in which they studied history by discussing readings from newspapers and books or by debating the merits of presentations made by invited speakers. Libraries became social and political centers, featuring historical exhibits of African artifacts and items from places in the diaspora that were nearer the United States, such as Haiti. City streets provided spaces that formal institutions such as universities failed to foster, especially in the black metropolis of Harlem. There, men atop soapboxes and ladders discoursing with their audience on Africa's past were a staple of the soundscape. Many individuals, both men and women, devoted their lives to altering the prevailing view of blacks in academic history. They were led by the indefatigable Carter G. Woodson, who in 1915 began the Association for the Study of Negro Life and History (ASNLH), which ran conferences, published a journal, and particularly targeted those responsible for the education of black children.

Black adults were very keen to ensure that their children did not suffer the same lack of insight into the heroic black past as they had endured. They campaigned hard to reform school curricula to include black heroes through the ages and toiled to make materials available to children, for example, by getting books published and writing plays and pageants suitable for children to perform. Black teachers, especially those in the South, whose own education in the field of black history was usually quite limited, now found organizations established to help them. Activists also targeted tertiary institutions so that all graduates, but especially teachers, would be better trained in black history. Alongside these efforts, to make up for the shortcomings of formal education, mothers were encouraged to teach children in the home, and community and church organizations were mobilized to assist in making sure that black youngsters knew they had nothing in their past of which to be ashamed. Knowledge of the truth about Africa's glorious past and the contributions made by black people to both world and American civilization could prevent "soul murder" or "social death" in children and therefore break a cycle of psychological damage that dated back to enslavement.[1]

Increasing urbanization, in both south and north, a burgeoning print media, with black train porters distributing newspapers and journals nationwide, and increasing levels of education for many Americans made it possible to pursue knowledge about black history in forums other than folklore and religion. Though the widespread focus in the interwar years on the study of history was unprecedented, such efforts at community building drew on a rich tradition that animated black life throughout the years since emancipation.[2] Even before the end of slavery, communal modes of agitation were widespread and fed into the abolitionist movement. The period of Reconstruction was characterized by political, social, and cultural organizing, drawing on and extending what had taken place during slavery and the campaigns to end it. In the 1890s, women continued the tradition in an arena they termed racial uplift, which revolved around the mobilization of local chapters of national organizations, most notably the National Association of Colored Women (NACW). Recognizing that nobody else would do the work to advance their causes for them, black Americans formed self-help and mutual-help communities. Efforts to encourage all black Americans to take pride in their ancestry grew out of just such traditions. Specifically, the push to educate children came out of a long-standing belief that freedom was defined by the ability to protect one's children from harm, and by the choice, unlike during slavery, to learn to read and write.

In spite of these concerted efforts, and partially because of their success, by the mid-1930s interest moved away from the study of African history and emphasized instead contemporary conditions in colonial Africa. Several new circumstances, but particularly the effects of economic depression and the impending attack on Ethiopia by fascist Italy, seemed too difficult to interpret using history as the only lens to do so. Increasing numbers of black individuals were attending college and taking higher degrees, and they, too, followed the more general trend away from history toward the social sciences. Black history remained important, and indeed the expansion of the study of African history in the interwar years provided the basis for the Afrocentrism of the black power movement in the 1960s, 1970s, and more recent years. But at the same time, sociology, anthropology, political science, and economics became the tools with which to understand Africa. By becoming, in the 1930s, African American in a way that connected them to Africans in the present day, black Americans were able to protest, as kin, the continuing colonization of the continent by various European, and increasingly American corporate, interests. Paying attention to contemporary Africans also offered black Americans a new way to think of themselves: as subjects of an internal colonization, whose experiences linked them to Africans, and to colonized peoples everywhere.

Academic history's scope had broadened since the Great War, but not enough to produce the kind of scholarship about black history that cohered with what black Americans knew from their own experience and the stories told to them by their parents and grandparents. Rather, academic attitudes toward Africa remained unchanged. Since nothing, apparently, ever happened there, there was no need to study its history. Anthropology was the discipline for understanding the dark continent. In U.S. history, some historians had begun to mull over conflict in the past and to turn their attention to experiences of ordinary people, including those in minority groups. This "New History" movement was about studying the past, in the words of Frederick Jackson Turner, "from the bottom up."[3] Such expansion of social and minority history, in contrast to political and elite history, might suggest a concomitant opening up of new ways to historicize slavery and even of teaching positions for black scholars. Although, to be sure, there were increasing numbers of minority students attending "white" universities, and individual black historians were read more widely across the discipline, the status of black Americans in the mainstream education profession remained largely unchanged.[4] With alternative voices confined to the margins of academe, racist and Southern studies of the past continued to hold sway. Ulrich Phillips's *American Negro Slavery* (1918) and *Life and Labor in the Old South* (1929), though challenged from the 1930s on by various monographs, remained the standard until the 1950s for understanding slavery as a relatively benign institution. Likewise, most Americans continued to view Reconstruction as a terrible mistake that sowed discord and disunion.[5]

In order to make an impact on entrenched history and to promulgate quickly and widely the version of the past favored in black history, its practitioners had to establish their studies as legitimate by conforming to standard historical methods. Whereas black history had earlier depended on the oral tradition, it now needed to be written down and substantiated by documented evidence, which readers could verify independently. Even in Afrocentric histories of black people's contributions to civilization, which were often polemical in style, there was a new demand for written words and hardback binding. The written word was now so treasured that artist Winfred Russell went so far as to paint a still life of a collection of books about black history. Black newspapers, magazines, and academic journals all ran extensive book review sections and greeted new books with fanfare. As a measure of black history's growing visibility, by the second half of the 1930s, reviews of books on race relations and black history appeared more frequently in mainstream academic publications. A search for the word "Negro" in the digital archives of the two leading historical journals indicates a jump from eighty reviews in the 1920s to 225 in the 1930s. Nearly seventy percent of the latter were published between 1935 and 1939.[6] Further evidence of the profession's newfound awareness of black history came when W. E. B. Du Bois chaired an interracial panel at the 1940 annual meeting of the American Historical Association, a historic event. *Black Reconstruction* (1935), Du Bois's major work, however, had not yet been reviewed in the organization's journal.[7]

Accurate accounts of black history, including African history, were needed to counter
Western stereotypes about the so-called Dark Continent and to assure black children that
they could be proud of their heritage. This *Shelf of Books* (1927), by Winfred J. Russell,
featured *Heart of Africa;* Du Bois's *Darkwater; The New Negro,* edited by Alain Locke;
Alone in West Africa, by Mary Gaunt; and P. Amaury Talbot's *In the Shadow of the Bush.*
(Art & Artifacts Division, Schomburg Center for Research in Black Culture, The New
York Public Library, Astor, Lenox and Tilden Foundations.)

Intransigence in the profession inspired black Americans to try to beat
mainstream historians at their own game. The single most important en-
deavor in this regard was Carter G. Woodson's 1915 founding of the ASNLH.
A Virginia-born son of former slaves, Woodson was twenty years old when
he began high school in 1895, going on in 1912 to become the second black
person to be awarded a doctorate from Harvard University (Du Bois was the
first). After teaching in high schools in Washington, D.C., and briefly at
Howard University, he struck out to establish the ASNLH. Woodson and a
cohort of historians devoted to him and the cause worked tirelessly with
meager resources to establish the *Journal of Negro History* in 1916 and the
Associated Publishers soon afterward. With funds raised from magazine
subscriptions, black patrons, and, initially at least, white donors, Woodson

and the ASNLH subsidized the work of a generation of scholars, whose research in turn provided material for the journal. Woodson recognized that one of the most severe hindrances to redressing American history was a lack of readily available resources. The *Journal* therefore had a section dedicated to the printing or reprinting of key materials, and Woodson donated documents generously to the Library of Congress.[8]

Other individuals, too, built up impressive collections of materials relating to black diaspora history. Most prolific was Arthur (Arturo) Schomburg, an immigrant from Puerto Rico. Born in 1874, he arrived in New York City at the age of seventeen and around the turn of the century began collecting material on black people's struggles worldwide.[9] His huge collection of documents, pamphlets, books, and artworks was purchased in 1926 to form the nucleus of the special collections of the Harlem branch of the New York Public Library. In explaining why he gave over his life to collecting, Schomburg likened the predicament of black Americans—indeed black people everywhere—to that of Jewish people. Each group existed without a nation to call its own, he wrote, and lived within "the very groups of nations who destroyed them. . . . The Negro must strive to follow in the good example of the Jews—they cling to their customs and traditions, no matter whether they live in [Timbuktu] or in the highest peaks of the Andean mountains."[10] Schomburg believed that just as scattered Jews shared a text—the Torah—so ought those in the African diaspora create their own text, their own national archive.[11]

Inspired by the same desire to overturn accepted truths about their past, Dorothy Porter took a job at Howard University library in 1930. There, she catalogued collections left to the university by abolitionist Lewis Tappan in 1871 and Jesse Moorland, a trustee of the university and general secretary of the YMCA, in 1914. Ferreting through the shelves of the main collection, Porter siphoned off for the special collection any material relating to black American, Caribbean, or African studies. Befriending book dealers and publishers, she convinced many to send the library free copies, or bought them herself and donated them to the Moorland Foundation: A Library of Negro Life. In 1946, Porter engineered the acquisition of Joel Spingarn's private collection of some 30,000 items. Her library was then renamed the Moorland-Spingarn Collection, to reflect its two main benefactors. Like Schomburg, Porter recognized that accepted and erroneous historical truths could not be challenged without appropriate archival material. Her interest in black history, like that of her peers, extended to international themes and transnational trends. It was impossible to tell black American history, it seemed, without at least one eye focused on events and developments outside the United States.[12]

Collectors without institutional support found alternate means to make accessible their archives of black history, and in doing so contributed to the building of black communities well apart from any desire to change white Americans' attitudes toward black people. L. S. Alexander Gumby arrived in New York in the earliest years of the century, having abandoned his legal studies at a Delaware college. Working various jobs to support his habit, and with the assistance until 1929 of a wealthy white partner, a stockbroker, Gumby amassed a serious, and by all accounts marvelous, rare book collection, earning him an entry in the 1922 Private Book Collectors' Who's Who. Combining the sober art of collecting with the tradition of the salon, he exhibited his finds for selected friends in a second-floor Harlem apartment known as the Gumby Book Studio, on Fifth Avenue between 131st and 132nd Streets. There, Gumby also exhibited annually work from the nearby Art Students' Club. The titles of these lost artworks, including "Hearts in Africa" and "King Christophe," indicate the interest Harlem residents had in an international black world. Alongside the rare books and artworks was Gumby's ever-growing collection of scrapbooks, comprising newspaper and magazine clippings on topics and individuals significant to black life. Gumby's sense of the importance of creating an archive for future use has been borne out by the popularity of the collection, which he donated to Columbia University's Rare Book and Manuscript Library in 1950. Like other collectors, Gumby's interests went beyond the United States, with scrapbooks on major figures who traveled internationally and ones devoted to Ethiopia, Haiti, and Africa.[13]

Closely related to the task of collecting was that of learning about the past. When John Henrik Clarke, later a significant historian in the Afrocentric tradition, arrived in Harlem in the early 1930s, he found multiple avenues for pursuing knowledge about Africa. Informal, ad hoc discussions could be had on the streets, while more formally organized groups met at libraries, public halls, and private homes. Together these venues formed a vibrant community of people interested in understanding their origins and their connections to people in Africa and around the diaspora. For Clarke, this was a huge relief. Raised in Alabama, he came to New York to escape stifling conditions in the South, where every single thing he had been taught as a child pointed to the conclusion that black people "had no place in history, no place in religion, had contributed nothing to civilization and, therefore, could not exist or be acknowledge[d] as of value as human beings in the present."[14] As a young man, he was affected profoundly by Schomburg's essay in *The New Negro* (1925), an important Harlem Renaissance anthology. Clarke was moved especially, he said, by two sentences: "The American Negro must remake his past in order to remake his future. History must restore what slavery took away."[15] Thus, he abandoned all he knew and traveled alone to New York, where he nervously sought Schomburg out. "My daddy wanted me to be a farmer," Clarke wrote, to "feel the smoothness of Alabama clay and become one of the first blacks in my town to own land. But, I was worried about my history being caked with that southern clay and I subscribed to a different kind of teaching and learning in my bones and in my spirit."[16] Harlem, like Chicago and other black urban communities, was exciting not only because the past was being rediscovered there, but because of the civic institutions sprouting up everywhere for that purpose.

Interwar organizations whose members studied Africa had direct antecedents in the American Negro Historical Society of Philadelphia and the American Negro Academy in Washington, both founded in 1897. An immediate predecessor was the Negro Society for Historical Research, inaugurated in 1911 by Schomburg and John E. Bruce, a journalist and lay historian who was later a major figure in Marcus Garvey's Universal Negro Improvement Association (UNIA). By the interwar years, however, such organizations had become central to black life in Harlem and other major centers of black American life. Their membership was no longer restricted to elites and university graduates, and the type of history they pursued was more varied.[17]

Such groups convened in cities and towns all over the country. Members of the Circle of Knowledge met regularly in New York City and, indicating their seriousness of purpose, kept minutes of each meeting. They debated the location of mankind's origins and gathered to consider the legend of Noah and the possibility that he was a black man. Herodotus's observations about the Egyptians' appearance were recorded by the secretary, who also noted discussion of "the Caucasian Race being savages once when the dark race ruled Egypt." Adding to the legion of "firsts" in Africa, members discussed the smelting of iron, astrology, and the beginnings of religious thought. These and other achievements were covered up by white Westerners, who denied Africa had offered anything to the world, a topic that itself was one of members' abiding concerns. At the group's third meeting, a member gave a speech "on who Cush, Ham, and the Queen of Sheba were, our place in historical books to-day as to the Caucasian Race, and how history is written."[18] The shortcomings of present-day history writing were thus the prime motivation for the Circle of Knowledge and other such groups.

Other groups focused on both African and more recent black history in North America. Diverse in its historical interests but more elite in its membership was a Washington, D.C., study group attended in 1921 by writer Jean Toomer, the Saturday Nighters. Toomer's motivation in the Saturday night salon was personal: he wanted to come to grips with "the actual place and condition of the mixed-blood group in this country."[19] This could be achieved only by looking back at historical roots. Influenced by tenets in the emerging science of psychology, he believed it necessary for personal well-being to be reconciled with the past. In his view, no black person had such peace. "External pressure," he wrote, had forced black people from their "racial roots." They were ashamed of the slave past and, in the case of mixed-blood people, were further denied their heritage by whites' refusal to acknowledge the familial relationship. Thus, Toomer argued, "the Negro, psychologically and spiritually has been literally uprooted, or worse, [had] no roots at all."[20] In order better to understand their personal and collective pasts, the group discussed written histories of slavery, including *Captain Canot, or Twenty Years as an African Slaver* (1854), an account of slave trading on Africa's West Coast; T.R.R. Cobb's *Historical Sketch of Slavery* (1858), a world history by the author of the single most influential legal defense of slavery; and sections of H.G. Wells's bestseller, *An Outline of History.*[21] Perhaps this group also talked of their family histories or tales they had heard from others, but they relied mainly on written accounts of African enslavement.

The endeavors of librarians, archivists, and the innumerable individuals who contributed in so many ways to the pursuit of black history meant that the Harlem in which John Clarke arrived in 1933 had a much richer array of materials on which to draw than were available even ten years earlier. Clarke devoted himself to studying black history, and his experiences provide insight into the existence of countless clubs and societies, formal and informal, in Harlem, around the country, and throughout the diaspora. Through Schomburg, Clarke signed up with the Harlem History Club. The club met Sunday mornings at the Harlem YMCA on West 135th Street. Dr. Willis N. Huggins's lectures focused discussion on pre-assigned readings in black history and on popular synthetic works such as Wells's *Outline of History.*[22] As a result, Clarke acquired a strong grounding in history despite the fact that he spent little time in school because he had to work.[23] The club also attracted members of the nearby African Students Union, perhaps including the future first president of Ghana, Kwame Nkrumah, who spent summer holidays in Harlem while studying at Lincoln University.[24] Reputed to be an inspiring teacher, Huggins spent most of his waking hours teaching and learning black history. He worked in the school system by day (he was the sixth black American to be hired in the city's schools) and in alternative education at night and on weekends.[25] His efforts to integrate black history in school curricula failed to convince the New York City Board of Education, but he encouraged a generation of Harlem residents and visitors to explore their past.[26]

Those fortunate enough to attend school still needed to augment their studies with further reading about Africa. The Universal Ethiopian Students Club, later Association (UESA), formed in New York in 1930, was designed to fill the gap. Its application form asked where potential members attended school and, if they did not, when and where they planned to. Admission required a short essay of between 300 and 500 words.[27] Its members, initially self-defined Garveyites, intended to "study the Africans' history in a systematic way."[28] They invited Huggins to lecture at summer evening classes and sought his advice on an appropriate textbook.[29] Huggins's previous appearance had been a huge hit, and his account of Africa's contribution to civilization "b[r]ought cheer to the hearts of the students as he entered."[30]

Garvey's desire that black Americans align themselves with Africans rather than Americans was reflected clearly in the proliferation of clubs and societies oriented toward Africa and the black diaspora. Clubs designed specifically for the study of history were only two of several organizations with which Clarke was in contact. Others included the African Patriotic Students Club at 114th Street; the Liberian Research Society in Los Angeles and Buffalo, New York; the Liberian-American League in Chicago; and the Cape Palmas Club in Harlem, whose members had purchased 300 acres in Liberia on which they were currently building three of many "American bungalows" to attract emigrants. Clarke also corresponded with members of the Dumas Literary Club in Harlem, devoted to "things progressive in the creation and uplift of the 'New Negro'"; the nearby Yoruba Literary and Debating Club; the Istmo African Pioneering Club in Panama City; and finally, Harlem's Ethiopian Social Club, whose logo featured three pyramids flanked by palm trees. Members of the last were busy organizing the Arabian Night Ball, while the Yoruba Club sought the aid of at least twenty further literary and social clubs for a fundraiser to enable J. A. Rogers to continue his research and publish *World's Greatest Men of African Descent.*[31] This array of organizations attests to the determination of Harlem's residents—and black people elsewhere—to rediscover their history and to restore connections between descendants of Africans separated by the slave trade. In the process, these groups made Harlem the most exciting black community in the nation, with a well-developed public life and a sense of itself as distinct from white America and connected instead to black communities throughout the world.

Clarke and others did not confine their history-making activism to indoors. On the streets, too, the struggle to find and define the past was often top billing for speakers on soapboxes and stepladders. In its heyday, the northeast corner of 135th Street and Seventh Avenue was known as "The Campus."[32] Clarke's recollections referred to the "junior or 'undergraduate' speakers" on Lenox Avenue, who after cutting their oratorical teeth, sometimes for years, in front of demanding audiences in this secondary location, graduated to the prime spot on Seventh Avenue.[33] William Pickens of the National Association for the Advancement of Colored People (NAACP) likened public speaker Hubert H. Harrison to Socrates and lamented that racism alone prevented Harrison from joining the faculty at Columbia, some of whom, he asserted, cribbed from Harrison's speeches for their own lectures.[34] Another Harlem resident recalled that Harrison was attached to the 135th Street branch of the public library "as a kind of unofficial lecturer-in-residence" and dubbed him the "Dean of the Harlem Street Orators."[35] Another local reminisced that "this was the time when the soap box orators in Harlem sounded like Harvard professors" and that speakers were taken very seriously.[36] The practice of lecturing and listening was a common occurrence on the streets and a means of bringing black topics and opinions that had little currency in the white public sphere to the black community.[37] Not only history but also current topics on race relations were grist for the soapbox mill. Ella Baker, later an important organizer in the civil rights movement, used her position as a member of the Adult Education Committee at the 135th Street Library to organize discussions on the street on topics such as lynching.[38] For black Americans who were routinely excluded from public institutions, including universities, street speaking provided an open classroom.

Less intellectually edifying but equally popular were the mystics and quacks who lined Harlem's streets, peddling cures for ailments and potions for remedying unrequited love, exacting revenge, or figuring out the three-digit number that would allow punters to triumph in the local "policy" game. Styling themselves as Oriental doctors, natives of Africa, Mohammedan brethren, or a mixture of all three, sometimes with a dash of Hinduism or Buddhism, these street salesmen were abundant both on the street and in newspapers, where their advertisements appeared weekly.[39] Professor Akpandac (who adopted several other similar identities over the years), shown in a photograph wearing a black suit and turban, at other times a fez, claimed to be African born and a "Professor of African and Oriental Occultism, Psychic Science, White and Black Magic, etc." From his studio on West 129th Street, he offered "Psychic and Scientific Readings and Advice Given—Egyptian and African Formulae Used."[40] Though mocked frequently by members of Harlem's intellectual elite, the longevity of these mystics in Harlem suggests that others took them seriously. Whether or not their treatments were successful, such characters formed an institution internal to Harlem. Just as older women, during the days of slavery, had competed with slave owners to treat the ailing, drawing on medical knowledge either brought with them from Africa or inherited from others, so, too, did Harlem's residents create their own cultures of remedy, which drew on a purportedly African heritage.

Into the 1930s, fierce labor activists combined the radical elements of street speakers such as Harrison and A. Philip Randolph with the mysticism of those claiming to be occult scientists, such as Akpandac. Born Eugene

Brown in Lowell, Massachusetts, Sufi Abdul Hamid championed black labor, black-owned business, and black separatism. For a brief spell, Hamid was enormously popular.[41] Late one Thursday evening, "thundering to a crowd of about 400 persons, he was said to have advocated atheism and sweepingly ridiculed all form of religion."[42] Despite his seeming lack of faith, in earlier years he called himself "Bishop Conshankin, mystic and Oriental philosopher."[43] His new moniker, turban, and leadership of the Universal Holy Temple of Tranquility indicated a continuing investment in mysticism. Doubtless this religiosity accounted in part for his appeal: his boycott of white-owned businesses may have failed eventually but not until after he had rallied the support of thousands to the cause. Novelist and poet Claude McKay certainly thought so, writing about Hamid in his 1940 non-fiction account, *Harlem: Negro Metropolis*. McKay also transformed into fictional characters those soapboxers who mixed advocacy of black workers' rights and of black-owned business with a faux African mysticism. "Sharp-age," wrote McKay,

> appeared on the streets of Harlem wearing a turban, a belted leather coat, boots and spurs and announcing himself as Omar, The African, founder of a new religion and a new idea of labor for the colored masses. . . . Haranguing Harlem from a step ladder on the street corners, Omar, more than any other soap boxer, drew the crowds. Young men, high school kids among them, stopped to listen and decided to follow him.[44]

African heritage was central to the making of Harlem as a separate space for black Americans, where they could feel relatively autonomous from the intrusion of white America.

Making a virtue of a necessity, black Americans came to regard street speaking—and noise of all sorts—as characteristic of the black diaspora and its subjects and as something derived from Africa. Many regarded themselves as having inherited from their ancestors an aural sensibility, which distinguished them from their white fellow citizens, who relied on sight. As singer, actor, and activist Paul Robeson put it, "my ancestors in Africa reckoned sound of major importance; they were all great talkers, great orators, and where writing was unknown, folk tales and an oral tradition kept the ears rather than the eyes sharpened. I am the same. I always hear, I seldom see. I hear my way through the world. I always judge by sound."[45] Harlem's streets became the locale, as did public space in other cities and the front porch in Southern towns, in which to assert a collective identity that went beyond the borders of the nation. In writer Wallace Thurman's estimation, there was always something happening on Harlem's streets: "A Hindoo faker here, a loud-voiced Socialist there, a medicine doctor ballyhooing, a corn doctor, a blind musician, serious people, gay people, philanderers and preachers. Seventh Avenue is filled with deep rhythmic laughter. It is a civilized lane with primitive traits. Harlem's most representative street."[46] It was not just that the topics discussed were concerned with a global black world, nor just that the most striking figures characterized themselves as from a mythical place somewhere between Africa and India, though these facts were significant in the creation of a transnational black identity. Moreover, as Robeson's words suggest, there was a self-consciousness about the very mode of comporting oneself, about belonging to a group that was separate from America and an integral part of an international black world.

It was one thing to find in Harlem's public life—or black culture in general—a refuge from the vagaries of American race relations. It was quite another to try to prevent in one's children the kind of psychological damage that racism exacted. In what has become a trope of black autobiography, memoirists invariably recall the psychic injury of discovering that being black was not desirable. Writer Maya Angelou described how as a child in the 1930s she fantasized that she was actually white and would eventually awaken from her "black ugly dream," to the surprise of her cruel white neighbors. She knew her dream was just that; her simultaneous awareness of her "displacement" was the "rust on the razor that threatens the throat."[47] Difference was not something most Americans celebrated; it was something they feared.

The wish to prevent such trauma extended to black parents in all regions and activists of all political affiliations. Marcus Garvey was one of the most vocal commentators on the subject, exploring the issue in an imagined dialogue in which a father tells his son not to take to heart that which he has been taught in school, because the curriculum was dictated by an assumption of white superiority. "Historians who have written have all twisted the history of the world so as to show the inferiority of the blacks," the father says. "The Blackman has not written recently his own history . . . and so, for the last hundred years, he has been learning out of the white man's book, thereby developing the white man's psychology."[48] Black people had poor self-esteem as a result of self-serving versions of history imposed by white educational institutions and their written texts. For Garvey, who was so keen to promote men as family heads, this was a double tragedy, because schooling led to the boy not only feeling badly about himself but also doubting the veracity of the things his father told him, which he could not find in books. Such pressures on individuals and on families made it difficult for children to inherit a positive racial identity.

Garvey's view was echoed constantly in every forum of black public life. Reviewing a new 1921 book for children, the *Journal of Negro History* asked, "Can anything be more dangerous than the continual subjection of our children to the influence of books, magazines, and newspapers in which their race is being held up constantly to pity or contempt? . . . If the psychological influence of such endlessly reiterated and therefore inescapable slurs is bad for adults, how much worse must it be for children."[49] *Unsung Heroes,* by Elizabeth Ross Haynes, contained illustrated summaries of the lives of seventeen notable black men and women of African descent, thirteen of them American and four from elsewhere. The *Journal*'s reviewer called for its inclusion in every black home and all libraries. Jessie Fauset, literary editor at *Crisis,* agreed, adding that it ought also to be a textbook in schools. "It is just the sort of book we need," she wrote, "to offset the tendency of American schools to impress upon children of both races that the only heroes in the world have been white heroes." Moreover, Fauset rejoiced that these tales were collected in a *book:* "The influence of the printed word is so great that these stories gain greater authenticity by the mere placing of them between the covers of a volume, instead of leaving them as we have for too long in the form of anecdotes and personal recollections to be handed down from father to son."[50] Oral history was no longer sufficient, in the modern era, for keeping up the spirits of young folk.

Parents in every part of the country, both urban and rural, were disappointed and frustrated when they sent their children to school, often at some cost to themselves, only to have them learn nothing of black history.

"We hope," said a 1923 newspaper article, "that the day will come when we will have in our schools, colleges and libraries, a history of the United States, giving the Negro his rightful place in history."[51] Eleven years later, Paul Robeson was still despairing that "the younger generation of Negroes in America looks towards Africa and asks 'What is there *there* to interest me?'" Robeson worried that "at first glance the question seems unanswerable. He sees only the savagery, devil-worship, witch-doctors, voo-doo, ignorance, squalor, and darkness taught in American schools."[52] Racism blinded teachers, and in turn their pupils, to the greatness of Africa's past and the variety of its present-day inhabitants and cultures. The quality of American schooling remained an abiding concern throughout the interwar period and, for that matter, beyond. Desegregating schools—a measure it was hoped would improve the education received by black pupils—became a centerpiece of the struggle for civil rights during the 1950s and 1960s. Before that, however, realizing that state school systems would not reform themselves voluntarily, black parents and activists took it upon themselves to transform curricula and teaching.

Concerned parents with the funds to do so subscribed to *The Brownies' Book,* a magazine for children ("brownies"), which ran monthly under the auspices of the *Crisis* between January 1920 and December 1921. Circulation, at 5,000 subscribers at most, was 8,000 short of breaking even.[53] The periodical featured histories and biographies of black people in the United States (including Sojourner Truth, Crispus Attucks, Harriet Tubman, and Paul Cuffe) and those under the yoke of white domination elsewhere (for instance, Haitian revolutionary Toussaint Louverture and Mahatma Gandhi). Heroes need not be famous; "The Bravest of the Brave" gave details of Elizabeth Blakesley, a slave girl who stowed away on a ship to escape from North Carolina to Boston and from there went to Canada via the Underground Railroad. That tale was not sugarcoated; rather, its author revealed to her audience that "Betsy" endured sexual slavery because her light skin was attractive to others and that she left behind a baby in the South.[54] Letters to the editor demonstrate that the children who read *The Brownies' Book* were delighted with its depictions of black people in history. Specifically, according to one letter writer, these pieces augmented what was a disappointingly Eurocentric curriculum at school.[55] Through biographies, fiction, poetry, drama, essays, news, columns, and imagery, the magazine encouraged children to identify with the experiences of black children around the world, as in the story of Olive Plaatje, a young South African girl whose experiences of segregation were likened to those of black children in the United States.[56] Both before and after the run of *The Brownies' Book, the Crisis* itself ran tales and images designed to be read and shown to children. Many took iconic fairy tales and replaced the white characters with black boys and girls—for example, one in which a Moroccan princess, descended from Hamites (and therefore darker, gentler, and of better character than her Berber and Semite cousins), kissed an ostrich who then transformed into a prince and rescued her from her wicked guardian.[57] These efforts all aimed at the same outcome: to ensure that black children developed a protective coating, as it were, that would deflect the slights and worse of racism.

Some of the most concerted efforts at altering the kind of schooling American children received was in the arena of book publishing. Without resources, there could be no wholesale change in either what was taught or the attitudes young people acquired as a result. The high hopes people pinned on rewritten textbooks were evident in a pageant, written for children to perform, in which a white boy and black boy converse. White Gilbert is unconvinced by black Sam's insistence that "my people" contributed to the growth of the United States into a great nation, retorting, "Well, it isn't in these books. The only thing that I saw that your people have done was to work as slaves on the plantations."[58] Just as Woodson and others in the historical profession knew that their history would be regarded as legitimate only in written form, with footnotes that cited other written evidence (as opposed to oral history passed down through generations), so, too, was it important to have documentation to change the mindset of young people in school.

Hundreds of books aimed at schoolchildren were written and published in the interwar years. The sheer volume of materials produced during the 1920s and 1930s is suggested by the lengthy bibliographies in Willis Huggins and John Jackson's 1934 *A Guide to Studies in African History: Directive Lists for Schools and Clubs.* It recommended to teachers and instructors that they divide historical studies into thirteen themes, arranged geographically and chronologically. Any course using the guide could expect to cover the bulk of black diasporic experience, from ancient Africa to the present day. Many of the texts it recommended had been written in the ten years prior, including Woodson's *Negro Makers of History* (1928), an adaptation for children of an earlier book for adults, and *Readings from Negro Authors for Schools and Colleges* (1931), edited by Otelia Cromwell, the first black woman to graduate from Smith College; Lorenzo Dow Turner, who pioneered research into Gullah language; and Eva B. Dykes, one of three black women who were the first to be awarded doctorates in 1921. Lists of readings for the study of various parts of Africa, the Caribbean, South America, and Central America were also dominated by black American authors. The breadth of materials now available, compared with ten years earlier, let alone twenty, stood as a testament to the determination of black Americans in all areas of history reform.

Book authors and publishers hoped to have their works placed in school libraries and, ideally, on school curricula. In 1924, the International Council of Women of the Darker Races focused its attention on curriculum reform. Formed in 1920 as an offshoot of the NACW, the council intended that one-quarter of its 200-strong membership be foreign. African, Sri Lankan, and West Indian women were present at its founding. Local groups of members met regularly to extend their own knowledge about political, social, and historical conditions of people of color worldwide.[59] In "Committees of Seven," members campaigned for black history, including knowledge about men and women of color worldwide, to be taught in schools.[60] They had some success: in one Virginia school, the president reported in 1924, pupils had learnt about Haitian women in February and would turn to Chinese, Indian, and African women in the coming three months.[61] In 1925, the Commission on Race Relations engaged historian Charles H. Wesley to prepare a dossier of "facts from Negro history" to present to school boards in northern cities. A New York newspaper reported enthusiastically on its purpose: "to create a sentiment which will lead to a better text-book treatment of Negroes, particularly in America, and ultimately to a fuller appreciation of Negro contributions in the making of America."[62]

In spite of poor teacher training and poverty, many teachers nationwide found in the general neglect by boards of black schools a space in which to teach their pupils "pride and tradition," as one student recalled.[63] Black Americans had long linked freedom to literacy and to education more broadly, so sometimes teachers' motivation to go beyond set curriculum came from students themselves or from the community in which they taught.[64] Freedom theoretically meant the opportunity to improve the lot of one's children, including protecting their self-esteem from the abuse they were bound to receive in a divided society in which even poor whites could improve their social standing by adhering to, and reinforcing, racist norms. The desire to teach children something about their past was aided by a general improvement in conditions in black schools prior to World War II, although white schools improved comparatively more.[65] Improvements came, too, from the increasing numbers of black Americans attending high school and college and, as a consequence, from better prepared teachers who raised the standards of elementary school education.[66]

None of these changes would have been possible without the unflagging work of Woodson, the ASNLH, its publishing house, and the *Journal of Negro History*. Woodson believed that the single most important factor in changing race relations in the United States was education. To this end, in 1926 he inaugurated Negro History Week as a vehicle to push for a full program of black history. For seven days each year, pupils would devote themselves to the study of the Negro's past, including the international and transnational dimensions of black history. Negro History Week also gave Woodson a chance to raise the profile and coffers of the ASNLH. Readers of the *Journal* were asked to ensure that their local community had a branch of the organization, which required at least ten people paying an annual due of three dollars apiece.[67]

Negro History Week was an opportunity for Woodson to appeal for the production and purchase of materials suitable for children to learn history. In its first year, he requested donations to provide schools with "pictures of distinguished Negroes, plays visualizing the life and history of the race, and stories of the Negro in the language of the child."[68] He was pleased to report in 1934 that schools were "asking for more books bearing upon the Negro" and wanting pictures of "outstanding Negroes."[69] Woodson called, too, for enterprising writers to pen pageants depicting black history in a "short snappy fashion." The pageants available, Woodson declared, were too cumbersome for young actors. As he put it, they "[undertook] the impossible for a school in trying to stage a pageant depicting the life of the Negro in Africa, the enslavement of the race, the struggle for freedom, emancipation, and the battle for social justice, all at the same time."[70] His request resulted in scripts targeting junior and high school students, collected in *Plays and Pageants from the Life of the Negro* (1930) and *Negro History in Thirteen Plays* (1935), both issued by the publishing wing of the ASNLH.[71] Woodson's intentions for the volumes were made clear in the introductions. He described watching an elementary school production of a pageant in which two young boys were told the truth about the "great men of African blood who had done much for the benefit of mankind. The Negro boy, thus enlightened, becomes inspired to do something great; and the white boy, rid of his prejudice, joins hands with the lad to help him do his part. Thus," Woodson concluded, "we see dramatized a new America."[72] This was an America that had listened to an alternative black history and thus discarded its nativism, xenophobia, and, most of all, its antiblack racism. This America celebrated the diversity of its many citizens.

Though Negro History Week was Woodson's initiative, its success relied on teachers' willingness to implement the program in schools.[73] Immediately after he launched Negro History Week, Woodson was pleased by the participants' enthusiasm, the number of inquiries received by the ASNLH, the broad spread of activities, and, increasingly as the years unfolded, the interest of the press.[74] He used the association's journal to communicate with teachers, ministers, social workers, and businessmen and to thank them for their support.[75] Allen B. Ballard, later professor of history at the State University of New York at Albany, recalled that at his segregated Philadelphia primary school, black history was important all year round but that Negro History Week was a special time for the principal, Nelly Bright. For her, "it was a time for skits about the Underground Railroad, poetry readings of the works of Paul Laurence Dunbar, art contests for the best Negro History poster, and a special chorus to sing such spirituals as 'Walk Together Children,' or 'Steal Away.'" By week's end, children knew they were "important," with fine traditions to uphold. This knowledge, reflected Ballard, was undeniably useful when each morning and afternoon the black students walked past the new, well-equipped white high school.[76]

For others who were not as swift as Nelly Bright to implement the programs of Negro History Week, the ASNLH provided the impetus in the form of a 1934 custom-made play. "The High Court of Historia" (1934), by playwright Randolph Edmonds, featured representatives of the United States, Great Britain, France, Germany, the American South, and black America. Named Samus, Johnus, Francus, Aryanus, Dixianus, and Afriopus, respectively, they are flying to an international history meeting when their plane hits an "air pocket." They find themselves before the bench of the High Court in the land of Historia, a place where people speak Ye Olde Englishe and claim to be absolute authorities on all things historical. The comedy's high point, when it was performed at Dillard University in 1939, was surely when Uncle Sam said to a comely young woman, "You know I think I'm going to declare a Monroe Doctrine around you." Forced to defend their various versions of history before the king and queen, each of the white men assures the august leaders that his own account, which favors his people, is correct. When Afriopus claims lamely that he teaches English, American, and ancient history, because those are the ones with "facts recorded," he is threatened with the ceremony of "Trarefirpun." The dastardly effects of this curse are evident in the character Traitorius, who "held the wrong views of history" and has been made an exhibit to warn those who would share his nonchalance about the past. Only after the torture begins does Afriopus see the error of his ways, beg for mercy, and announce, "I will reform. I will do as all other historians do. I will look at life from the standpoint of my own people. I will join the Association for The Study of Negro Life and History. I will buy all the books of Woodson, Wesley and DuBois and teach my children pride of race as well as of nation. Give me another chance, O High King!"[77] The play ended soon after, Edmonds offering no account as to how these eminent historians returned home from Historia.

For those teachers who were enthusiastic about black history but lacked training and materials, Negro History Week, and the ASNLH more generally, was a boon. Primary documents printed in the monthly *Journal of Negro History* were aimed at them, to expand their knowledge and for use in classrooms. Each year, the historians who had gathered around Woodson, younger men including Charles Wesley, Lorenzo Greene, and Luther Jackson (significant figures in their own right), went out to teacher training summer schools across the South, where they lectured and sold books and subscriptions to the ASNLH (including the *Journal*). Teachers' attendance at such schools was subsidized by the General Education Board, a philanthropic organization begun by John D. Rockefeller in 1902, which worked closely with the Jeanes Foundation, named for its benefactor, Anna T. Jeanes.[78] Both organizations were interested first and foremost in vocational training for black boys and girls, and so it was an uphill battle for the ASNLH staff. Contrary to the central plank in Woodson's study of the past, the Jeanes supervisors believed that when black people emerged from slavery, they "had long since been stripped of their African heritage."[79] Nevertheless, materials for the study and teaching of black history were being distributed throughout the South.

Though activists such as Woodson had only limited success in having black history inserted into general school curricula, and though the broader aim to transform ideas about America's past may have been only partially realized, they managed to bring the study of black history out into public light and, importantly, into black schools, colleges, and universities. By 1929, many books on black history were accepted by state school boards, including in the South. The greatest success was Woodson's own book, *The Negro in Our History,* in use in twenty-one states, including some in the South, with a further six Southern states considering its adoption in public schools.[80] The "our" of the book's title reflected Woodson's focus on an inclusive American nation. True history, he believed, told in an unbiased fashion, gave credit to various people and nations for contributions they made to world development.[81] It was in the best interest of all Americans to learn and integrate black history, including that of black people in Africa prior to their enslavement. On this latter point, Woodson became increasingly convinced, wanting both white Americans and Europeans to come to grips with the fact that their origins, too, lay in Africa. In the preface to the book's fourth edition in 1927, he despaired of a public not ready for the inclusion of more material on the "early history of Africa" but gradually became more bold.[82] After a summer spent in Europe, he wrote something of a prequel to *The Negro in Our History,* already in its sixth edition: *The African Background Outlined* (1936).[83]

Negro History Week was enormously successful within black communities. Parents' desire to shield black children from racism was trumped by the conviction that it was more important to give them the tools to deal with life in the United States and that one of those tools was a good knowledge of black history. Moreover, because the week's format relied on local communities putting together its own events, in whatever venues were available, history itself became something around which the community was organized. Community building and the study of the past were therefore quite closely linked. Negro History Week nationalized the pursuit of black history at the same time that some of its study and celebrations were focused on African and diaspora history, reinforcing black Americans' sense of themselves as having connections with people beyond the frontiers of the United States. The very process of learning and institutionalizing black history was integral to black Americans' transformation of themselves into subjects of the black diaspora who were also essential members of the United States.

Black public history efforts to bolster children's self-esteem went well beyond school classrooms. Woodson used Negro History Week to exhort pastors to focus on historical themes in their sermons. If schools could not be convinced to acquire books favorable to Negro history, then communities were to use Book and Picture Fund Day to appeal for money to buy them and then to place them in either public libraries or churches.[84] Community leaders were to speak publicly to their youth, to open children's eyes to the possibility of success. In this, Negro History Week went beyond an emphasis on the famous men and women of black history, heralding lesser-known folk, whose triumph over adversity was cause for celebration enough. Even during this annual celebration, schools were only one of the locations and the institutions called upon to steel children for life in the United States.

Librarians in particular played a key role in enabling black children to access images of themselves beyond caricatured picaninnies. At the 135th Street branch of the New York Public Library, a Boys' Club of high-school-age students met twice monthly in 1921 and 1922 to study black history.[85] Their younger brothers and sisters may have been among those who took advantage of the well-patronized children's room in 1924, when it was run by novelist Nella Larsen, then the children's librarian. Children were encouraged to read and to enjoy story hour each afternoon. Their activities extended to art classes, with the library mounting a display of children's artwork at least once.[86] Funds for the children's collection were tight, so in the 1930s a group of Harlem women joined forces with Arthur Schomburg and James Weldon Johnson in the James Weldon Johnson Literary Guild to raise money for the purchase of books. Their main criterion, as was often the case, was that the books ought to contain characters who would inspire black children and counteract the stereotyped comic young characters in most children's tales.[87]

Churches and civic organizations were also instrumental in children's learning. The NAACP's Junior Organization and the UNIA's Juvenile Division, to take two examples of groups created by national organizations, aimed to educate young members to participate in civic life.[88] Adult leaders in the NAACP received instructions on exercises that included a "how-to" guide for dramatizing the Boston Massacre, important because the first man to die in the conflict was Crispus Attucks, a black man. The history children were to learn went beyond a narrowly national framework. They were encouraged to perform songs from Africa, taken from *Songs and Tales from the Dark Continent* (1920), as well as tunes by contemporary black composers, including the unofficial black anthem, "Lift Every Voice and Sing." Children were divided into activity committees. One group took charge of cutting out all newspaper pieces "pertaining to the achievements of Negroes to be read at meetings and to be pasted in a scrap book which will be the property of the group." Clippings were arranged by content: "educational, art, music, science, industry, athletic, etc. including foreign as well as American." Another group of children formed the Library Committee to ascertain what books were in the local library and to ask to borrow from local individuals any books relevant to black history that were not housed in the library. A third group, assisted by an adult, selected music for each meeting.[89] The intention was to encourage in children a curiosity and pride in their past and present, by focusing on topics that ranged from African cultural heritage to the achievements of Crispus Attucks to contemporary athletes.

Acting and singing were central to children's history education, as the NAACP program and Ballard's recollections of Negro History Week suggest, whether inside school or out. All over the United States, in fact, pageantry was an extremely popular means of learning and representing America's past and of taking part in civic culture, especially during the Progressive era leading up to World War I, but also in the two decades following the war.[90] These public expressions of identity were important at a time when many Americans felt their nation to be in turmoil as a result of the large numbers of immigrants entering the country. As in historical discourse more broadly, however, black Americans played little or no part. When pageantry was at its peak, black people were excluded even from those scripts portraying the ethnic mix of the nation's past.[91] Israel Zangwill's *The Melting Pot* (1908), into which all newcomers stepped and from which they emerged "Americanized," included no black American characters; its author believed that "white and black are as yet too far apart for profitable fusion."[92] Into the 1920s, pageants depicted slavery as a benign institution and Reconstruction as a tragedy, adhering to the Southern white memory of the nineteenth century. Three pageants in North Carolina in 1921, 1925, and 1929, for instance, felt no need to offer any excuses or apologies for slavery, let alone introduce any sympathetic black characters.[93]

Playscripts for black children were available in collections after 1930; prior to that, they were created and sometimes circulated locally. One evening in New York, children transformed music and poetry into pantomimes and pageants under the direction of the children's librarian at the 135th Street branch of the Public Library.[94] Elsewhere, Miss Ada Crogman penned the pageant "The Milestones of a Race." When staged in Rockford, Illinois, with a cast of two hundred, the auditorium was fully booked for two nights. When it moved on to Dayton, Ohio, the *New York Amsterdam News* ended its long report with high praise: "In this production, the spectators were given a more sympathetic understanding of America's colored people and their contribution to her national life than ever before. Said one colored citizen: 'I never felt so proud of the fact that I'm a Negro until I saw this pageant.'"[95] Black Americans at last were center stage, and they welcomed the novelty.

Written mostly by women, and almost always directed by women, pageants employed an oral dimension of history making by performing anew the telling of historical tales and passing them down from generation to generation. As a genre, pageants were somewhere in between oral and written histories. Although they were sometimes recorded, even published, and could be repeated in different places and times, they were not footnoted nor subject to the "scientific" disciplinary requirements that were fast becoming the hallmark of publications by Woodson and others. Each performance of a scripted pageant was different, as they strived to be dramatic and entertaining, rather than scholarly and fact-based. They were nevertheless supported by activists, Woodson primary among them, as an outstanding way to teach children and to boost their psychological health.

Teachers and activists hoped that, in donning costumes and declaiming scripted lines, children would learn from their black predecessors, both American and African. Most pageants and short plays dramatized the achievements of notable men and women of the past. Activists hoped that, by standing, just for a moment, in the shoes of these historical greats, children would develop empathy for the men and women of their race as well as a degree of racial pride. It would make them feel good about themselves and would reverse the trend whereby each black pupil, in Woodson's words, "easily learns to follow the line of least resistance rather than battle against odds for what real history has shown to be the right course."[96] Teachers, in short, hoped that their pupils would imbibe the character traits of those whose lives they impersonated on stage.

Some black pageant writers were keen to extend the picture painted of black history beyond a focus on the achievements of famous individuals and the glories of Africa's ancient past. Though writers hoped that their pageants would shield children from racism's harm, they did not think it sufficient merely to furnish the young actors with heroes. Dissidents sought to expand what was thought of as "positive" history. The incessant replaying of that which had been lost—those glories of the past hidden beyond what Clarke called "slavery's curtain"—indicated an unhealthy melancholy.[97] Dominant forms of black history making might be seen as an "acting out" of a traumatic past without any resolution. What was needed, some averred, was a "working through" of that past to reach a stage of mourning that would bring about reconciliation.[98] Coming to terms with their loss would enable black Americans to maintain a healthy separation between past history and present circumstances. Importantly, in their view, coming to terms with the entirety of black history would bring about a recognition of those decidedly not-famous people in the past who had survived adverse circumstances with dignity.

History makers' emphasis on glory and contribution was coupled with relative silence on the painful legacy of enslavement. It was comparatively rare to find in popular histories of the era accounts of Africans' engagement in the slave trade, the journey known as the Middle Passage, or even the violence of enslavement on the American mainland. It was not that these accounts did not exist but that painful aspects of the past were overshadowed by popular, entertaining histories, and they were underplayed in texts aimed at children.

Many female pageant writers, by contrast, wanted children both to know about the hardships endured by their ancestors and to be proud of their predecessors' tenacity in surviving. From 1920 to 1924, a pageant by Alice Holdship Ware, the wife of Atlanta University's president, played around the country, garnering effusive notices wherever it went.[99] According to newspaper reports, it emphasized the progress from barbarism to enlightenment, as former slaves came through the "open door"—the pageant's title—of American education and civilization. Although all mainstream newspapers noted the progress narrative, the show did have its large cast perform scenes of the travails of "the dark days in Africa, through slavery and oppression."[100] According to its program, the pageant enacted "Four hundred years, of agony and pain, / Beaten and cursed, transplanted, forced to serve, / Under the lash of Greed."[101] The point of many of these pageants was to demonstrate how far black Americans had come since the degradations of enslavement, but whatever their intentions, pageants were rare in extending depictions of black history beyond a litany of contributions to world and American civilization.

Pageants around the country similarly emphasized the progress of the race while depicting the horrors of enslavement. Dorothy Guinn's *Out of the Dark* (1924), included in a 1930 collection published by the ASNLH's Associated Publishers, offered a fulsome treatment of the black past. In this production, the narrator alluded briefly to the Middle Passage while documenting poet Phillis Wheatley's arrival in North America.[102] Staging represented the hardships of slavery; props included a bullwhip and the costumes were "burlap sacks."[103] An unnamed pageant performed in 1934 at the Mother Zion church in Harlem shied away from the slave trade but did portray American slavery. It was

an historical pageant of Negro progress . . . accompanied by hymns and song. In the role of historian Miss Kelly told of the race's beginning, its glory and grandeur from the days of Ham and his sons, as related in the Christian Bible, through the days of mighty Egypt with its black Phar[ao]hs; then through the days of slavery in America, the long years of the Negro's travail under the pitiless yoke of bondage, then freedom, followed by the Negro's comparatively swift rise to full citizenship and culture in America, and delineating some of the race's prominent characters of today as published in "Who's Who in Colored America."[104]

The attention paid in these performances to the experience of enslavement made the rise of the race since even more remarkable and made it abundantly clear that circumstances, not biological inferiority, accounted for the present-day situation of black Americans.

Activist Mary Church Terrell in 1932 wrote a pageant that even more thoroughly defied the convention of avoiding the horrors of the Middle Passage. The "Historical Pageant-Play Based on the Life of Phyllis Wheatley" was an unusual pageant in that it featured a single figure whose experiences were followed in some depth. Terrell opened with a scene depicting the capture of slaves in Africa, then in Act II dramatized the Middle Passage. The narrator spoke: "The ocean voyage was terrible, they say. There was an awful storm. The waves were so high they almost touched the sky. The people were packed in that ship like those little fishes you buy in a can." Several characters make the description a kind of refrain: "They were packed in that ship. . . . They could hardly move. . . . Many of them died on the way over and were thrown overboard. . . . Hundreds of them died on the way over, you know."[105] Terrell's dialogue was uniquely explicit about conditions during transportation.

The "they say" of Terrell's text was also atypical in pageantry. Rather than scripting the usual pious narration accompanied by children in tableaux, Terrell drew on the oral tradition of black American history, told generation to generation. She introduced on stage the narrative dimensions of an understanding of the past. The pageant's unusual form reflected its striking content: the story of the Middle Passage, as passed down orally through generations of slaves and free black Americans. As in other pageants written by women, Terrell implicitly critiqued the idea that meaningful and useful history had to commemorate forgotten contributions to civilization. The focus was still on positive aspects of the past, but here "positive" also meant the strength required to survive the adversity of enslavement. Children ought to be as equally proud of their enslaved ancestors as they were of being descendants of the first humans on earth and the great pharaohs, kings, and queens of Africa. Terrell's pageant, like all pageants, also served an important and related function: to reclaim oral history as a valid method of remembering and recording the past.

Home and family were potential sites of resistance and political mobilization as much as were those institutions established in the black public sphere. Black Americans' struggle to gain some control over their history took place at the personal, psychological, and domestic levels, as well as in public institutions. Black historians and bibliophiles became quite literally household names among readers of black American history, including newspapers and magazines, because the impact of these scholars' work resonated through black homes as parents undertook their children's historical education.[106]

Institutions dedicated to reshaping views of the African past advised women to take a leading role in their children's education. Amy Jacques Garvey, married to UNIA head Marcus Garvey, encouraged women to develop a "'taste for serious reading.' Do not throw away newspapers but 'put a wrapper on it and mail it' to others." On special occasions, women ought to send books as gifts, and they should read stories to their children every day. Reading should be something families enjoyed together. In an editorial, Jacques Garvey admonished mothers: "Meek docile women usually rear puny, effeminate men, and ignorance certainly begets ignorance."[107] Emphasis on the home as the place for learning continued into the next decade, when the ASNLH urged families to ensure that they acquired "the best newspapers, magazines, and books which record the significant achievements of the Negro" as well as accounts of the achievements and histories of other races.[108]

Olivia Pearl Stokes, born in 1916, remembered that she and her siblings learnt about "the African contribution and of the African pattern of life" from their mother.[109] There were few other places for children to learn about their own history and traditions. As one New York letter writer to the *Negro World* said, she "knew of no institution to which Negro children may be sent to learn the facts about themselves." She sought remedies for the difficulty of "acquir[ing] education along racial lines" and was eager "to hear what other readers, especially mothers, have to suggest along these lines."[110] Women understood that black history could help root their children in the community and the larger nation by showing them how and why they belonged. Deborah Wolfe, also born in 1916, recalled that her parents

> were determined that we know who we are and what our background and heritage is, and so we always had all the books by and about blacks in Africa and the United States. We were concerned to know and document whatever we said about it. . . . We have a great heritage. And I knew this because my parents began to teach me. We didn't used to get this information in school, going to white schools, as I did all my life.[111]

There was a pervasive sense that mothers needed to take seriously their role as a rearguard, as it were, to back up schools in the fight against ignorance about black history. A study of black American women's reading habits in Chicago had as its rationale the fact that these women could potentially be responsible for children's learning and therefore the advancement of the race. Published in the *Journal of Negro Education,* the study aimed to determine whether the women under scrutiny had been schooled sufficiently "in the art of selecting types of reading material during the formative period" of their lives. If not, then the same error needed to be offset in the present and avoided in the future. Though the conclusion was that libraries ought to "improve the reading interests and tastes" of poorly educated women, the implicit suggestion was that women themselves needed to prevent ignorance from being passed down from generation to generation.[112]

Even if mothers had the best of intentions, there were shortcomings to relying on the home as a place where children could learn the history they were missing out on in school. In Jessie Fauset's fourth and final novel, *Comedy, American Style* (1933), the curiosity of the two elder children in the Cary family is nurtured when they are young. "For a brief while Christopher's hero was Crispus Attucks; Teresa's brave Sojourner Truth. But later, through lack of nourishment, their interest in this phase of history died."[113] Early education at home could not overcome outside forces that asserted that black people had made no contribution to civilization and were lesser human beings. Through a lack of understanding of her own past, Teresa comes to feel that she is "a girl without a country."[114] Fauset put into fiction

the fear among most parents that as their children grew and ventured beyond the home, white perceptions of black people would prevail. The family
setting was insufficient for teaching a history of Africans and their scattered
descendants. Public institutions had to come to the fore if children's interest
in and knowledge of an African past was to be sustained as they grew older.

Not every effort to reform what children learnt about black history was a
success, especially in the South, where the major sources of funding were
philanthropic organizations bent on agricultural and industrial education.
In rural areas, schools for black children remained extremely poor, with
teachers of varying levels of training and enthusiasm.[115] Even those who
wanted to teach children about the black past had limited resources. Rare
indeed was a set of matching textbooks; most written materials were
hand-me-downs from nearby white schools.[116] Teachers faced the challenge
of one-room schools with students of different ages and abilities. Urban
schoolteachers in the South dealt more directly with the constraints of
white superintendents and school boards.[117] Arthur Parker, long-time principal of Birmingham's black high school, was able to introduce black history
into the curriculum only in the late 1930s, shortly before his death, and even
then he faced "keen opposition."[118] Black historical education in Southern
schools was stymied further by the desires of white benefactors, who advocated "industrial education" for vocational purposes, rather than a more
classic liberal curriculum. With precious funding linked to compliance,
"practical education," as urged by various philanthropic organizations, won
out over history lessons.[119]

   Even with resources and willpower, teachers faced the challenge of there
simply not being materials for children to learn black history. The *Wilson
Bulletin for Libraries* for 1933 published a list of twenty-seven books about
"The American Negro" that ought to be in "*all* school libraries." Of these,
only four were written for children.[120] Many more existed by then, but
those who compiled such lists were either not aware of them or not impressed by them. In most cases, librarians did not seek out such resources.
A survey conducted by the American Library Association in the early 1920s
discovered that in sixteen public libraries in the South, there was not one
black American library school graduate. This was undoubtedly due to the

lack of access to professional training and then the difficulty of finding employment in segregated towns and cities. Not until 1925 did black librarians begin training at Hampton Institute, a black college. In the late 1920s, 419 Southern schools, funded by philanthropist Julius Rosenwald, purchased books from a list prepared by the Hampton Institute library and thus began their own collections on black studies. The General Education Board and other philanthropic organizations provided funds around the same time for library buildings and resources for major Southern black institutions at lower levels. The Depression stalled these activities.[121] A 1944 survey showed that of the nation's 7,100 public libraries, only 802 were in the South, and of these only 121 would provide any sort of service to black Americans.[122]

Activists also battled to institute the study of African history at the tertiary level. Alain Locke, a professor at Howard University, waged a constant campaign from 1924 to the early 1930s for a Department of African Studies. Like Schomburg, Locke was a collector, though his passion was for African art rather than books. Born in Philadelphia, he was educated at Harvard University and, as the first black Rhodes Scholar, at Oxford. At Howard University, where he taught from 1912, he was the chair of the Department of Philosophy from 1921 until he retired in 1953. Howard, he asserted, could become the world leader in the field and perform an enormous service to its main constituents: black American students and their families and communities. "Slavery," he wrote "cut the Negro off almost completely from his roots. Its greatest damage was not the bondage of those generations that bore the physical brunt of it, but the damage to the group tradition, the self esteem and morals of these people,—which spiritual loss and handicap grows rather than diminishes as the Negro struggles on toward intellectual and cultural development." If Locke's argument was contentious, none of the activists discussed here would have disagreed with him that "one of the peculiar functions and duties" of black universities was to remedy this wrong.[123] Locke was unsuccessful; he would not have been surprised when he received from Woodson a letter describing the latter's fury when a faculty member at a black college treated the request to mount a course in Negro history "as a joke."[124] Locke's vision of the study of black life and history, in its broadest and most expansive geographical and chronological sense, came to pass only after the black studies movement of the 1960s.

Motivated by that very experience, and striving to overcome barriers to better history teaching, in 1927 Woodson's ASNLH introduced correspondence classes through its Home Study Department. By doing so, the organization cut out the middle man, who was so often difficult to convince of the merit of including black experience in history education. Aimed initially at "those who would like to study the aspects of African civilization which were neglected in the schools in which they were trained," on offer were courses in history, social history, church history, literature, African art, education, social psychology, sociology, and anthropology, each custom-made by experts associated with the ASNLH and Howard University. The latter two disciplines would focus on black people in Africa.[125] Courses such as these—in which the "Negro" was always considered in a framework beyond the borders of the United States and that intended to raise the self-regard of black individuals—could be instituted only by an organization such as the ASNLH, because by then it was operating independent of white philanthropy and of white university trustees. Upon review of the initiative's progress over the first couple of years, it was clear that only a few people had enrolled in 1928. In 1929, Woodson put a very positive spin on what looked like only a few individual teachers, and perhaps a couple of clubs and societies, who had banded together to pay the tuition fees for one person, who would then lecture the others.[126] Irrespective of an offer to tailor further courses for individuals or groups, however, there was clearly not enough interest to sustain the home study program beyond the onset of the Depression.

Whatever the limits of changes in the education of black youngsters and youth, these labors barely touched white institutions. As Woodson, Clarke, Fauset, and countless others feared, black history remained outside the mainstream of American public life and made few inroads into traditional school and university curricula. By 1934, when Huggins and Jackson compiled their *Guide* for teachers, they trumpeted the absolute necessity that black children learn their "thrilling story" but conceded that "the time when America will regard us as members, in full and regular standing in its industrial and cultural society, is far distant. We cannot, we dare not," the authors averred, "continue to remain indifferent to our own cultural heritage, in the well nigh vain hope of being grafted into that of another."[127] Even if Africans were the originators of democracy and civilization, and despite black Americans' myriad contributions to the homeland to which their ancestors were transported by force, their descendants would never simply be seamlessly interwoven into the American nation-state. By the mid-1930s, it was clear that America had to be changed radically, not merely reformed.

The emphasis placed on history in black public life yielded in the mid-1930s to a preference for social science or interdisciplinary approaches to understanding Africa and black diaspora experiences. As in children's pageants, celebratory histories of progress and triumph began to give way to more considered accounts of conflict in America's past. This change came partly from an emphasis on "scientific" history. *Journal of Negro History* reviews disdained work by Du Bois and others as vague, sentimental, and "unscientific".[128] No higher accolade could have been given Woodson than a review praising *The Negro in Our History* as having "used the principles of historical investigation which safeguard accuracy, proportion, and judgment to record in a sympathetic way the story of his race."[129] Accurate accounts could not brook racial chauvinism and therefore required a wider account of black people's history than just a record of their positive achievements. Ultimately, these would serve the race better than simplistic, if therapeutic, renderings. Even though the *Journal* published work mainly about black people, Carter Woodson's vision was for world history that recognized the contributions made by all peoples and favoring no single race. This, he believed, was a more scientific approach to the past. The move toward scientific history paved the way for social science approaches to understanding Africa.

Racial romanticists came under increasing ridicule. Bibliophile and scholar Arthur Schomburg derided them in no less a publication than *The New Negro* (1925), the first major literature anthology of the New Negro Renaissance, edited by Alain Locke. Schomburg condemned as counterproductive the "rash and rabid amateur who has glibly tried to prove half of the world's geniuses to have been Negroes and to trace the pedigree of nineteenth century Americans from the Queen of Sheba."[130] Writer Zora Neale Hurston was the most damning. She observed, in typically caustic yet affectionate fashion, that those "Negroes who claim that they are descendants

of royal African blood have taken a leaf out of the book of the white
ancestor-hounds in America, whose folks went to England with William the
Conqueror, got restless and caught the *Mayflower* for Boston, then feeling a
romantic lack, rushed down the coast and descended from Pocahontas."[131]
Not only was the trend to link one's personal history to important historical
figures scientifically bogus, Hurston seemed to say, but it was ineffective to
do so. The result was to confirm one's Americanness, rather than one's
Africanness.

Interest in Africa began to move more firmly into the present day. Black
Americans, most famously singer and actor Paul Robeson, began to learn
African languages.[132] A "striking African program" given in 1934 at International House in New York City listed mostly missionaries and Jeanes
education supervisors as its speakers. In keeping with this focus on contemporary Africa, an American woman was slated to give an illustrated lecture
on "native life and leadership," while an African graduate student, studying
in the United States, was to "speak on Africa for Africans."[133] Nobody spoke,
at least according to the newspaper's brief outline, on African history. Such
an omission would have been unthinkable five years earlier, let alone ten, in
the aftermath of Marcus Garvey's heyday, when Africa's past dominated
black American public life.

The general change in approach was well illustrated by the changing interests of UESA members. Inspired by a Garvey-like "Ethiopianism," the
group initially celebrated Africa's past glories and anticipated eagerly the
fulfillment of the biblical prophesy that Ethiopia would rise again. But when
fascist Italy threatened to invade Abyssinia, UESA members' consciousness
of Africa was brought quickly into the present day. Just four years earlier,
the revelation that Liberians were engaged in slavery was insufficient for
UESA club members to shift their gaze from Africa's glorious past. The society's president in fact condemned George Schuyler, who unearthed the
scandal for America's newspaper readers, as a race-hating Uncle Tom.[134]
UESA members preferred, like Du Bois, to keep their gaze fixed firmly on
the past, portrayed in such a way that black people were always victims of
white colonizers and slave traders, who destroyed their majestic king-
doms.[135] Even in 1933, when UESA members corresponded with Liberian
students and teachers, members' delight at this exchange was expressed as
though the Africans were the same as the slaves from whom the black

Americans were descended: "words from the Motherland . . . [for the] Sons of Africa."[136] With Mussolini's encroachment upon Ethiopia, however, it became apparent to many black Americans that history, especially that specializing in black people's contributions to early civilization, did not provide the analytic tools needed to survey this crisis. A circular letter sent out sometime after the war broke out noted that the UESA would be "fostering a 'National Ethiopia Week,' during which every effort will be made to dis[s]eminate authentic informations about Ethiopia."[137] The organization's 1936 pamphlet *The Truth about Ethiopia* opened with two pages of general history about Africa, then a few pages dealing with the Ethiopian past. Most of the document concerned events in Ethiopia since 1896, that is, the relationship between Ethiopia and Italy leading up to the invasion and occupation.[138]

This disaster crystallized a changed attitude toward Africa that was partly the product of a new generation of students and scholars exposed to changes in American academia as well as world politics. Sociologists transferred their attention from topics and questions close to those studied in anthropology—namely, primitive, non-Western societies. Instead, practitioners tended now to pursue questions about urban environments. Sociology became a tool to examine contemporary society.[139] For black students and scholars, who already had a "global vision" of the past, sociology, with its questions about the present, became an ideal methodology through which to think about Africa.[140]

Sociology, like all the social sciences, did not necessarily lend itself easily to critiques of American race relations; the social sciences were steeped in beliefs held widely among Americans that their nation was exceptional, on an ever-improving, forward-moving path to greatness.[141] Nevertheless, these new disciplines displaced history as the mode for examining questions about the relationship between black Americans and Africa. When Ralph Bunche, a talented young man who later went on to win a Nobel Peace Prize, came to pick a discipline for doctoral study, he opted for political science. Completed at Harvard in 1934, his dissertation was entitled "French Administration in Togoland and Dahomey." Bunche dealt swiftly with the history of these two areas since the sixteenth century and moved on to focus on the present-day colonial administration. He aimed to enlighten administrators about each place, because "Africa is the 'mysterious continent' to many of the Europeans who invade it because they make so little effort to understand it."[142] Greater knowledge, Bunche hoped, would lead to the withdrawal of colonial administration. Access to that knowledge, it was now thought, came through disciplines other than history.

Research and teaching in black universities were heading in the same direction. Charles S. Johnson was lured away from the Urban League to Fisk University in 1928 to help the university's president, Thomas Elsa Jones, establish a social sciences department. Johnson emphasized sociology and economics in order to focus the department's attention on "the Negro and Race Relations in the United States."[143] By the mid-1940s, Johnson's vision extended to make the research comparative. He and his colleagues compared race relations in the South with those in the North, the West Indies, and Africa. Johnson's faculty was one of two in the South distinctive for its insistence on scientific methodology. At the second, run by Howard W. Odum at the University of North Carolina, race relations were but one of many factors under scrutiny in a focus on the South and, into the 1930s, American regionalism more generally.[144]

Black scholars sometimes chafed against the expectation that they would focus their attention on matters linked to race.[145] Nevertheless, in the growing social science disciplines, many did just that. The *Journal of Negro History* marveled in 1934 at the potential for change that came with the proliferation of fields in which to study "the Negro." With increasing numbers of colleges moving toward graduate work (and with increasing student enrollments), the *Journal* asserted that "the departments of History, Political Science, Anthropology, English, Education, Sociology, and Economics can very easily find places for courses dealing definitely with the Negro."[146] Woodson's journal itself was now joined—and challenged—by the *Journal of Negro Education*, begun in 1932 under the auspices of the College of Education at Howard University. The newer publication's editors aimed to rise above other organizations focused on black education, which tended toward "inspirational talks rather than critical appraisals." History, they stated explicitly, was not up to the task.[147] The editors conceded it was crucial to know the past so as "to show the proper place of the race in history" but suggested that students ought to learn "the history of ancient, mediaeval, and modern Africa."[148] Contemporary African life and politics were moving center stage.

Nor, it seemed, was history sufficient to the task of addressing worsening conditions among black Americans during the Depression. The new journal's editors shared with colleagues throughout Howard University a desire to analyze and improve the economic situation of working-class black Americans. Economist Abram Harris Jr., sociologist E. Franklin Frazier, and political scientist Ralph Bunche were all also connected to Howard. It was a Howard-run conference on the economic situation of black Americans in 1935 that led to the establishment of the National Negro Congress, which had close ties to the Communist Party.[149]

A generation of scholars in the new disciplines rejected the racial ideology of black nationalism evident in so much history writing of the interwar years. The school of anthropology led by Franz Boas, which asserted that racial differences were cultural rather than biological, planted deep roots in the 1920s. In the ensuing decade, some black intellectuals ignored, or publicly denounced, black unity, which they now saw as racial chauvinism based on false assumptions about biological difference.[150] Their number included sociologists who descended, as it were, from Robert Park and other researchers at the University of Chicago. Park announced that "the Negro, when he landed in the United States, left behind him almost everything but his dark complexion and his tropical temperament. It is very difficult to find in the South today anything that can be traced directly back to Africa."[151] These two approaches to black American culture were used to fight for racial equality and desegregation, respectively.[152] Liberal disciplines were skeptical about the biological basis of race and therefore challenged the assumption that ancient Africans and present-day black Americans were linked. As a result, in the new environment of the mid-1930s, a celebration of African history was no longer instantly meaningful.

Du Bois recognized the shortcomings of histories of contribution, coming to emphasize instead a Marxist approach to American and colonial race relations, and breaking with the integrationist NAACP. In 1935, he published his powerful *Black Reconstruction,* which broke the mold of idealist histories that looked forward to a time of racial harmony in a genuinely pluralist American society. Du Bois came to argue (publicly) that the ideals of the Declaration of Independence and the Constitution would never be implemented without economic change.[153] The impetus for such change could come about only through a radically altered American historical consciousness, one based in an ethical approach to understanding the past that included a confrontation with conflict, especially around the question of race.[154] *Black Reconstruction* signaled a shift from Du Bois's earlier stated hope (even if it was one he was dubious about) that an appeal to conscience alone would bring about an egalitarian America. "Blackness" could no longer be understood as simply racial difference; it was also an experience of difference designated by a distance from wealth and the means to acquire it. This shift was to have significant effects on black identity, reorienting it yet again, away from the hard-fought alliance with Africans (at least of the past) and toward oppressed people worldwide.

History's waning influence was evident in landmark publications in the 1930s and beyond, whose methodologies were derived more from social sciences than from tales of the past. Many black Americans contributed to a massive compendium, *Negro* (1934), put together in France by wealthy British heiress Nancy Cunard. The anthology employed myriad approaches to its topic, drawing on geographic regions spanning the globe.[155] Back in the United States, black academics and intellectuals discussed at length a proposed "Encyclopaedia of the Negro." It had been Du Bois's dream for decades to document in an important, lengthy, and authoritative volume all of the difficulties faced and triumphs achieved by black Americans.[156] Typically, it would place black Americans in a global context:

> It is proposed that the Encyclopaedia be devoted mainly to the American Negro, but that it should include important related topics regarding the Negro in Africa and elsewhere. It is believed that an Encyclopaedia of about four volumes of the general type of the "Encyclopaedia of the Social Sciences," each volume containing about 500,000 words, would be suitable. It should include all important phases of Negro Life and History—anthropological, ethnographical, biographical, historical, educational, industrial, economic, political, religious, psychological (including race relations), artistic, etc.[157]

The encyclopedia, in which new disciplines fell under the overarching banner of "Negro Life and History," was never published. (Du Bois kept the dream alive, going to Ghana in 1961 to head a project to write it there.) Instead, the personnel who might have written it were recruited to take part in a $300,000 Carnegie-Myrdal Study published as *An American Dilemma: The Negro Problem and Modern Democracy* (1944). Targeting an implicitly white male audience, Swedish author Gunnar Myrdal implored readers to fix the American problem of race relations, presenting it as a moral dilemma rather than an economic one. "The economic situation of the Negroes in America," Myrdal asserted confidently, "is pathological."[158] Where black activism—drawing on history and now other disciplines—had placed "the Negroes" and American race relations in extra-national perspectives, and always as actors in the pageant of their own destiny, Myrdal proclaimed a narrowly national account that foresaw an end to injustice once the "American Creed" was made to live up to its ideals. Myrdal's vision of the so-called Negro Problem came to prevail in mainstream America, animating much of the struggle for civil rights in the 1950s and 1960s, at the expense of a more radical vision of social change.[159]

The 1920s saw an explosion of interest in black American history. Accounts of black people's terrific achievements in the past were rich fodder for refuting so-called scientific claims of black inferiority. The desire to protect children from psychologically damaging racism made the study of history an imperative. It motivated activists to concentrate their efforts on schooling and on the creation and distribution of materials appropriate to children.

What had for a long time been a marginal pursuit—the telling and retelling of Africa's glorious history—became instrumental in the development of black civic life. Across the country and with ties to others abroad, black Americans organized themselves into societies and clubs to learn and disseminate black history, starting with Africa and carrying through to the present day, taking in places around the diaspora along the way. Even those societies not expressly devoted to such study evinced an interest in the topic, naming themselves after ancient black heroes, inviting speakers with expertise in history, and discussing with gusto their heritage. Black Americans' reorientation toward Africa was a process that involved institutions as well as individuals. At an individual and collective level, the discovery of a rich past, both in Africa and in the New World, made for a more positive black identity.

Woodson would have been disappointed that all this work had only limited success in changing attitudes among white Americans. He had "looked forward to the time when it would not be necessary to set aside a 'week' to call attention to the contributions of Negroes to this country."[160] Yet, this still had not happened by the time of his death in 1950, nor, in fact, today. Woodson's reservations about Negro History Week and separatist black history notwithstanding, his work and that of others were essential in nationalizing and institutionalizing an interest among black Americans in their heritage and in fostering a positive relationship between black Americans and black people elsewhere.

4

The Artistic Capital of Africa

Africa was "poetic capital of the first order" according to Alain Locke, philosopher at Howard University in Washington, D.C., and a key promoter of writers and artists during the 1920s and 1930s.[1] The "motherland" certainly preoccupied many of black America's creative elite, who were the luminaries of a cultural movement known at the time as the New Negro Renaissance or Awakening. These names for the movement—now more commonly known as the Harlem Renaissance—referred to the hope that the brilliance last seen at the glittering peak of the Ethiopian and Egyptian civilizations would shine once again. Protagonists and lesser lights felt that they were in the middle of something special, with their profiles high due to America's burgeoning culture of celebrity combined with the emergence of black urban centers. They were buoyed along by support for black writers at new publishing houses in New York, an expanding print media in Harlem and other cities, and an interest in African art not only in black creative circles but in modernist painting and sculpture more generally.

The New Negro Renaissance spanned roughly the years from 1919 to 1935, though its start, finish, and high points differ depending on whether the emphasis is on literature, visual arts, stage productions, or music. It was made possible by the same confluence of events and ideas that gave new license to black public life in general, with a few additional conditions unique to New York. The willingness of black Southerners and migrants from the Caribbean to pick up and move, combined with white Northerners' distaste for mixed neighborhoods, resulted in the formation of ever more crowded black areas in all major Northern cities. Harlem, with its sweeping wide boulevards and well-maintained brownstone buildings, was one such community. Not yet the ghetto it would famously become, Harlem afforded newcomers an unprecedented sense of freedom, while tales of the "all-black" city spread far and wide. Though businesses were owned mostly by non-black Americans—Jewish and Italian Americans especially—and the majority of Harlem's residents lived in shocking poverty that has been captured better by novelists than by historians, its symbolic importance cannot be overstated. Nor can the feeling of freedom many of its residents enjoyed, especially compared with their former lives. It was, in the words of Locke, the "Mecca of the New Negro."[2]

The "New Negro" was a figure who emerged from black activists' concern over public representations of the race. During the decades when "Jim Crow" segregation was at its height, caricatured images of black Americans adorned everything from breakfast cereal to toothpaste. Activists were keen to expose these mammies, Sambos, and picaninnies as fantasies of white Americans' imaginations, not grounded in reality.[3] Booker T. Washington, a famous Southern educator, was the first to popularize the term, proclaiming "A New Negro for a New Century" in a 1900 anthology of the same name, which he edited with two others. Subtitled "An Accurate and Up-to-Date Record of the Upward Struggles of the Negro Race," it aimed to prove to white readers just how far black Americans had come since slavery (and to chide some black readers into pulling up their socks).[4] Washington's "New Negro" was produced by particular strategies for improving black Americans' future. These tactics aimed to create a black elite, or "Talented Tenth" as W. E. B. Du Bois called it, that would prove to white Americans that beliefs in black inferiority were groundless while simultaneously lifting the rest of the race up to the elite's standards.[5]

Come 1919 and beyond, the "New Negro" continued to perform as a representational figure for some, while others began to chafe against the expectation that their public statements (including creative arts) would always have in mind a white audience and the ultimate goal of improving the condition of "the race." Speaking broadly, Du Bois, Locke, and Charles Johnson, who edited the Urban League's journal, *Opportunity,* an important publication for the movement, sought full inclusion in American life, not through a simple assimilation but by transforming the United States into a genuinely pluralist place. A younger generation of writers, artists, and musicians professed to care less about their audiences and were more interested in mining the "real" of black life (often conceived of as Southern folk and vernacular culture) for their art. In the words of writer Langston Hughes in the conclusion to a long piece he penned for the *Nation* in 1926, a year that saw a great deal of debate about what constituted valid public expression:

> We younger Negro artists who create now intend to express our individual dark-skinned selves without fear or shame. If white people are pleased we are glad. If they are not, it doesn't matter. We know we are beautiful. And ugly too. The tom-tom cries and the tom-tom laughs. If colored people are pleased we are glad. If they are not, their displeasure doesn't matter either. We build our temples for tomorrow, strong as we know how, and we stand on top of the mountain, free within ourselves.[6]

Members of this younger generation wrote "blues poetry" and racy novels that made Du Bois "feel distinctly like taking a bath."[7] Their stage productions focused on the seamier side of life, while their visual art productions explored themes relating to identity that Du Bois and others would rather not have had aired in public.

Visual artists and creative writers featured Africa extensively in their work. Some echoed the preoccupation of those more overtly intent on activism, namely, an emphasis on Africa's glorious past and a possible return to the so-called motherland. Many artists and writers, however, probed the limits of an alliance between black Americans and Africans. Feeling no particular bond to Africa or Africans, they found that lack of emotional connection significant. Artists and writers may not have cared whether their work was representative, but their words and images are extremely useful in determining the full spectrum of black Americans' attitudes toward Africa. Their sentiments, expressed in myriad forms, allow access to emotions that are less apparent in other types of material, such as newspapers and organizations' files.

Five poets, for instance, mused on the degree or quality of the connection between black Americans, Africa, and Africans, by penning verses titled "Heritage." One of these was the era's best-known poem, by Countée Cullen, darling of the artistic movement and married, albeit briefly, to the daughter of Du Bois, Yolande. His poem opened with a question: "What is Africa to me?"[8] The answer was by no means straightforward. His poem's quest to describe and define black identity was typical of much of the art produced during the time. Not feeling any innate connection to Africa, in the face of widespread debate in black public life about the relationship between black Americans and the "motherland," creative types explored the nature of black identity. Was it local, national, African, diasporic, global, or something else entirely?

If writers and artists did not much feel like Africa's sons and daughters, nor did they feel part of an American family. Such a sense of estrangement had long been part of the experience of black residents and citizens in the United States, but in the postwar period these sentiments took on a new cast. National self-determination became an abiding theme of politics worldwide, and individuals had come to think of themselves in national as well as local or global terms. In the wake of World War I, American patriotism came to mean both accepting the policies of the nation-state and identifying with them, strong regional affiliations notwithstanding.[9] When the nation demanded loyalty of its members and yet rejected its black citizens, those in the latter group were left asking questions about their allegiance. By the end of Cullen's poem, it is clear that the poet was also addressing another question: "What is America to me?"[10] To be alienated from one's own nation meant either looking elsewhere for somewhere to call home, or redoubling efforts to transform the United States.

Given their sense of displacement, it was nothing short of a boon to black artists when the most cutting-edge of European artists took up African forms in their work. Pablo Picasso was the European modernist probably best known for his importation of African forms into his painting and sculpture, most provocatively in a painting of five prostitutes, *Les Demoiselles d'Avignon* (1907). Picasso kept company, formally speaking, with painter Georges Braque, sculptor Constantin Brancusi, Amedeo Modigliani, who worked in both media, and many others. Such work was quite well known in the United States, thanks to the efforts of Alfred Stieglitz, who exhibited it from 1908 at his New York City gallery, 291, and whose influence was instrumental in the gathering of 1,300 works for the International Exhibition of Modern Art, known as the Armory Show, in 1913. Successive and bigger shows from the 1910s through 1930s, combined with controversy over so-called degenerate art, ensured the increasing fame of these works and, in turn, of the original source of their inspiration: African sculpture.[11]

At first, most Americans, like most Europeans, were shocked and even horrified by the images produced by modernist painters and sculptors. Over time, however, as the artists' reputations grew, the kudos they accorded African art meant that it, too, rose in estimation.

Changing attitudes toward African artifacts and changing ideas about Africa's relationship to modernity were also a result of very significant academic and public debates over the meaning of race. Columbia University anthropologist Franz Boas led the way in introducing into mainstream thought a critique of racial ideology in which people were cast into categories on the basis of biological traits. Boas took issue with the idea that characteristics such as skin color and hair texture could indicate something about a person's place in the evolution of humanity, with black people considered more primitive than white. Instead, Boas asserted, people who belonged to—or claimed allegiance to—a particular race would come to share cultural traits with other members of that race. The case for race as a cultural form rather than something biological and determined made obvious sense to a group who rejected assertions that they were racially inferior but who continued to feel an affinity toward other black people and who could see the utility in continuing to act as a group in order to struggle against oppression. Regardless of the origins of such ideas, Boas's articulation of them helped interwar Americans to reassess African culture. These ideas were of great value to black intellectuals, who took them and ran with them, to use a sporting metaphor, aiming to discredit entirely the scientific basis of American racism.[12] In the arts specifically, new ideas about the non-hierarchical relationship of cultural forms to one another meant that foreign cultural forms could, in theory, be appreciated on their own merits, and not relative to Western civilization.

Even as academics gave up their belief that cultures, like the human race itself, developed along discernible lines, they remained fascinated with the processes by which people adapted to new surroundings. Sociologists and anthropologists were intrigued by the degree to which black Americans had "retained" African culture. Their debates proved useful to artists—and black Americans in general—who were interested in an African dimension to their own sense of self and collective identity. Leading white Chicago sociologist Robert Park was convinced that the process of enslavement meant that black Americans were divested of "anything that can be traced directly back to

Africa."[13] Park wrote as a liberal; as far as he was concerned, black Americans' adaptation to their new homeland was a good thing and provided evidence that discrimination ought to end. For him, the cultures of peoples thrown together invariably clashed, and after a struggle, one would be assimilated into the other. In the case of black Americans, the white man's culture had prevailed. Park's interpretation of black culture left something to be desired, and his conclusions were much challenged by the New Negro Renaissance. (Of particular note is Park's conclusion that slaves had no wish to return to Africa, based on a conversation with one of the last Africans to be transported across the Atlantic, who told him dryly, having survived the passage once, "I made up my mind then never to trust myself in a boat with a white man again.")[14] Writers and artists proved thoughtful commentators on the so-called retention of African culture in black American life, and they influenced in turn academic ideas. Their work also both reflected and encouraged an expansion of black consciousness that looked beyond the borders of the United States for its roots and, eventually, its modern-day ties.

In a nation in which they never felt quite at home, black Americans' exploration of identity was a political act. Black Americans were, of course, citizens, but their experiences were far from those associated with the status of citizenship. In truth, black Americans were more like "alien citizens," whose race, like that of certain Asian and other immigrant groups, marked them as not quite deserving of the full rights and duties of U.S. citizenship.[15] Black Americans' political protest centered on the injustice of being treated as though they were aliens; their activism revolved around issues of belonging and identity. Any poetic or artistic exploration of identity was therefore caught up in both the comparison of black Americans' experiences with those of aliens and the insistence on being accorded the rights and responsibilities of citizenship. Most artists and writers resisted the expectation, stated explicitly by Du Bois, for instance, that they be spokespeople for political campaigns, propagandists.[16] But their refusal to become propagandists did not, as they themselves recognized, change the fact that the questions in which they were interested were exactly those that formed the basis of black Americans' political struggle: Who are we? Where do we belong?

Black Americans had ample opportunity to survey African art, touted as an authentic expression of an unchanging culture and therefore the same as objects their ancestors might have produced. In 1923 in Brooklyn and in 1935 in midtown New York, major museums mounted large exhibitions of works from Africa, inviting visitors to appreciate what they were seeing as art. Both "Primitive Negro Art" at the Brooklyn Museum and "African Negro Art" at the Museum of Modern Art (MoMA) borrowed from eminent collectors in the United States and Europe and from major European institutions. The former exhibit held some 1454 items; the latter, 603. Unlike art exhibitions of African sculpture in New York in the 1910s, the pieces were not exhibited alongside paintings or sculptures by European modernists. Rather, they were displayed as objects with an intrinsic artistic value, irrespective of their relationship to European art.

The Brooklyn show was displayed as art, not anthropology. Curator Stewart Culin celebrated the decontextualized nature of the pieces exhibited. Specifically, he distinguished the 1923 collection from that displayed in the American Museum of Natural History's "vast hall of African ethnology."[17] "The entire collection," he wrote on the first page of the exhibition catalogue, "whatever may have been its original uses, is shown under the classification of art; as representing a creative impulse, and not for the purpose of illustrating the customs of African peoples."[18] Divesting the works—including cups, bowls, masks, and so-called fetishes—of details of their creation was done in an effort to free them from the baggage of ethnological research into their original function and what that might reveal about the people who created and used them. Instead, these objects ought to be valued like any other art form. Despite this effort to move viewers away from interpreting the objects as artifacts that would reveal the primitive soul, Culin also claimed that African art was timeless, that it literally "had no chronology." It was impossible to know "whether the objects exhibited be new or old." Something of this belief was captured in the exhibition catalog's cover, with its undated, unattributed androgynous figure and just the simple exhibition date of "1923." When curator James Johnson Sweeney came to write an essay for the 1935 MoMA exhibit catalog, he emphasized, as many reviewers noted, that most of the pieces in the collection, being wood, could not be more than 150 years old. Yet even those reviewers regarded these recent pieces as evidence of an ancient culture that had remained unchanged, aloof from the rest of the world.[19] Without any context to guide them, most reviewers (and perhaps most visitors) fell back on the image they had of Africa in their minds: ahistorical, unchanging, a static foil to Western civilization's progress.

In 1923 the Brooklyn Museum hosted an important exhibition of African art. Most of the pieces exhibited were fewer than 150 years old, but they were taken by the curator and most white reviewers to demonstrate an age-old, unchanging, "primitive" racial mindset. (Brooklyn Museum Libraries. *Primitive Negro Art: Chiefly from the Belgian Congo.* Department of Ethnology, Brooklyn Museum, 1923. Call number: ARL N7397.5 C76 B79.)

At the same time, these African objects were never simply art—at least, not in the way the curators intended, with attention paid purely to their aesthetic qualities. Tension lingered between art and ethnology, even among those who championed the former. Revealingly, in popular parlance the exhibitions' contents remained "relics" or "artifacts." Collective nouns were "specimens," "objects," "pieces," and "items," rather than "works," the common designation for art from, say, Europe.[20] In the catalogs, items were classified under such subheadings as "Fetishes" and "Masks." The Brooklyn

Museum's exhibition catalog came out of the Department of Ethnology, with some items displayed with no commentary at all, while others had numbers corresponding to a catalog description.[21] Such entries ranged from simply "218: Woman standing at top" to the much more detailed, such as "203: Carved and painted wooden bowl sustained by four human figures, male and female alternating. Yoruba. Used to hold the palm nuts in the practice of divination."[22] During the process of viewing the object and checking its number against its catalog entry, viewers were invited to link aesthetics to function and thereby interpret the objects ethnologically.

Inconsistency in the display of the collections also reflected an overlap between aesthetics and anthropology. In Brooklyn, the works were displayed mostly on white walls, indicating their status as art, rather than in glass cases as was more commonly the style in natural history or earlier museums. But again this transition was not complete; many of the wall hangings were collections of objects deemed similar in some way (type, purpose), hung together within a single frame.[23] Of course, the arrangement of the items did not necessarily mean that viewers did not consume them as art, just that the objects' display was reminiscent of ethnological and natural history collections. This dilemma in presentation extended beyond New York. For instance, when the African Art Sponsors of Cleveland donated $1,000 for the acquisition of African materials, a newspaper reported that the "African art objects" would ultimately be divided between institutions, including both the Museum of Art and Cleveland's Museum of Natural History.[24] The continuing confusion came from the slippage between the assertion that the objects reflected a timeless creative impulse and the idea that nothing changed in Africa anyhow, and that artistic genius was therefore a part of the static culture.

Debates about how to exhibit art from Africa reflected a more widespread contest over the nature of African culture and, for that matter, culture more generally. The work of Boas and others was fast transforming, at least in academic and associated circles, the definition of culture itself. Was culture, like biology, evolutionary, moving from lowest to highest? Or was culture nonhierarchical and inherently valuable because it reflected something of the people who created it?[25] When Paul Guillaume and Thomas Munro published *Primitive Negro Sculpture* (1926), their stated intention was to analyze the objects as "pure art." Guillaume was a famed French collector of African sculpture whose collection was said to have inspired

Picasso, while Munro worked in the educational unit of the Barnes Foundation in Merion, Pennsylvania. Albert C. Barnes had purchased a huge collection of African art from Guillaume in 1923 and now supported young black artists with fellowships. Barnes engineered the writing and publication of the book, and it reflected his very fixed ideas about the necessity of an aesthetic approach to African art.[26] This approach, Guillaume and Munro argued, would render void any discussion about whether African art was inferior to Western art. The breakthrough of *Primitive Negro Sculpture,* as far as Western art reviewing was concerned, was its treatment of African sculptors as sentient beings, whose achievements were not mere accidents of instinct, as English critics Clive Bell and Roger Fry had argued only a few years earlier.[27] Guillaume and Munro, however, never quite escaped the idea that cultures were related to one another through time, arguing that contrary to the usual interpretations, African sculpture was not the beginning of modern art but rather "perhaps a stage in advance of European evolution."[28]

This landmark publication was divisive: according to the critics of the "pure art" school, divorcing African objects from their original context emptied them of all significant meaning. If they were simply objects to be admired as pretty or ogled as barbarous and primitive, what use were they in understanding African culture? In a scathing review, anthropologist Melville Herskovits, a significant figure in a growing debate about the degree to which black Americans had retained African customs and tradition, condemned the project. First, Herskovits claimed, the authors' aim to analyze the objects in a purely artistic, formal way, was impossible to achieve. "Such an art," he wrote, "cannot be appreciated or understood outside its cultural setting." Locke likewise took Munro to task for his "arbitrary distinction between art and handicraft [which] is a vicious misinterpretation of African art. The distinction did not exist in that culture itself, and recognition of that fact is basic in the competent study and appreciation of African art." By following such criteria, Locke continued, half the photographic plates in the book (of bowls, cups, and so forth) should have been deleted.[29] The distinction between art object and object for use would have simply made no sense to the Africans who created the items. Herskovits further criticized the book's authors for failing to live up to their own expectations, providing cultural background for each piece included and doing so, he complained further, with no "factual historical data."[30] On this point, Herskovits was spot on: Guillaume and Munro stated erroneously that African art had died out long before European colonization. The sculptures featured in the book, which were produced probably no earlier than the nineteenth century, were dated as far back as the fifth century.[31]

Even if Guillaume and Munro had been able to interpret the objects as "pure art," their judgment, as Herskovits and others suggested, would simply impose the aesthetic taste of the European or Western viewer upon the thing or collection being examined. Decontextualization was a form of primitivism, derived from imperialism. "Art" was not an innocent category; what counted as art was wholly bound up in Western history, including the colonization of the non-West with its attendant ideologies of racial difference and racial hierarchy.[32] Regardless of these critiques, books such as *Primitive Negro Sculpture* helped transform the reputation of African art in the Western world.

Harlem's residents paid attention to the two downtown exhibitions. At up to 150 years old, some of these pieces were created when the British dominated the slave trade and many black Americans' ancestors were being transported across the Atlantic to American slavery. Newspapers and journals reported on both exhibitions, with editor Charles Johnson commissioning a long piece for the Urban League's journal, *Opportunity*.[33] Black commentaries differed in one significant respect from the mass of other press attention given to both exhibitions: they were concerned with the relationship between the art on view and black Americans. This great art was black Americans' inheritance. Black critics were quick to emphasize what Culin and Sweeney had downplayed in their effort to have the objects appreciated in their own right: the debt modern European artists owed to Africa. It was, after all, the interest of increasingly famous artists, foremost among them Picasso, that prompted institutions such as the Brooklyn Museum and MoMA to reappraise African art as worthwhile. A 1923 *New York Amsterdam News* article ended with a short paragraph appended to what was otherwise cribbed from Culin's press releases and essay: "The present vogue for African carving in New York, coinciding with the success of Negroes in the theatre, is lending new interest to the cultural background of the race."[34] Given the total absence of any such discussion in the extensive reportage in the mainstream press on both the 1923 and 1935 exhibitions, this was a case of wishful thinking.

Culin himself was far from interested in the connection between African art and black Americans, not mentioning it at all in his many interviews. Though perfectly cordial in his correspondence with Locke, staff at the 135th Street branch of the New York Public Library, Charles Johnson, Walter White at the National Association for the Advancement of Colored People (NAACP), and other black Americans, Culin never accepted their invitations to address a Harlem forum, nor did he attend uptown events.[35] And although he authorized the loan of a few pieces from the Brooklyn show for use in a lecture that Locke was to give in Harlem, there is little evidence that Culin wanted to draw any attention to a connection between his exhibition and black America.[36] Coverage of the 1923 Brooklyn exhibition in black newspapers and magazines came after the show opened. There was no advance notice in *Crisis* of the display, which is surprising given the magazine's eagerness to run stories about black people's illustrious past, and a short piece and article in *Opportunity* appeared after the show ended, suggesting that its editors did not know about the exhibition until it opened. Any association between the brilliant art that Culin was keen to have his audience appreciate and modern black Americans was left to the latter group to make for itself.

Activists seized on this excellent opportunity to draw attention to the wonderful legacy black Americans had in African art. Locke orchestrated the mounting of a 1928 exhibition consisting of items from the Belgian Congo alongside the Schomburg Collection of Africana, which had been recently acquired by the 135th Street branch of the New York Public Library, where the lot was put on display. The African objects were chosen from one thousand pieces, originally assembled over a twenty-five-year period from 1885 by Raoul Blondiau, a Belgian in the Congo, and then brought to the United States by Edith Isaacs for the Theatre Arts Monthly, which exhibited the collection in New York's midtown in early 1927. This small slice of the Blondiau-Theatre Arts Collection was to have become the nucleus of the permanent collection of a newly established Harlem Museum of Art, but it was never to be. Instead, the collection eventually found a permanent home at the 135th Street branch of the library.

Some seventy-one other items purchased from the Blondiau-Theatre Arts Collection went on tour nationwide.[37] Curators in many major northern and western cities contacted Locke to express their interest in exhibiting the collection, so much so that he mapped out a tentative itinerary to begin in the fall of 1928: Detroit, Cleveland, Minneapolis, Seattle, San Francisco, Los Angeles, and San Diego.[38] Pieces from the "Travelling Collection" were displayed at the Chicago Art Institute, Memorial Art Gallery of Rochester in upstate New York, Albright Art Gallery in nearby Buffalo, and Hampton Institute, a black college in Virginia, by 1929.[39] Black tertiary institutions were very keen to host exhibitions; the Traveling Collection was divided, and items sent simultaneously to Fisk University, Tennessee, and Howard University, Washington, D.C., and possibly to Atlanta University and the Tuskegee Institute.[40] The last was eventually the recipient of a gift of thirty-one objects from the original one thousand-piece collection, purchased and donated by trustee George Foster Peabody.[41] These objects fascinated black Americans across the nation.

One of the rationales for the New Negro Renaissance (though by no means one to which everyone subscribed) was that creative work could prove that assumptions about black racial inferiority were unfounded. No race, said the NAACP's James Weldon Johnson, that has ever produced great art or literature could be regarded as inferior.[42] Exhibitors of the Blondiau collection hoped that the "public presentation of a little known and representative side of African life and civilization" would evoke "a real popular interest" when viewed in those "centers interested in promoting the cultural interests of the Negro."[43] Like Culin before them and Sweeney after them, the Blondiau organizers hoped that exposure to black people's creative genius would reform bigots of their racism. According to an *Opportunity* editorial, the strategy worked. The author praised the exhibition for supplanting an evolutionary model of culture with cultural relativism. "A revision of concepts about the African has been forced," it read; "their unintelligible rites assume the dignity of a meaningful even if strange culture."[44] Not everyone was so convinced; many white newspaper reviewers saw such exhibitions through the lenses they used every day and were far from free of their preconceived ideas about the racial inferiority of the creators of the works before their eyes.[45] These attitudes notwithstanding, now stamped with the imprimatur of European experts and with home-grown support from figures such as Barnes in Philadelphia, African art moved from being a fancy of the avant-garde to being supported by mainstream American institutions.

Locke and other activists aimed to capitalize on changing attitudes toward African art by displaying African plastic art alongside recent works by black American artists. A two-week exhibition at the Chicago Art Institute featured "Primitive African Sculpture, Modern Paintings and Sculpture." It was advertised with a poster whose image was dominated by an Egyptian mummy, holding a scroll on which details of the exhibition were inscribed. At the foot of the image, tuxedoed musicians and singers gathered around a grand piano, representing modern black art.[46] Similarly, the traveling slice of the Blondiau Collection was coupled with paintings by Henry Ossawa Tanner, Hale Woodruff, William Edouard Scott, and others; some drawings; and a few three-dimensional pieces, some by leading sculptors Edmonia Lewis and Meta Warrick Fuller. Details on the full contents of each mounting of the collection are scarce. What information remains indicates that the items selected were the least edgy of what black American artists were producing, that is, those least associated with what were taken to be African forms and avant-garde modernism. Rather, the paintings, for instance, were portraits and landscapes notable for their attention to brush strokes, following by now famous models provided by French impressionist painters.[47] The one exception may have been at Fisk University, where it is possible that a wider range of black American art went on display. According to the university's president, the show was such a hit that the Nashville Museum of Art committed itself to re-exhibiting the African pieces alongside an even bigger collection of American artists, including Aaron Douglas, Laura Wheeler Waring, and others. Even before the Nashville exhibit opened, people expressed a keenness to purchase the pictures, and there started "a little controversy in the local press about whether the Negro is capable of doing artistic work."[48] Attending the exhibition, it was hoped, would settle that question—and by extension refute claims about black inferiority—once and for all.

Given the burgeoning number of small societies, organizations, and lecture groups in Harlem, it is reasonable to assume that a fair number of black Americans attended exhibitions in Harlem, downtown Manhattan, and Brooklyn. No museum records survive from the Brooklyn and Blondiau exhibitions that might tell us anything about the number or composition of guests, let alone what they thought. Some 45,000 people went through the 1935 MoMA exhibition, and according to the museum's *Bulletin*, efforts to bring the exhibit to the attention of black Americans increased attendance by six percent.[49] Figuring out what black Americans thought of the art is difficult. Did they regard it as a series of ethnological displays or as pieces of art? Did they feel any connection to the pieces? Did they bemoan the lack of any sense of an innate link to them?

Pondering such questions proved rich fodder for one best-selling white French author, who, like many white Westerners, assumed that an unbreakable link of savagery remained between Africans and their distant New World relatives. In Paul Morand's short story, "Syracuse, or the Panther Man," a well-to-do black American visitor to the Tervueren Museum in Brussels catches sight of a Congo mask and, as summed up by one reviewer, "promptly goes native."[50] The 1929 translation of the collection of which it was part received a great deal of critical attention in the United States.[51] None of its black American reviewers liked it, save for an appreciation of the accompanying illustrations by premier Harlem Renaissance artist Aaron Douglas.[52] They singled out "Syracuse," along with another story with a similar theme, for particular ridicule. As Walter White put it, "imagine, if you will, a Negro such as Dr. Du Bois or James Weldon Johnson going 'witch-doctor.'"[53] Certainly Du Bois and Jessie Fauset of the NAACP were two notable visitors to the Brussels museum who managed to survive their brush with the primitive, at least long enough to publish their impressions in the *New Republic* and *Crisis,* respectively.[54] Black Americans were curious about African art, keen to claim it as the progenitor of European modernism, and perhaps delighted at some of it, but they resented enormously the idea that it would send them screaming back to the jungle. "Paul Morand's theories may seem plausible to some," concluded another black American reviewer, "but Harlem is a long, long way from Africa."[55]

In an image to coincide with the 1935 MoMA show, cartoonist E. Simms Campbell pilloried the assumption that black people had retained something of the jungle. Set in a museum gallery, an elegantly dressed black American man in the foreground looks on with some surprise at an African sculpture, the face and head of which are not unlike his own. The cartoonist captured the distance many black Americans felt from their ancestry, with the man clutching an open catalog, as if desperate to learn something about the confronting figure. Campbell's parody was enhanced by the likeness between the man and the sculpture: the static figure was a mask, after all, created in a nonrealist aesthetic style. That the sculpture looked like the man gazing upon it was a little joke Campbell had at the expense of those white Americans who considered both groups alike and each little more than savages or animals. Such unthinking assumptions were mocked further in the depiction, in the background, of two fashionable and wealthy white women in fur coats, swanning through the exhibition with their noses in the air, their skittish attention caught only by the exaggerated buttocks on a statue of an African warrior. Their attitudes about race were unlikely to be altered by attending the exhibition, as black activists hoped. The material of the exhibition, in short, was as shocking to black American visitors as it was inconsequential to white attendees.

According to some, being confronted with these artworks only confirmed black Americans' distance from Africa. An *Opportunity* editorial suggested that the Blondiau exhibition and the subsequent art collection in Harlem were "evidences of an overcoming of the first shock of unfamiliarity" to African art. Its writer witnessed no sense of recognition from black American "lovers of art." He or she claimed that "there is no more convincing evidence of the cultural assimilation of American Negroes than in their own response to this art in sections remote from authentic enthusiasms. The shock of its bold self-assertion, if anything, is even greater with them."[56] For this author, writing in the organ of the Urban League, an organization committed to reform in the United States and still refuting the challenges laid down by Marcus Garvey years earlier, such responses demonstrated that black Americans were just that, Americans, with no inherent connection to black people elsewhere. At the same time, there was no reason that black Americans could not be proud of this lost heritage; hence, the magazine featured in the same issue—a special on art—various articles on African art and a long, detailed survey of European artists' use of African forms and ideas.

Black American artists were fascinated by the New York exhibitions. The art they saw, already given a sort of legitimacy in the avant-garde circles of Paris, both inspired them and in a way pained them. Given the cachet of African art, and the pride so many black Americans were now taking in their ancient heritage, it seemed a great shame that European artists had got to the source, as it were, of modernism, before them. To some, it seemed an unfair robbery of a heritage they had already been denied once. Many

Cartoonist E. Simms Campbell took aim at white Americans' unthinking assumption that black Americans and Africans were of a piece. (*New York Amsterdam News,* June 1, 1935; used by permission.)

claimed that European artists who had been inspired by African art forms lacked a certain something that black artists, the true inheritors of those traditions, could bring to their creations.

As black artists began importing African themes into their artwork in earnest, questions about the relationship between their work and European modernist art became pressing. Alain Locke wrote of the traveling exhibit that "the work of some of our contemporary Negro artists has already begun to show the influence of African art, very much as modernist painting and sculpture in Europe . . . benefited by its influence."[57] Locke evaded the issue of the influence of European artists on Americans by implying that black artists derived inspiration from African forms just as Europeans had before them. African inspiration was primary, Locke suggested elsewhere in 1927, because it, rather than the mere imitations by European modernist painters and sculptors, was the genuine and original source. Native African art, he averred, could revitalize not only art but life, with values truly important in society. "Most of us today," he invited readers to agree, "will concede the superiority and desirability of an art that is native, healthy, useful as well as ornamental, and integral with life, as contrasted with an art that is artificial, borrowed, non-utilitarian, and the exclusive product and possession of cliques and coteries."[58]

Locke's comments notwithstanding, European modernist art was an entrée into African art for many artists. Soon after arriving in New York City from Kansas City in 1925, Aaron Douglas studied painting and drawing under the tutelage of Winold Reiss, a German immigrant who illustrated the first major anthology of the New Negro Renaissance, *The New Negro* (1925). Douglas borrowed from Reiss the skyscrapers, smokestacks, and concentric circles that became a hallmark of his work.[59] Years later, Douglas recalled Reiss's unease with his own, very successful, work. It never had "the proper kind of feeling," Reiss thought, and so he was pleased when Douglas adopted some of his signature motifs.[60] The geometric and repetitive forms made Douglas's work instantly recognizable within a couple of short years. His illustrations, woodcuts, and paintings developed a reputation for their use of "African" forms, with contemporary critic Benjamin Brawley calling him "a pioneer in the so-called African style."[61] Douglas's acclaim stemmed from his eye-catching and distinctive combination of art deco shapes and African and black diaspora themes. He was a modernist, just like his mentor, Reiss.

Other artists cited a combination of African and European influences on their early work. Hale Woodruff, a printmaker and painter of the era, recalled later that his interest in African art was given legitimacy in 1923 by a book given to him as a gift: *Afrikanische Plastik* (1921) by Carl Einstein, a German Dadaist. "You can't imagine the effect that book had on me," Woodruff told his interviewer:

Part of the effect was due to the fact that as a black artist I felt very much alone there in Indianapolis. I had heard of Tanner, but I had never heard of the significance of the impact of African art. Yet here it was! And all written up in German, a language I didn't understand! Yet published with beautiful photographs and treated with great seriousness and respect! Plainly sculptures of black people, my people, they were considered very beautiful by these German art experts! The whole idea that this could be so was like an explosion. It was a real turning point for me. I was just astonished at this enormous discovery.[62]

In Paris a few years later, Woodruff collected African art, beginning with a small Bembe sculpture he picked up at a flea market. Like Douglas, Woodruff's interest in African forms was bound up with his exposure to European art, in this case French impressionism. He was particularly taken with Cezanne's *Boy in a Red Waistcoat* (1888–1890), a straightforward portrait in one way, but with colors and repetitive shapes that anticipated the cubists' fracturing of their canvasses. "I went back again and again and, between the Cézannes and the African work, I was off and winging."[63] In later years, Woodruff came to think that Modigliani was the only artist of the early Paris school "who really [went] deep into the essentials of African art and then, by integrating it with his own vision, made something of his own." In his early years, however, Woodruff drew on many European artists' use of African forms.[64] Fellow printmaker James Lesesne Wells, whose woodblock designs often featured African scenes, also credited both African and European influences on his early work. He listed among his inspirations the woodcuts and lithographs of German expressionists, the Norwegian Edvard Munch, and the 1923 exhibition of African sculpture at the Brooklyn Museum.[65]

Many visual artists spent time in Europe, especially Paris. Loïs Mailou Jones recalled, "when I arrived in Paris, African art was just the thing. All the galleries and museums were featuring African sculptures, African designs, and I sketched, sketched everything."[66] Jones was one of a long stream of black artists to cross the Atlantic only to find the best examples of their own black heritage. The black painter Albert A. Smith was commissioned by Arthur Schomburg in New York to scour the Paris markets for rare books and other valuables. Smith lamented: "As to ivory or wooden statues I shall look about—but artistic pieces of African origin are decently quoted at this moment because of the modernistic movement in Art,—which had its origin in such pieces."[67]

Whether acquired in Europe or in the United States, many artists were ambivalent about the extent of European influence on their work. Aaron Douglas, although he thought Reiss exceptional, came to resent that modernist painters in Europe collected the kudos for what was an African sculptural form. "Cubism," he wrote in the mid-1920s to his future wife, "no longer exists as an active artistic force." It was only because cubists took from African sculpture, or "the womb of art," that it came "to live as modern art."[68] Douglas was also exceedingly frustrated by artistic standards that continued to privilege European art over African "primitive" forms. Most irritating of all were black artists who adhered to those same ideals. He wrote bitterly, "they (White America) believe that a black artist is impossible. They have good grounds for their beliefs. Most of us are utterly despicable. Most of us feel that we have reached the heights when we have depicted their chalky faces and disgusting sentimentality or filled yards of canvas with feeble imitations of the second rate 'little masters.'"[69]

Douglas's desire for a set of criteria that derived from within blackness and did not adhere to the standards set by "White America" was widespread. Black American artists drew upon the significant cultural capital African art now provided, while explaining that their use of the forms came direct from within black life, not via Europe. West Coast sculptor Sargent Johnson, never drawn to the heady scene in New York, echoed Douglas's private sentiments in the *San Francisco Chronicle*. Appraising the impact of famous modernist painters on black Americans, he was brutal, declaring "the slogan for the Negro artist should be 'Go South, young man!' Too many Negro artists go to Europe and come back imitators of Cézanne, Matisse, or Picasso, and this attitude is not only a weakness of the artists, but of their racial public." Johnson concluded: "in all artistic circles I hear too much talking and too much theorizing."[70] Painter Jacob Lawrence was the most insistent of black artists that he was not affected by European modernism. It is possible that Lawrence sought to make a virtue of the tendency of art institutions and critics to segregate black artists, continuing to exhibit black painters separately, as if they lived in a world separate from all sorts of currents of artistic expression. Lawrence always said that he was influenced early in his life by Mexican artists, but beyond that, any external effects on his work came from within the black race. Lawrence's artwork reflected, he said, the impact of everyday life in Harlem, of training by black teachers (especially Charles Alston), and if the cubists had any effect on him at all, it came only through his exposure to African art.[71] His wife, Gwendolyn Knight Lawrence, shared these sentiments, recalling "we all . . . knew about Picasso, but . . . we thought about Picasso in terms of African sculpture."[72]

Making assertions about the genealogy of one's artistic endeavors was one thing; exploring it in the art itself was something else. Malvin Gray Johnson hailed from Greensboro, North Carolina, but migrated north to Harlem where he came to public prominence in 1928, when he won an award at the annual Harmon Foundation exhibit of black artists. Over the following six years until his death, he was prolific. Johnson mused in his art on the role played by European artists in mediating the relationship between black American artists and an African heritage. A 1932 painting, *Negro Masks,* neither straightforwardly mimicked Picasso's use of masks, especially in *Head of a Sleeping Woman (Study for Nude with Drapery)* (1907), nor did it ignore the already iconic work, made famous particularly by *Les Demoiselles d'Avignon* (1907). Rather, Johnson probed questions of influence and inheritance.[73]

The most sustained consideration of the question of influence came in Johnson's 1934 *Self-Portrait.* In the foreground sits a figure—"Johnson"— staring directly at the viewer, surrounded by a mismatch of furniture, in a room that looks to have been ransacked by a cubist. On the wall behind the seated figure hangs a framed painting of two masks, very much like Johnson's earlier *Negro Masks* and very like the sort of thing Picasso and others had been producing in the previous twenty-five years. The relationship between "Johnson" and these representations of Africanness was difficult to discern, and that was really the point. Further, the artist invited viewers to reflect on their impulse to make any connection, as the painting on the wall in this work is of masks, themselves intended to conceal and distort rather than to provide any mimetic representation of the real. Johnson's realist representation of himself was itself provocative, begging the question of whether we can know any subject. Johnson provided one hint as to his own feelings about his relationship to both African art and European appropriations or adaptations of that art: his clothing and setting. The figure's sweater is tight, and the furniture crowds him, constricting movement, much as artists felt constrained by a need to represent an authentic experience of

Many artists and writers, including Malvin Gray Johnson, who painted this *Self-Portrait*
in 1934, and author Langston Hughes, were deeply committed to forging links between
black Americans, others in the diaspora, and Africa. They nevertheless provided the most
sustained treatments of black Americans' ambivalence about Africa, because their
connection to the continent often seemed tenuous. (Smithsonian American Art Museum,
Gift of the Harmon Foundation.)

blackness, including a link to Africa. Wealthy patrons, those individuals
and institutions responsible for the grants on which artistic livelihood depended, wanted to see images they thought of as "black." Mainstream critics were disappointed with Harmon Foundation shows between 1930 and
1933, which included Johnson's paintings, because, aside from the presence

of black subjects, the pieces might have come from any contemporary artists.[74] Such demands stymied creativity.

Johnson's paintings expressed the broader problem of trying to resurrect a past to which black Americans felt a sometimes tenuous, sometimes ambivalent, connection. He portrayed the lack of pure connection to African art forms that he and other black artists of the time experienced, because their work was also influenced by the work of European modernist painters and sculptors. For visual artists, reclaiming the African heritage was tricky because they felt as though others had already been there, already "discovered" it. They could never simply include African masks in a painting to represent their African heritage without then becoming part of the broader conversation of modernist artistic expression and identity. Their specific experience is instructive in considering more broadly how black Americans related to the past whose importance they intended to resurrect.

Reaching for ways to express their distance—physical, temporal, and emotional—from Africa, artists and writers in America confronted the geographical space between the two places: the Atlantic Ocean. It was an immense space, difficult and sometimes impossible to traverse, metaphorically and in fact. Though many artists and writers of the interwar years managed to garner sufficient funding to cross this expanse to reach Paris, London, and occasionally other European cities, few made it to Africa itself. But they wanted to. Their correspondence and diaries burned with a deeply felt desire to reach Africa, to see for themselves the land of so much myth and conjecture. Writers Claude McKay and Nella Larsen got as far as Morocco; Du Bois went to both Liberia and Ethiopia, George Schuyler to Liberia. Best known of all, Langston Hughes in 1923 traveled to Africa as a ship's messmate. Few of the Harlem Renaissance luminaries spent much time in Africa, and none beyond these few places.

The Atlantic Ocean became a poetic and visual motif to symbolize the division black Americans felt from Africa and Africans. Take this poem, published in the newspaper of the Universal Negro Improvement Association:

O Africa, blest motherland –
    I long to be with thee;

I fain would grasp thy loving hand,
    And to thee nearer be.
The florid sea divides us now,
    I cannot reach thy shore;
But soon at Afric's shrine to bow,
    And the living God adore.[75]

In poet John Smith's hands, the Atlantic Ocean divided individuals, here imagined as scattered members of a family whose existence survived the passing of several centuries. He ignored the temporal division of Africans and their descendants, preferring to think of the separation as a physical estrangement. But that gulf was unbridgeable; the ocean was not simply a large body of water; it was a "florid sea." Smith chose a striking adjective, one commonly meaning blooming or in flower, but which also referred to the bright red color of blood in the arteries. In describing the Atlantic Ocean as impassable, it was not just its enormity or the cost of travel Smith found daunting. The potential journey also contained within it a memory of the last time Africans crossed the ocean, coming toward the Americas in slave ships, the ocean colored red with blood. Smith's touch was light, typical of the veiled and oblique reference to the traumatic effects of enslavement and the Middle Passage on those who experienced it. Such trauma had secondary effects on the descendants of those transported across the ocean.

When artists portrayed the contributions made to the New World by black men and women, they investigated, too, the price paid, psychologically speaking, by enslaved Africans and their descendants. Artist Laura Wheeler took up the legacy of the Middle Passage in her depiction of the ocean as a divider between the two continents. "Africa in America," at first glance, was a positive rendering of the contribution made to American life and culture by its black inhabitants. The figure, garbed in classical robes and jewelry, had also a flapperish quality about her, particularly in the head scarf and bangles. Modern life owed something to its classical heritage—understood here as originating with a black foremother. Wheeler's image was also a melancholy one. The female figure stared resolutely, even longingly, to the east, unable to return to her homeland because of the turbulent waters separating the continents, with the currents between Africa and the United States bearing west. A sailing ship, a relic in the age of fast and

Africa left her legacy all over the Americas, this image suggested. Rooted now to the American continent, it was hard to leave for Africa. (Laura Wheeler, "Africa in America." By permission of the Crisis Publishing Co., Inc., the publisher of the magazine of the NAACP; image first published in the June 1924 issue of *The Crisis*.)

comfortable steamship travel, reminded the viewer of the days of slave transportation, a memory that was impossible to shake when contemplating, as this woman did, the return journey.

Artists depicted the hope that the ocean, impossible to breach in life, could be traversed in death. A woodblock print by James Lesesne Wells, published in a collection of plays for schoolchildren to perform, suggested that the United States owed a huge debt to the enslaved Africans on whose labor and lives the nation had been built. The bottom section of the image reminded readers of the hull of a ship, replete with chained bodies gesturing upward for salvation. At the picture's top, iconic skyscrapers of modern New York provided the background for a large black person pleading with a God. American modernity's bedrock was the labor of those shackled bodies, forced into transportation and enslaved. Similarities between the postures and actions of the main figure and those below deck connected the suffering of those transported Africans and their descendants in New York, implying that the latter were likewise integral to the American nation. At first glance, however, the illustration was about religious faith. The prostrate figure and caption would have put readers in mind of Jesus' power to cure illness, especially leprosy, and to offer salvation to even the most wretched. In this case, salvation took the form of a reunification of the diaspora, in the afterlife. But Wells took his argument about Africa's role in American society further. In the top left corner, beyond the borders that contain modern America, stood dwellings, or temples, in a North African architectural style. For all the contributions they had made to the making of America, in ascending to heaven America's black folk would return to other shores. Just as artists and writers such as John Smith explored a lack of a connection to Africa and a sense of dislocation, many also suggested that peace would come—could only come—with some sort of reconciliation with Africa.

Philosopher Alain Locke saw the retention of African life and culture in some traits but not others and held the experience of the Middle Passage in particular responsible for the loss. The 1927 Blondiau exhibition was an act of "bringing over the cultural baggage of the American Negro that was crowded out of the slave-ship."[76] Nearly ten years later, Locke argued again that the Middle Passage constituted what he called a "painful gap" between the African artist and the black American artist. For Locke, the physical dexterity he thought key in African arts was "lost in the nakedness and horror of the slave-ship, where families, castes, tribes were ruthlessly scrambled."[77] By 1936, he was quite forthcoming about the remove at which American artists found themselves from Africa, stating directly that the "art mode" of "extreme modernists" among black artists "began, as we have seen, through European art being influenced by African art. It is, thus, an African influence at second remove upon our younger Negro modernistic painters and sculptors; in being

"Faith builds in the dungeon and lazarhouse its sublimest
shrines; and up through roofs of stone, that shut out the
eye of heaven ascends the ladder where the angels glide."

Woodblock artist James Lesesne Wells drew on a belief held dear by many Africans who
were transported to the New World, suggesting that in death, enslaved Africans and their
descendants would return to Africa. (From *Plays and Pageants from the Life of the Negro*,
1930.)

modernistic, they are indirectly being African."[78] The exception to this terrible loss was rhythm, which Locke argued inhered in the body in a way that could not be deleted, not even by the Atlantic slave trade.[79]

The Middle Passage constituted for many artists and writers a break in the relationship between Africans of the past and black Americans of the present and was itself something many found nearly impossible or difficult to represent in their work. It was indeed that "painful gap," as Locke called it. In reviewing a 1928 edition of a slave-ship captain's memoir, the accomplished writer Wallace Thurman found the "jolly tone" of the prose completely inappropriate. By contrast, he was extremely moved by illustrations by Miguel Covarrubias, a Mexican immigrant prominent in the New Negro Renaissance. It was the drawings, not the words, Thurman said, that "[made] one realize just what a brutal and indescribable experience it really must have been."[80] It was not up to historians, or even writers, he implied, to capture the horror of the journey; rather, that task fell to visual artists. As if to confirm Thurman's implied preference, scholar Rayford Logan's review of the book in *Opportunity* was accompanied, most unusually, by two of Covarrubias's illustrations.[81]

One writer who did attempt an extended treatment of the role of the Middle Passage in determining the relationship between black Americans and Africa was Jean Toomer. Growing up in Washington, D.C., and New Rochelle, New York, Toomer attended both all-black and all-white schools. After checkered studies in several fields in many tertiary institutions, he taught in Georgia and eventually returned to Washington. In 1923, Toomer published *Cane*, a poetic novel that strung together tales connected occasionally by repeating characters but more by theme. The book explored how individual memory might be haunted by a collective violent past. Toomer had been thinking about this topic for some time. In 1921, he commended Eugene O'Neill's play *The Emperor Jones* for representing "an unconscious which is peculiar to the Negro. Slave ships, whipping posts, and so on."[82] In Toomer's reckoning, the unconscious was far from universal; rather, its character depended on experiences in the past shared by particular groups of people. The unconscious, then, was racial, though shaped by culture, not biology. King Barlo, a preacher in *Cane*, gave voice to the trauma of enslavement and the Middle Passage in particular. He described for an audience an African man, "big an black an powerful," captured, enslaved, and transported across the ocean into the New World. Barlo concluded that "the old coast didnt miss him, an th new coast wasnt free, he left the old-coast brothers, t give birth t you an me. O Lord, great God Almighty, t give birth t you an me."[83] In suggesting that those left behind did not miss those taken away, Toomer went against the popular image of the weeping woman waiting for centuries at Africa's shoreline for the return of her missing children. Those descended from transported slaves were instead effectively orphaned, left to create their own new family. That it was men, not women, who gave birth to the offspring suggests that this was definitely an American patriarchal family, rather than the matriarchal African one so prevalent in black public discussions of Africa.

Despite its powerful depiction of the disconnection of black Americans from Africa, *Cane* concluded with an optimistic portrayal of black Americans coming to terms with their history. The main character, Kabnis, reconciled with the past, represented by Father John, who inhabited a cellar known as "the hole." Located at the bottom of the building, "the hole" was an architectural metaphor for the material Toomer believed had been repressed. Spatially, the hole, or hull, represented specifically the trauma of the Middle Passage.[84] In embracing John, Kabnis came to recognize the beauty of black folk culture and to regret his repudiation of his Southern past, with its African connections. In Toomer's words, "the Dixie Pike has grown from a goat path in Africa."[85]

Almost immediately following its 1923 publication, Toomer himself rejected the vision of black folk culture, including the link to Africa, depicted in *Cane*. It would be a mistake, he believed, to wallow in history when the quick pace of change in modern society was rendering the past utterly irrelevant. In Toomer's view, it was too late to go back to Africa, either physically or metaphorically. Black Americans were just that, American, and no longer African. He came to regard *Cane* as an elegy, a swan song, as he renounced any definite "black" or "Negro" identity for himself, preferring to embrace a mixed identity he called "American."[86] Other times, Toomer said, he preferred to think of himself as a member of the human race.[87] He foresaw—and hoped to create—a national identity that was ethnically diverse and sprang from many sources, including Africa.

Toomer's insistence on being classified as neither white nor black was not unique. Nella Larsen, another Harlem Renaissance writer, for one, shared his stance.[88] People beyond the literati lived likewise, but existing between the color line—or as if it did not exist—became harder and harder as the decade bore on and that line became fixed. The sad story of Alice Rhinelander, née Jones, proves the point. A working class New Yorker, she married the youngest son in a wealthy family, Leonard "Kip" Rhinelander. Only days after their wedding, the groom's father insisted the marriage be annulled, on the basis that Alice was colored and had hidden the fact from Kip. At a sensational court trial, Alice was subject to all manner of indignities, including being forced to disrobe for the judge and jury, who could therefore adjudicate whether or not her white husband might reasonably have not understood that she was "Negro" before they married. Alice and Kip wed in 1924, the same year in which tightening ideas about racial identity resulted in the enactment of much-debated immigration restrictions into federal law. The jury decided in favor of Alice, concluding that Leonard Rhinelander must have known she was not white and therefore that she was "Negro." It was no longer possible to live between the color line; people had to be either white or black.[89]

Lives of the kind that Alice Rhinelander and Jean Toomer lived became less likely as the color line held fast. Their experiences suggest something about the ever-greater connection black Americans made to Africa. In a climate in which blackness remained a category of racial, and still largely biological, difference—when that difference had, in fact, hardened into a seemingly insurmountable "problem"—connecting to Africa became, if not a necessity, something of a forced phenomenon. Disenfranchised still in the United States, even as second- and third-generation migrants were becoming assimilated, the diaspora provided a lifeline. This is not to say that black politics and culture were defined by white racism but that the longevity of the exclusion of black Americans from full participation in national life certainly contributed to their desire to seek a meaningful collective identity beyond the borders of the nation.

Black vernacular culture found its greatest champion in writer Langston Hughes, and throughout his long career, he linked that culture to Africa. The 1921 poem with which he arrived on the New York scene, "The Negro Speaks of Rivers," was about the retention of a memory of Africa. Four decades later, when decolonization in Africa and freedom movements in America rekindled his faith, Hughes gave a speech about the strengthening links between black Americans and Africans, both endeavoring to bring about true liberty in their respective lands. This 1962 talk included a recitation of his famous 1921 poem.[90] Despite this certainty at either end of his career, in the years following the young poet's debut, Hughes, like fellow writers and artists, became steadily more skeptical about connections between the Old and New Worlds.

In his 1921 poem, the rivers of Africa coursed through black Americans' bodies, as it were. Imagine editor Jessie Fauset's excitement at receiving through the mail this gem for the literary section of *Crisis:*

I've known rivers:
I've known rivers ancient as the world and older than the
    flow of human blood in human veins.
My soul has grown deep like the rivers.
I bathed in the Euphrates when dawns were young.
I built my hut near the Congo and it lulled me to sleep.
I looked upon the Nile and raised the pyramids above it.
I heard the singing of the Mississippi when Abe Lincoln
    went down to New Orleans, and I've seen its muddy
    bosom turn all golden in the sunset.
I've known rivers:
Ancient, dusky rivers.
My soul has grown deep like the rivers.[91]

Hughes catalogued here memories of both African rivers and the Mississippi, which were contained and made sensible by the body. These were memories of bathing and building, listening and watching. This bodily sensibility was neither destroyed nor overtaken by the experience of crossing a much bigger body of water, the Atlantic. Hughes drew on what was a very modern conception of the past, one quite different from the formal historicism of the nineteenth century. The past was now thought to inhere in individuals' bodies, to persist "in germ cells and muscle tissue, dreams and neuroses, retentions and involuntary memories, guilt and ghosts."[92] Africa remained in black Americans' bodies.

Hughes's attitude came to seem very romantic by the time he actually met some Africans. In 1923, he traveled along the west coast of Africa while working on board the SS *West Hesseltine.* Far from feeling any innate affinity to these coastal Africans, Hughes was jolted by how unfamiliar they were, and by the degree to which he was obviously foreign to them. In a letter home to his mother, he commented on their appearance:

You should see the clothes they wear here, everything from overcoats to nothing. I have laughed until I can't. No two people dress alike. Some have on capes, some shawls, some pants, some wear blue clothes fastened around their necks and feet blowing out like sails behind. Some have on preachers' coats, others knee pants like bloomers, with halfhose and garters. It's a scream![93]

Despite Hughes's alienation from Africans, he never published anything like this epistolary account. Rather, he continued for some time to write in romantic terms about his fond attachment to Africa.

It was not until 1940 that Hughes committed to print his repudiation of a pulsating bodily memory of Africa, though his turn to the left in the early 1930s also signaled at least a disaffection with the themes of his previous writing. In his 1940 memoir, *The Big Sea,* even the very title gave away his changed attitude. The rivers that linked Africans of the diaspora were replaced by "the big sea" that separated continents and cultures. There was nothing resembling a familial relationship between Hughes and the people he met in Africa. He managed only to skirt the continent's coast, unable to overcome the divide represented by that "big sea." Instead, Hughes was confronted by an Africa that inspired in him no feeling of recognition, let alone kinship or a desire for repatriation. Hughes recounted meeting an African boy, Edward, who desired Hughes's companionship and wrote to him, but Hughes did not return the mail. As he wrote in 1940, he came to realize in 1930 that "I was not Africa. I was Chicago and Kansas City and Broadway and Harlem."[94]

Langston Hughes's reluctance until 1940 to admit in print his lack of emotional connection to Africa reveals just how important an African-inflected identity was to black Americans in the interwar period. Hughes, politically sensitive regardless of his exhortations against propaganda, continued to strive to make connections to Africans, eventually succeeding in the final years of his life, when travel became easier and cheaper and the invitations to writers of his stature began to flow from the continent.

Writers and artists of the Harlem Renaissance helped to effect a broader reconsideration of the relationship between black Americans and Africa. The conversion of anthropologist Melville Herskovits is a case in point. Herskovits believed passionately, following Robert Park, that black Americans were utterly acculturated and published an essay presenting his case in the foremost anthology of the era, *The New Negro* (1925). He made similar claims in a 1927 article and then in a 1928 book, *The American Negro: A Study in Racial Crossing.*[95] As the Renaissance hit its peak, and coinciding with Herskovits's research trip to Suriname in 1928, he began to reverse his position. Herskovits transformed himself into the world's leading authority on the so-called retention of African culture and traditions in the New World in a book still read widely, *The Myth of the Negro Past* (1941).[96] In the decades since its publication, most anthropologists, historians, and sociologists of black experiences have come to a position that more closely resembles the point that Aaron Douglas and others made in their artworks: culture is a process that takes from various legacies and new experiences, making something new and something that changes, not necessarily "forward" or "backward" at every turn. That development notwithstanding, it was in no small part the efforts of black writers and artists that transformed the academic landscape—and ideas more broadly—about the longevity of Africa's effects on the United States.

It was hard to embrace Africa from such a distance and when the continent's reputation was so poor. The fact that black Americans, in this case writers and artists, felt compelled nonetheless to explore the legacy left to them, not just for nostalgic reasons but because they actively sought the sense of contentment that could come from feeling they belonged somewhere, was a serious indictment of American nationalism, which excluded them so thoroughly. Taking their cue from European modernist painters and sculptors, they celebrated their tie to a culture that, in truth, seemed foreign and strange to them.

Writers and artists provided some of the most cogent meditations on what Africa meant to black Americans. Collectively their work demonstrates above all the difficulties of thinking transnationally at a time when national borders—unless one were a wealthy tourist—were becoming increasingly difficult to traverse. Without actually going to Africa, imaginative flights of connection were difficult to sustain. Even among those who could travel, to think of oneself as having binding ties to people from different nations was a radical step, out of sync with the kind of patriotism required of Americans in the era after World War I. Irrespective of these constraints, most black authors and artists did think beyond the nation. The difficulties they encountered in doing so underscore the bravery and determination of black Americans in their quest to transform the United States into a place where their heritage (and that of immigrant groups), and multiculturalism, could be celebrated.

5

Haiti, a Stepping-Stone to Africa

If connecting to Africans proved a challenge, there was a place closer to home that offered black Americans fertile ground for thinking about what it meant to be black in America. Haiti had long been regarded as the jewel in the black world's crown. At the dawn of the nineteenth century, after fighting tenaciously for over thirteen years, enslaved Haitians had overthrown their French colonial overlords.[1] This unique revolution inspired black Americans, and at mid-century, some two thousand free people emigrated there, hoping for a better life.[2] Come the second decade of the twentieth century, Haiti was fresh once more in the minds of black Americans because in 1915 the U.S. Marines invaded and began an occupation that would last until 1934. The American government cited potential interference from Germany as a justification for intervention in the republic.[3] When that reasoning failed to convince, U.S. officials offered instead a picture of a tiny nation in terminal decline, inhabited as it was by black people, who, as everyone knew, could not possibly govern themselves.[4] Ideologies about race were central to the U.S. occupation, as to all modern colonial exercises of power. In this case, those ideologies had a particularly paternalistic cast. Abandoned by its French father, ill-kept by its single African mother, Haiti required the protection of Uncle Sam, who had a duty to step in and shepherd it into adult nationhood.[5] Though the occupation began in 1915, it was really only after 1919, with the disappointment of the lack of recognition afforded their wartime service still stinging, that Haiti came to occupy an important place in the politics and culture of black Americans.

It is hard to overstate the presence of Haiti in interwar American culture, especially when compared with the inconsequential consideration given to most places overseas. Throughout the period of the U.S. occupation of the republic, Haiti appeared in American culture in books, on stage, in film, in newspapers, and even on "scenic wallpaper." The phenomenal expansion of mass consumer culture occurred alongside the rise of American imperial power, producing a particular fascination among Americans with the exoticism of conquered territories.[6]

For many Americans, white and black, Haiti was the Africa of the New World. Its physical accessibility meant that many Americans could travel there, unlike Africa. Haiti also seemed accessible for other reasons: it was small and manageable, especially when compared with Africa. The so-called Dark Continent was vast, dangerous, and impenetrable in the minds of most Americans, whose exposure to Africa was limited to popular tales of explorers who went missing in its jungles, whether based on real-life characters such as David Livingstone or on fictional ones such as Allan Quartermain in the best-selling Victorian novel *King Solomon's Mines*. Haiti, occupying just one-half of a small island close to the United States, was much easier to fathom.

When white Americans traveled to Haiti, their contact with the place, its people, and its customs almost always confirmed for them their prejudices. Racial difference and scientific ideas about a racial evolutionary ladder seemed proven by a culture that to white visitors looked to be permanently rooted in the past. White Americans' travel accounts were saturated with voodoo, cannibalism, and the ever-present menacing sound of drumming. Such interpretations of Haitian culture were also part and parcel of the occupying forces' rhetoric about the Haitians, as the former attempted to subdue the latter on behalf of the National City Bank of New York and in service of an ideology that held that Haitians were in need of help. Whether directly involved in the occupation or not, these accounts rendered Haiti as the missing link between black Americans and Africans and proof positive in the minds of white Americans that the primitive traits of black races could never be overcome, no matter how civilized some of their black American fellow citizens appeared.

Some black Americans had likewise regarded Haiti as a place where they could gain access to undiluted African cultures, but such attitudes altered quickly over the 1920s and 1930s. Writer Pauline Hopkins called it a "stepping stone" to Africa in 1900.[7] Alain Locke, philosopher at Howard University and editor of the important 1925 anthology *The New Negro*, called Haiti "the most favorable reservoir now left of that original primitive earth religion and fetichism which was transplanted from the old world of Africa in the wake of the slave trade."[8] On visiting Haiti and interpreting Haitian culture in their own creations and nonfiction writings, however, most black Americans moved away from the sentiments expressed by Hopkins and Locke. Instead, Haiti became something of an anvil on which to forge a diverse and vibrant African American identity. This identity took in an affinity to people around the black diaspora, based on shared histories of enslavement and experiences of racism. It also encompassed a recognition that diasporic groups had responded in similar ways to these conditions, including the development of black cultures that stressed a deliberate continuity or connection to things African, rather than a biological racial connection.

Black Americans' efforts to engage politically and culturally with things Haitian or African chafed against the assumption widely held by white Americans that black Americans were already connected biologically and temperamentally to black people worldwide. This belief was a means to exclude black people from American life. If they were connected to people elsewhere by race, then they could not fulfill the requirements of citizenship as it was defined in the era. Postwar patriotism demanded of U.S. citizens that they pledge allegiance to the American flag alone, that immigrants give up their prior nationality and culture, that they become "100 percent" American. The insistence that "Negroes" were already different, that their race made it impossible for them to be American, made forging a transnational black identity, while remaining in the United States, a very difficult undertaking. Nevertheless, in their protests against the occupation of Haiti, black Americans came to appreciate the similarities of their own experiences with those of Haitians and, by extension, with other groups in the diaspora. In a series of plays depicting Haitian culture, black Americans negotiated the obstacles posed by the assumptions of whites that they were already linked to Africans and other blacks in the diaspora. Focusing on music, dance, and religion, black Americans demonstrated that any relationships that existed between the various groups had more to do with similarities in the process by which these vibrant cultures were created, in spite of the most inimical conditions.

Haiti fascinated white Americans, who regarded it as the Africa of the New World. Close by, small, and under American military control, many tourists regarded it as a safer option for travel than Africa, with its daunting fauna, hot temperatures better suited to natives than to whites, and, of course, those natives themselves. But in Haiti, they reassured themselves, they could find the "real" Africa. No less a figure than Secretary of State Robert Lansing assured them it was the case. "The experience of Liberia and Haiti," he argued, "show that the African race are devoid of any capacity for political organization and lack genius for government. Unquestionably there is in them an inherent tendency to revert to savagery and to cast aside the shackles of civilization which are irksome to their physical nature."[9] In Lansing's mind, as in the minds of many white Americans, Haitians, Africans, and black Americans were all the same.

For those who did not actually make the journey, Harlem-Haiti-Africa was a route well traveled in the mind. French writer Paul Morand, popular in the United States, put it most baldly in his 1930 account of New York City. In Harlem, he wrote, black citizens found a refuge from civilization, and yet order was maintained, just: "Standing erect at the street crossing, symbolic of white civilization, the policeman keeps his eye on this miniature Africa." If "that policeman happened to disappear," however, "Harlem would quickly revert to Haiti, given over to voodoo and the rhetorical despotism of a plumed Souloque."[10] Poor leadership by self-styled rulers became a symbol of Haiti's backwardness for many white American writers, whose lurid treatments of Haitian culture, sold as "reportage" by conscientious and intrepid travelers, were frequently best sellers.[11] As it was for Morand, in these writers' accounts Haiti was just a stone's throw away from Africa. Mass paperbacks and the increasingly popular medium of film enabled the production and consumption of a Haiti packaged to thrill. Tales and images of voodoo ceremonies, cannibalism, child sacrifice, and zombies, not to mention of drumming and half-naked bodies, became popular books and films.

Such prurient interest in Haiti came partly out of a new value being placed on so-called racial primitivism. The catchword for the nineteenth century and early twentieth had been progress, but the devastation wrought during the Great War forced people to rethink the steady march forward. Many white Westerners became nostalgic for a time before civilization had deteriorated into decadence and sterility. Hoping to revivify Western life, they sought inspiration from those they considered free from the symptoms of "overcivilization." Black people, held by science and popular belief to have not climbed as high on the evolutionary ladder, became models of how to live life happily. Long disdained for their supposed attachment to nature and their inability to move forward in time, Africans now found themselves valorized for their lack of modernity. Closer to home, black Americans provided the necessary link to a prior level of civilization. As well as being likened to Haiti, Harlem was sometimes referred to as "Little Africa" or "a negro colony."[12] The impulse to rejuvenate tired Western culture ensured that Harlem's nightclubs and cabarets were full, night after night, with white patrons who hoped their proximity to the rhythms of the jungle could somehow cure them of their modern malaise. Although such favorable regard spared some black Americans the violence and viciousness of more conventional forms of American racism, it was straitening in its imposition of romanticized racial attributes.

Such attitudes, like more garden-variety racism, assumed a consonance among black people worldwide. Black Americans might appear to be civilized, so this thinking went, but race would ultimately tell, revealing them to be just the same as their African brethren, rather than distantly related to their continent of origin. Certainly the plan by white supremacist groups to send black Americans "back" to Africa assumed that no dissonance would result.[13] As with earlier advocates in the American Colonization Society who wanted to "repatriate" former slaves to Liberia, it did not cross the minds of white Americans that their black fellow citizens might find Africa foreign or that Africans might regard the newcomers as aliens. Rather, many whites assumed that all black people, whether American Negro, Haitian, African or from elsewhere in the diaspora, shared an essentially similar primitive nature.

Visual imagery was often used to argue for the inherent barbarism and atavism of black people (think of the familiar rendering of "the ascent of man" from animal to human, each figure annotated with a racial category). Equally important in the casual association between black Americans and Africans was sound, and in particular, the sound of the drum.[14] The idea that black Americans, like Africans, were closer to animals than to God was echoed—or perhaps parodied—in the cover for the sheet music for *Ringtail Blues* (1918), a collaboration between two well-known ragtime musicians, one black, the other white. The blues, so closely associated with black Americans, was depicted here as being performed by a band of monkeys, enjoyed by an audience of carefree jungle animals. Linked to rhythm, a supposedly lower-order cultural attribute possessed by all black people, in this aural economy a single beat of the drum was enough to transform the most elegant and sophisticated black American into a chest-thumping savage. All white Americans' popular accounts of travels in Haiti featured the sound of the drum as a herald of racial primitivism.

Civilization was such a thin veneer in this measure of black Americans that with the merest hint of the right prompt, it would be stripped away to reveal the savage within. Although white Americans, enthralled by Sigmund Freud's theory of psychosexual development, considered it therapeutic to peel back a layer or two of civilization, there was a constant danger that any black person might backslide to Africa, might miss a rung and slide all the way to the bottom of the ladder of civilization.[15] The primordial forces within all people were simply closer to the surface in black people. In whites, it was very well, arguably too well, repressed. Reflecting on his 1920 trip to North Africa, Carl Jung proposed that the surroundings "awaken an archetypal memory of an only too well known prehistoric past which apparently we have entirely forgotten. We are remembering a potentiality of life which has been overgrown by civilisation, but which in certain places is still existent."[16] If black Americans had only just managed to cover up their inherent savagery, in Haitians, according to white Americans, it was just that little bit more obvious again. Where a drumbeat could provoke a black American to descend into primitive behavior and feeling, Haitians, in the depictions by white Americans, were rarely awake without a drumbeat accompanying their every movement.

In 1920, the powerful associations between black Americans, Haitians, and African primitivism were given dramatic form in *The Emperor Jones*, the second full-length play in the brilliant career of Irish American playwright Eugene O'Neill. The play centers on Brutus Jones, a Pullman train porter who has escaped jail in the United States and within two years becomes emperor of an unnamed Caribbean island. Jones's brutal exploitation of the natives ensures their wish to overthrow him. With rebellion mounting, Jones attempts to flee, but his progress is impeded by ghosts of his misdeeds. He is haunted at first by his recent sins, and then going back into his past, by a chain gang, a slave auction, and lastly a witch doctor in an African setting. Jones loses his clothing, his nerve, and his sanity. Ultimately, a native kills him with a silver bullet.

White Americans' ideas about the essentially primitive nature of all black people were reflected in the way they heard music performed by black Americans, as if it came from an earlier time, before civilization had so inhibited people that they could no longer enjoy life. Here, cheerful jungle animals communed in blues music. (J. Russel Robinson and Spencer Williams, *Ringtail Blues,* sheet music cover, 1918. Courtesy of the E. Azalia Hackley Collection of Negro Music, Dance, and Drama, Detroit Public Library.)

The play's audience assumed that the action took place in Haiti; the setting was, in O'Neill's scathing observation in the preface, "an island in the West Indies as yet not self-determined by white marines. The form of government is, for the time being, an Empire."[17] If O'Neill's stage directions did not give it away, the very character of a self-proclaimed black emperor put viewers in mind of Jean-Jacques Dessalines, the inaugural leader of the Republic of

Haiti who declared himself emperor in 1804. Some in the audience would have recognized, too, the bravado of the heroic character's claim that he could be shot dead by only a silver bullet. Another of Haiti's revolutionary heroes, Henri Christophe, who ruled the northern part of Haiti from 1807 to 1820, said the same thing and eventually, infirm and with his enemies fast approaching, took his own life in this fashion.[18] Extremely popular, *The Emperor Jones* was mounted first in 1920 in downtown New York, with Charles Gilpin playing the lead in a run of over two hundred performances. Three New York seasons followed by 1926, including one starring Paul Robeson in 1924, and several played in Europe. A film and opera came in 1933. Its popularity was derived from the fact that it played to white audiences' prejudices quite comfortably while also raising issues about the nature of black identity that were exactly those with which so many black Americans were concerned.

O'Neill's decision to portray the brutality of colonialism through the figure of a black despot confirmed for many white audience members the savagery they believed inherent in black people, which made them unfit to rule themselves. Reviewers could barely contain their excitement while watching Brutus Jones's descent into an earlier version of *homo sapiens*. Drums, the aural avatars of black barbarism, encouraged this opinion. A beaten tom-tom accompanied performers every step of the way, increasing throughout in tempo and intensity, whipping up Jones's frenzy and prompting his motion back through evolutionary time. Alexander Woollcott, a white reviewer of the original production noted, "from first to last, through all of the agonizing circle of his flight, he is followed by the dull beat, beat, beat of the tom-tom, ever nearer, ever faster, till it seems to be playing an ominous accompaniment to his mounting panic. The heightening effect of this device is much as you might imagine."[19] That was O'Neill's intention; stage directions stated that the tom-tom ought to begin at seventy-two beats per minute, to match the pulse, and steadily increase, presumably taking audience members' heart rates with it. What Woollcott's readers might imagine without seeing the show was not an undefined suspense but specifically the thrilling spectacle of a man's descent into atavism. This, after all, was what many white Americans expected from their black neighbors, and it was certainly the claim of the State Department that dictators such as Jones had ruined Haiti, making the invasion and occupation a necessity to ensure the nation's stability and rescue its people from tyranny.

In spite of such hackneyed representations of blackness, many black theatergoers found *The Emperor Jones* profoundly moving. Visual images of black people, whether on material objects ranging from piggy banks to pancake mix or in films that took their cue from immensely popular theatrical minstrel routines, were rarely complimentary. Long used to seeing themselves portrayed as buffoons, audiences appreciated that Brutus Jones, even if his traits included stereotypical criminality and dandyism, was a genuinely tragic character who occupied the stage the whole time in a full-length play. The play enabled serious black actors to bring to life a figure who drew on the Haitian heroes so dear to black Americans. Jones may have been immoral, but at least his decisions were his own, and his fate of his own making. His uniform might have been over the top, but according to the stage directions, he "has a way of carrying it off."[20] He may not have been likeable, but he was powerful, reminding his Cockney sidekick, Smithers, to "Talk polite, white man! Talk polite, you heah me! I'm boss heah now, is you fergettin'?"[21]

For black audiences, although Jones on paper was a brutally exploitative imperial master, in production the play was much more about the psychological torments that black Americans had experienced at the hands of white violence and subjugation. Writer Jean Toomer lauded O'Neill in 1921 for the playwright's achievement in portraying "a section of Negro psychology presented in significant dramatic form." For Toomer, each individual had his or her own particular unconscious, but all were subject to group conditions, so "in fact Brutus Jones lives through sections of an unconscious which is peculiar to the Negro. Slave ships, whipping posts, and so on. . . . In a word, his fear becomes a Negro's fear, recognizably different from a similar emotion, modified by other racial experience."[22] *The Emperor Jones,* for all its faults, took the psychology of a black man seriously. Promoting the 1933 film, Robeson said that O'Neill "dug down into my racial life and has found the essence of my race. Every word he wrote for *The Emperor Jones* is true to the Negro racial experience."[23] Black American intellectuals were not only relieved to see a dramatic character on stage but also thought that the psychological elements of the play had real merit.

Black Americans struggled not only against the discipline of psychology itself, which assumed a white subject in its studies of the individual in society, but also against "internal colonialism" (as black power advocates later termed it).[24] The genius of O'Neill's play in production, for some critics, was its portrayal of the similarities between black Americans' experiences of slavery and its aftermath and those experiences of people under colonial rule, whether Haitians under the thumb of the U.S. Marines or Africans subject to the rule of various European powers. Hubert Harrison, an immigrant from the Virgin Islands to the United States, concurred with O'Neill in calling the play a "psychological study" but, like Toomer, stressed that it was a study of a black man. In Harrison's view, "the external setting of the drama is really of no importance whatsoever. . . . It could just as readily be set in Africa or South Carolina."[25] Haiti linked Africans to their descendants in the United States, but the links were more than biological. Insisting on the similarity of experiences in Africa and throughout the diaspora, Harrison implied that racism in the United States was structurally like that of colonialism elsewhere, with similar effects on those under the thumb.[26] The experience of subjugation, justified on the basis of supposed black inferiority, was the same everywhere.

What was "true . . . racial experience" for Robeson was not to the tastes of all black Americans. Some had merely reservations, like an East Coast writer who called *The Emperor Jones* an unflattering but "necessary intermediary step."[27] Others, including a reviewer for the newspaper of the Universal Negro Improvement Association (UNIA), the *Negro World,* condemned the play, finding it utterly unsuitable to the task of representing black history, which should focus on the far more positive aspects of the past:

> The Negro, with the new thought of racial respect, cannot be proud of the Negro actor, who holds his race up out of the shadows in such a limelight as that which shines in "Emperor Jones." . . . The man who sells the spirit of his manhood and the soul of his womanhood for the electric lights of an American Broadway and the tainted medals of the white man, is not an ideal Negro for Negro history.[28]

Where that reviewer lamented the lack of uplifting themes, others found Brutus Jones's psychological torments unconvincing and were irritated by his predictable descent into an atavistic past, helped along by the constant drumming. The sound drove the "hot" rhythm that for white visitors to nighttime Harlem was the soundtrack to a rejuvenating trip into "pre-civilization." A poet in *The World*, tired of overdetermined depictions of black people's responses to drumming, called for the "Death of the Emperor Jones" in the title of a 1930 poem:

I'm tired;
Weary from drums
Pounding in my ears,
Banging in my head,
Drumming in my heart,
Drums—white drums
Bursting fear
Into my brain,
Sweating agony
Over my body,
Drums, drums driving,
Driving to madness.[29]

While, as time wore on, the black intelligentsia became disillusioned with the play, those removed from the hubbub of the Harlem Renaissance found it nothing short of ludicrous. Both the stage productions and the film were dependent on a primitivism that many in the audience found more amusing than tragic. They laughed at a parody, "Pudden Jones," by the hotshot Broadway team of Flournoy Miller and Aubrey Lyles.[30] Langston Hughes recalled being impressed with members of a 1930s audience in Harlem who had failed to admire Jules Bledsoe's rendering of the tragedy. They laughed without restraint and reportedly yelled out, "'Why don't you come on out of that jungle—back to Harlem where you belong?'"[31]

Such derision notwithstanding, O'Neill's play did a great deal to popularize an issue dear to the hearts of many black Americans: the dubious basis of the U.S. occupation of Haiti and the brutality of the Marines stationed there. Transforming people's ideas about Haiti through culture became paramount after it became clear that efforts to end the occupation in more directly political ways had failed. James Weldon Johnson, executive secretary of the National Association for the Advancement of Colored People (NAACP), lobbied presidential hopeful Warren Harding on the back of four widely read articles published in 1920 in *The Nation* under the series title "Self-Determining Haiti."[32] Taking the terminology used so extensively by Woodrow Wilson at the 1919 Paris Peace Conference, Johnson suggested that American democracy itself was being damaged by the abrogation of Haitian sovereignty. Responding to the articles and lobbying by Johnson and others, Harding courted the votes of black Americans and anti-imperialists by criticizing Wilson's administration. Soon into his own term, however, he dropped the matter, irrespective of damning findings by a Senate inquiry into conditions in Haiti, held in 1921–1922.[33]

Other than in black public life, where it appeared constantly in newspapers, journal articles, editorials, cartoons, and letters, American interest in Haiti declined for the remainder of the decade. It was only after a massacre of Haitians in the town of Aux Cayes in late 1929—coinciding with a move in foreign relations away from Theodore Roosevelt's "big stick" and toward the "good neighborliness" of the late Hoover administration and then Franklin Roosevelt—that Americans' interest turned again to Haiti. Throughout these years, however, black artists and writers in all genres, influenced by the press and urban organizations, kept their attention focused on Haitian history and culture. Their interest in Haiti had its historical roots in black Americans' delight at the successful revolution between 1791 and 1804 and the connections forged between Haitians and black Americans during the nineteenth century. It was renewed in the 1920s and 1930s as Haitians suffered under the direct rule of white Americans, an extension overseas, in the eyes of black Americans, of the racial ideologies that shaped life in the United States.

Although they drew on all genres to portray Haiti and its history, black cultural producers turned especially to modes of performance. The startling success of some black Broadway shows, combined with a strong tradition of locally produced theater, made it an attractive option. One of the first of these plays was *Genifrede*, written and first performed in 1922 and published in a 1935 collection for black schoolchildren.[34] Its author, Helen I. Webb, was a schoolteacher in Washington, D.C. *Genifrede* set the scene, so to speak, for plays by black Americans that were set in Haiti and explored themes relevant to the experiences of black people in both countries (and further afield). Tension built in the play with a booming cannon firing at very specific intervals, as the title character, daughter of revolutionary leader Toussaint Louverture, attempted to avert the execution of her lover, General Pierre Moyse, himself Louverture's nephew.[35] The taut atmosphere in Webb's play was very much like that in numerous one-act plays that focused on lynching and were written by black American women during the interwar period.[36] Webb's focus on the helplessness of Genifrede in the face of Moyse's death paralleled a central preoccupation in that other set of female-authored plays, which were often laid out in domestic settings with women anticipating in horror the imminent death of their sons, brothers, and/or lovers. Despite the differences between *Genifrede* and these plays—notably, that Moyse was murdered by fellow black men rather than by white lynchers—each counterposed the relative helplessness of black women in the face of such violence with a certain nobility among the men facing death. Webb thus linked black Americans and Haitians on the basis of a shared experience of violence. By referring to Louverture as a "courageous chief," Webb's exploration of masculinity further connected black Americans and Haitians to African men. Webb evoked tribal Africa in order to show that Haitian men and, in turn, black American men, were the descendants of proud Africans.

The search for a strong leader was an abiding theme in black American culture and politics.[37] During the 1920s and 1930s, Marcus Garvey was likened to Louverture in the pages of his organization's newspaper and, just as Louverture had been during the antebellum period, to George Washington.[38] A lineage of strong male nation builders, imagined to have originated with a redoubtable African masculinity, was a foremost preoccupation of Garvey's black nationalist organization, and it pervaded black American culture more widely, as the plays demonstrate. One of the most straightforward ways to protest the U.S. occupation of Haiti was to dramatize a diasporic family of black men, all capable of self- and collective government. Contrary to claims by the occupying forces, Haitians were not constitutionally incapable of leading and managing their own country, just as black Americans could live without the paternalism so many white Americans assumed they needed. Women's roles in these plays were almost always as adjuncts—usually wives or girlfriends—to active men. In Langston

Hughes's play *Emperor of Haiti* (begun in 1928; finished in 1935; produced for the first time in 1936; later the basis for the libretto of William Grant Still's opera *Troubled Island,* composed between 1936 and 1941; and revised again in 1963),[39] the focus was again on revolutionary leaders. Whatever their faults, they were paragons of strength and courage:

> *Dessalines:* Then remain on guard! But not inside.
> *Congo:* I got you, chief.
> *Dessalines: (laughing)* Chief!
> *Congo:* Like in Africa, Jean Jacques—Chief.
> *Dessalines:* Can you remember Africa, Congo?
> *Congo:* Sure. I was a big boy when that English ship got hold of me.
>   That's why I can do our dances so well. I learnt 'em in Africa.[40]

Taking charge during the revolution enabled Haitian men to restore putatively natural qualities associated with men in Africa.

Black playwrights depicted not only Haiti's leaders as strong and admirable, but also turned their talents to bringing to life those Haitian people whose names were not known. In contrast to O'Neill's play, which failed to give depth to any Haitian characters, Hughes's *Emperor of Haiti* dramatized everyday life. The continuing commitment to the principles of the revolution—freedom and fairness for all—animated those Haitians who sought to overthrow Dessalines. Hughes portrayed these characters as identified with Africa, while Dessalines was seduced by the Anglo-Western world:

> *Pierre:* I'd rather have a bugle, that's what I want.
> *Celeste:* For what?
> *Pierre:* A bugle blows pretty. All the white children have 'em.
> *Celeste:* The white children's free.
> *Mars:* Anyhow, a drum can sound twenty times as far as any bugle ever
>   blowed. Bugles don't belong to black folks.
> *Pierre:* That's how come I want one.
> *Lulu:* You can have one, honey, when we's free. . . .
> *Celeste:* Drums is what our gods like, though. Drums is for Legba and
>   Dambala, Nanna and M'bo.

Congo: African gods been knowin' drums a long time. Them tinny
  bugles just cain't reach they ears. . . .
Mars: The drum's a black man's heart a-beatin'. Tonight that beatin's
  goin' to set the Frenchmen's hair on end.[41]

The anemia of the "tinny" bugle was contrasted with the vitality of the
throbbing drums—the "black man's heart a-beatin'." As the moment of rebellion approached, "the drums beat louder, ever spreading."[42] At the end of
the second act, they beat again, this time to signal the overthrow of Dessalines's self-indulgent court. Hughes conveyed conflict between light-skinned
mulattoes and black Haitians aurally, with sound used to mock the upper
class's imperfect mimicry of white customs. During a Banquet of State, the
Bugle Boy (Pierre grown up) announced the arrival of the Emperor and his
light-skinned aristocratic cronies, but the sound of his instrument was lost
in the din of the drums. "The drum," the stage directions read, was "never
silent during the rest of the scene. Its monotonous beat continues, as if calling for one knows not what."[43] Drumming may have signaled black atavism
to some, but in Hughes's hands, it became a symbol of masculinity that was
a little closer to Africa and a lot less cowed than black men in the United
States, where Jim Crow racism and violence worked hard to enforce submis-
sion. Hughes, like Webb, effected something of a return to an imagined
place—"Africa"—where men's masculinity went unquestioned and their
lives and bodies unharmed. The plays were more than a protest against the
occupation; they also protested the emasculation racism wrought in the
United States.

Such a "reclaiming" of an imagined African masculinity was a problem-
atic enterprise. Brute strength may have become a treasured hallmark of
American masculinity by the early twentieth century, but in black men it was
always dangerous.[44] White supremacist ideology held that savagery hovered
just under the skin of black Africans, Haitians, and Americans, and that
therefore any show of unrestrained strength had to be checked at once. Black
militancy was therefore always a double-edged sword, at once enabling vehe-
ment protest against conditions in Haiti and in the United States (and especially forming the basis of a claim to proper and rightful citizenship, because
these men were appropriately strong and independent) but at the same time
confirming stereotypes about a lack of civilization among black people.

Black playwrights, like their white fellow citizens, were often fascinated with aspects of Haiti's culture they thought exotic and were not immune to the tendency to emphasize its sensational aspects. When two university teachers, Clarence Cameron White and John Frederick Matheus, traveled to Haiti, they were enthralled by what they respectively called "The Magic Isle" and "this luxurious island paradise."[45] White was also a well regarded composer and violinist. Matheus was a writer and expert in Romance languages. In *Tambour,* a play written just after their 1928 trip to Haiti, the female lead character, Zabette, objects to her boyfriend's preference for drumming over spending time with her. Her protests notwithstanding, Mougalou continues to drum, half-naked, because "when I make the drums talk they speak back to me. They whisper the long lost secrets of the Congo. They tell the story of black warriors crashing thru the African jungles." Zabette, in spite of herself, "suddenly begins to tremble and quiver, her whole frame undulating with the contagion of the vibrating drums."[46] Mougalou "thumps with a certain wild abandon, yet in perfect rhythm that is never once missed. At times he appears to fall into a trance state."[47] *Tambour* put into words and music the equation between drums, Haiti, Africa, and unshakeable savagery that had been implicit—even if equally well understood—in *The Emperor Jones.*

Drums were linked to rhythm, widely considered to be the most prominent "African" characteristic of black people in the New World. Rhythm in turn was linked to an easy sexuality, uninhibited by generations of civilization and all the healthier for it. On first reading, Zabette and Mougalou are staple characters, drawn from Westerners' fantasies about how black people spent their time. Her very proximity to a drumbeat seems to signal her descent down the ladder of civilization. And yet neither Mougalou nor Zabette was made out to be grotesque or comedic, which was usually the case in characterizations of black people on stage. Although the script was not explicit about the fact that drumming and dancing were skills learnt through years of training and practice, it did not fetishize these abilities as coming naturally to black people. Instead, drumming and dancing were signs of a culture that at the play's conclusion triumphed over the failures in Haitian politics since the reign of the "four great founders," Louverture, Dessalines, Christophe, and Pétion, and the chaos fueled by mercenaries known as "cacos." With Mougalou kidnapped, Zabette was about to be ravaged by his rival but was saved by a powerful voodoo curse. The play ended with the distinctive sound of Mougalou's drumming coming from the distant hills, bringing with it the hope that he remained alive. Written in 1929 but set in 1911, just before the U.S. Marines invaded, White and Matheus implied that the Haitian people of the countryside would triumph yet over all oppression.

Scripts such as *Tambour* reflected a new appreciation in anthropology for that which was different, without conventional denunciations of racial inferiority. Drumming was not necessarily a signal of racial atavism. When anthropologist Melville Herskovits traveled in 1931 to Dahomey, west Africa, with his wife and sometime co-writer Frances, he recorded in his diary the experience of watching the worship of "the tutelary spirit of Ibadan." He recognized that members of the ceremony heard the drum in a number of ways intelligible to neither him nor Frances. "The drum itself, the interpreter told me," Herskovits wrote, "can speak several messages on such occasions, it can call the praise of the deity, of the dancer, of some distinguished person who is looking, and it can also drum an invitation to sexual intercourse." As for the worshippers, the drumming accompanied a woman dancing, "her entire body representing the motions of the sex act," and the crowd shouting and laughing. In writing about the "talking drum (dudú)," which was played to give different tones, Herskovits concluded that "in this case it clearly took the place of the male." He ascribed a gender to the communicating drum by assuming it played the "male" "call," to which the explicitly sexual dances performed by the accompanying female dancer "responded."[48] Herskovits recorded all this in the relatively judgment-free language now available to anthropologists, in the wake of a monumental overhaul of ideas about race. Differences between people could now be ascribed to culture, rather than to biology.

Clarence White adopted anthropological discussions about African drumming into his Southern classroom. Teaching students at Hampton Institute, Virginia, White also classified drums by gender, arguing that the more acute sounds were produced by the masculine drum ("kossi linga" or "kolinga"), while the "big tom-tom" ("éguiri linga") produced the lowest note, called the "mother linga."[49] Focusing his class on the Banda-Linda in the district of Ouaka in what is now the Central African Republic, he told students simply that "the language of the linga [drum] is the banda dialect."

In White's lesson notes, he explained that "the Linda speaks by striking the linga so as to reproduce exactly the rhythm of his own words and the different tones of his dialect. . . . In addition to being 'spoken' by the tom-tom," White told students, "the Banda Language can be whistled as well by the natives and a linga phrase played on the violin is perfectly understood by them." Not everyone could transmit messages because it took training to drum out the language correctly, but everyone, White taught, even children, could understand the drum's messages.[50] Far from being a sound linked to primitive consciousness, the drum was an important means to communicate, and drumming a technology requiring much training. Drums, "speech tones," and the Bantu people's "polyphonic thought" were all interconnected.[51] Drumming was not an unthinking skill inherent to black people, nor was rhythm. Both required training and skill and were attributes treasured by those in the Old World as a means to distinguish themselves from their oppressors and to take pleasure in a shared culture.

When White and Matheus collaborated on *Ouanga!* (1932), an opera set during the revolutionary era, a more complicated score pit the tom-tom against other instruments to symbolize the clash between African culture, specifically voodoo, and the modernizing will of Dessalines; it was the drum versus the "passionate sweep of strings and woodwinds, which sound the theme of conflict between the old customs and the new."[52] Stage directions specified that the drumbeat have a similar effect on the audience as in *The Emperor Jones:* "The insistent, measured beat of the native drums from the distant mountains ominously strikes the ear as the flamboyant tropical scene with the full force flashes upon the eye. The orchestration expresses peace and the fresh beauty of nature in contrast to the veiled threat of the booming tom-toms."[53] But alongside this familiar portrayal of primitive culture, White, desiring to represent Haitian culture in all its variety, included méringues in the score.[54] And although voodoo was represented in the play by drums and dancing, it was not barbaric. Rather, Matheus's script and White's score dramatized voodoo as a serious belief system, integral to Haitian life. In their account of the revolution, Dessalines met his demise because he outlawed indigenous religious practice and tried to replace it with Catholicism.

When black American playwrights, librettists, and composers focused their attentions on voodoo, they intended to do more than simply titillate

their audience with exoticism and a view of life further down the evolutionary ladder. In these portrayals, it did not necessarily follow that just because
Haitians engaged in religious and musical practices that some assumed
harked back to Africa that they were therefore a backward people. On the
contrary, black dramatists' use of voodoo was a celebration of autonomous
black culture that was borne very much of the experience of enslavement in
the New World. For playwright Leslie Pinckney Hill, voodoo was one of the
"black man's necessary masks . . . a clever mystico-political organization
operating powerfully upon the minds of illiterate masses."[55] Far from being
a piece of "authentic" African culture and therefore evidence of black people's inability to move forward through time, voodoo was a terrific example
of the syncretism and adaptability that characterized black culture and
formed the basis of black political struggle.[56] Accordingly, given the environment in which culture was divided hierarchically into "high" and "low," the
forms black American writers and musicians chose for representing Haiti
fell squarely into the "high" category.[57] They created operas, librettos, and,
in the case of Hill, 120 pages of single-spaced blank verse, a mode he declared
"the only vehicle worthy of the dignity and elevation of my theme."[58] Black
American artists rejected the sensational "reportage" of Haitian customs in
newspapers, best-selling travel accounts by many white Americans, and the
increasingly pervasive figure of the zombie, who would come in the early
1930s to dominate a new genre of horror film.

Using these forms, artists challenged characterizations of black folk that
shored up the Haitian occupation by implying that black people were childlike, primitive, and in need of help. Instead, they called into question Americans' claim that their nation was an exceptional republican democracy by
implicitly critiquing the version of Haitian history offered by the conquerors. Cultural renditions of their opposition echoed the stinging words of a
white NAACP executive, who asked, "Which is worse, to eat a human being
without cooking him, as is alleged to be the custom in Haiti, or to cook a
human being without eating him, as we know to be a custom in Mississippi?"[59] Leslie Hill answered succinctly, "Haiti has come to be a sort of
challenge to the democratic sentiments and preten[s]ions of our time."[60] He
went so far as to claim the story of the Haitian Revolution as salutary for
white as well as black American audiences because Louverture was responsible for thwarting Napoleon's desire for empire and enabling, therefore, the

sale of the Louisiana territory to Jefferson and the birth of the modern United States.[61] Langston Hughes replied to the NAACP executive's question with a short satirical skit, *The Em-Fuehrer Jones* (1938). Hitler took the place of Emperor Brutus Jones but similarly stumbled about the stage as if frightened in a forest, haunted by the specter of sportsmen Joe Louis and Jesse Owens.[62] In a four-page script, Hughes replaced Brutus Jones with a more historically accurate white colonizing figure, drawing a parallel between the racial ideologies that prompted America's occupation of Haiti, its treatment of its black citizens, and fascist Germany's imperial designs.

Well-to-do Haitians and black Americans collaborated in cultural critiques of the U.S. occupation of Haiti. Where elite Haitians had previously disdained "peasant" culture, they now revered it in their efforts to demonstrate a cultural national sovereignty, in the face of an attack on their political sovereignty.[63] The revolution featured prominently in such collaborations, as when Dantès Bellegarde, the Haitian diplomatic envoy to Washington and the Pan-American Union, came at Arthur Schomburg's invitation to the opening of an exhibition of Haitian history and culture at the Harlem branch of the New York Public Library. "Nothing can better serve the cause of my country, so misunderstood, so particularly disparaged in the United States," wrote Bellegarde to Schomburg, than such an exhibition. Echoing the sentiments of many central to the Harlem Renaissance, Bellegarde claimed that the exhibition would show "how a people, freed from the most brutalizing slavery, has been able to overcome all the hostility which surrounded it and attain, by its own effort, the highest culture, thus avenging the black race of the accusation of inferiority which they have dared to place against it."[64] James Weldon Johnson had said almost exactly the same thing about what art could do for improving race relations within the United States, even to erase racism. Black inferiority could be disproved, Johnson argued time and again, by showing that black artists could match or even surpass the creativity, ingenuity, and aesthetic sense of their white compatriots.

Haitians and black Americans also joined forces to establish organizations designed to lobby the U.S. government into retreating from Haiti. These included the Union Patriotique and the Haiti-Santo Domingo Independence Society.[65] The basis of these societies was a new militancy that characterized postwar black politics, including, for example, better-known organizations such as the UNIA. This militancy was linked closely to a particular style of masculinity that was shared by cultural producers of the era, including those who wrote about Haiti. In both *Tambour* and *Ouanga!*, the characters associated rebellion with manliness, and in turn linked both to drums and therefore to Africa. By writing and performing works with such themes in the United States, artists completed the line of descent from African manhood to African American, via leaders and participants in the Haitian revolution. This relationship was given form in Clarence White's scrapbook of his trip to Haiti. A caption to a photograph of collaborator John Matheus sitting on the steps at the base of a massive statue of Dessalines read, "J. F. M. at the Feet of Dessalines."[66]

It was difficult, as many black thinkers noted, to reclaim a black history that stretched back in time, or to proclaim an affinity to contemporary black people, without confirming racist assumptions about the continuity of biological traits or cultural characteristics in members of any one race. Discussions of expressive culture, especially music and rhythm, were particularly sticky in the context of competing ideas about race. For black American artists, musicians, writers, activists, and intellectuals, similarities between black American and Haitian cultures were a result of historical and current circumstances.

Musician and academic Clarence Cameron White asserted that the folk music of black Americans was connected to that of Africa by using the term "Afro American" in his lesson notes and "Aframerican" elsewhere.[67] White drew a link between contemporary black American music and the folk music of Ancient Egypt. He cited as evidence the "musical pyramid" entombing King Ounsa, which had musical incantations inscribed on its walls. It was first in a line "down to the present [in which] each nation has left a record in one form or another of what we might reasonably suppose was its Folk Music, War Music, and Ceremonial Songs and Dances." White went on to list all the types of music and dance he knew of in Africa, past and present, and in "Afro American" culture.[68] White was not alone in looking to Egypt for the origin of North American black music. Maud Cuney-Hare, a pianist, teacher, folklorist, and writer born in Texas and residing in Boston, opened her 1936 book, *Negro Musicians and Their Music,* with an assertion that "Negro music traced to its source, carries us to the continent of Africa and into the early history of that far off land. We may even journey to one of the chief sections said to hold the music of the past—that of Egypt."[69] Black Americans' attachment to music and dance had a long lineage.

This lineage relied on more than just biology or romantic racialism. Work was fundamental to black music. White relied on an "old script" describing conditions under which folk music was created by slaves in Egypt: "'Half nake[d] men, with bodies of bronze, begin their endless task, starting it at the beginning of day and keep on singing until the evening hour of rest.'"[70] Several commentators shared White's view that work influenced style. J. A. Rogers had made a similar point in 1925 when writing on jazz. "The average Negro," wrote Rogers, "particularly of the lower classes, puts rhythm into whatever he does, whether it be shining shoes or carrying a basket on the head to market as the Jamaican women do."[71] By emphasizing the conditions of work under which each of them beheld this sense of rhythm, these writers complicated their simple assertion that the inclusion of rhythm into everyday style was a particularly "Negro" characteristic, where the connection was assumed to be biological. It became, instead, cultural and contextual.

The question of whether racial identity was cultural or biological, however, was never straightforward. Alain Locke, for instance, observed that "original jazz . . . [has] a distinctive racial intensity of mood and a peculiar style of technical performance inborn in the typical or folky type of Negro. It can be detected even in a stevedore's swing, a preachers' sway, or a bootblack's flick; and heard equally in an amen-corner quaver, a blue cadence or a chromatic cascade of Negro laughter."[72] At the same time that Locke attributed style to conditions, he also described that style as "inborn." Culture had a biological sting in its tail.

Nowhere was this jumble more visible than in discussions of rhythm's genealogy. For many, rhythm began in Africa and was too pungent an element of not only music but also everyday style to be erased, even by time, distance, and trauma. White taught his students that in all the places where "the African has either voluntarily or involuntarily gone . . . we find traces, in various degrees, of African idiom."[73] In this instance, there was no explicit sense that black workers or musicians were in any way deploying rhythm deliberately or that it was produced by cultural conditions. Rhythm was, once again, innate. White was not alone. Composer William Grant

Still similarly asserted that "colored people in America have a natural and deep-rooted feeling for music."[74]

Alain Locke explored the metaphor of musical trees and roots most fully. His 1936 treatise, *The Negro and His Music,* was held together by the idea that musical form was traceable. Though everything else was lost in the Middle Passage, Locke argued, rhythm was "intimately and instinctively . . . carried."[75] One could trace its divided roots "down" through the diaspora to "the common tap-root source in Africa."[76] The extent to which this essential and natural idiom existed in people in any one place depended on their relative distance from Africa. "Nearer" here meant not only relative distance from Africa but also how many stops on the slave-trading route a place was from Africa's west coast. Hence "African" characteristics were "strongest in the deep American South, the Carolina coast islands, Haiti, the Bahamas, the eastern provinces of Cuba, Vera Cruz and Yucatan and Guiana," all spots "close" to Africa, usually on or near to eastern seaboards. "The nearer to the source," Locke claimed, "the deeper and more torrid the idiom." He went onto say that the "[idiom] tinctures out hybrid in Brazil, the Spanish West Indies, the Creole area of America and lower Spain." African music "finally becomes only a faint tinge in the American Southwest, in the sophisticated Mexican and Argentine music and in that widespread dilution of cosmopolitan jazz. Yet it is strong enough to flavor distinctively almost any mixture."[77] Rhythm came down through the generations and persisted over vast geographical distance and yet was shaped by environmental factors such as work. Were shared characteristics biological or cultural? This was a question few addressed directly, and thus the confusion attendant on new cultural ideas about race was never quite clarified.

Figuring out how "African" was music in the New World meant reinscribing some of the basic premises of white Westerners' ideas about the essentially primitive nature of black people. Rhythm was that one thing they could never shake, that would always prove someone was black, if they should try to "pass" for white. Play a drum nearby, and they would start quivering with the effort not to break into dance. African music—specifically, rhythm—was contagious and unable to be contained. It was like blackness itself, which was still widely imagined to be contained in the "blood" and to be strong enough to contaminate any mixture of which it was a part. Moreover, these discussions of culture rested on an image of Africa as a place that did not change. Not only were African cultural attributes so pungent that they could never be shaken off, even if one wanted to, but because African culture was static, there was therefore an enduring connection between the descendants of those who had left Africa and those who had remained.[78] The problem Clarence White, Locke, and others faced in trying to disentangle race from biology was not unique to them. It is still with us today.

Fuzziness of analyses around biology and culture stemmed from the fact that it was impossible to escape one in favor of the other, logically speaking. Looking to a group of people in the past assumed some prior link between them and the present, whether or not that link was then characterized as cultural rather than biological.[79] Yet, given the force of biological arguments about race—and white supremacy—nobody wanted to give up the new cultural definition of race. It may have been illogical, but it had enormous political utility.[80] If Locke, White, Robeson, and others did not manage to separate biology and culture, to do so was not their aim. Rather, they sought to reach out beyond the borders of the United States in accounting for the nature and quality of black life and culture. They thereby both emphasized their distinctiveness and sought also to remake what was considered "American."

Perhaps an even bigger, and certainly more immediate, challenge for those who wrote plays and operas aiming to convey that Haitian culture was admirable, not depraved, was that relatively few people were interested in political art. The most commercially successful stage and film productions of the era featuring or created by black Americans were those that updated the minstrel tradition into modern musicals. Such shows offered up, for runs of months at a time, half-naked bodies and thumping drum rhythms for consumption by audiences whose responses were very different depending on who they were. Assumptions among white Americans about their black neighbors survived without challenge.[81] Staging productions that would contravene racial prejudice was very difficult. In Clarence White's unpublished autobiography, he recalled that after winning the 1932 David Bispham Memorial Medal for an American opera composition, he contacted many people to try to interest them in producing *Ouanga!* It was discouraging,

White wrote, to be informed over and over that "since the subject matter was not humorous, it might not be acc[ep]table as a vehicle for a Negro cast." A white patron organized a reading in New York for notables including Leopold Godowski, but as White discovered later, these producers were already keen to mount George Gershwin's score of *Porgy and Bess.* White concluded: "In fact I now think that American Producers were not interested in the idea of an all Negro Opera at this time."[82] *Ouanga!* had its first full production in 1949, by an all-black company in South Bend, Indiana. William Grant Still's opera, *Troubled Island,* waited until the same year for its first outing.[83] Things were little different for black Americans in Europe. White and Matheus hoped for a London production starring Paul Robeson as Dessalines and for a film version. They may also have hoped for a Paris production with Jules Bledsoe singing the role of Dessalines, but it all came to nought.[84] Trinidadian C. L. R. James's stage show, *Toussaint L'Ouverture,* with Robeson in the title role, played London for just two nights.[85]

Recognizing the limitations of stage performance as a means of improving ideas about black people, whether Haitian or North American, many black Americans instead attempted to mobilize the still relatively new cinema technology for their purposes. Forays into film, which along with music was the most widely accessed and popular form of American mass culture, were always difficult. Film of the classical era favored caricatures of black Americans, either as stock Southern plantation characters or as monsters of one sort or another. *King Kong,* with its obvious racial overtones, was the hit of 1933. Horror-filled "zombie flicks," set in Haiti, began screening in the 1930s.[86] Mainstream film portrayed others in the African diaspora no more sensitively than it did American blacks. The many movies of this ilk included Columbia Pictures' *Black Moon* in 1932, with over 250 extras running riot as a voodoo high priest prepared to sacrifice the pretty heroine.[87] *Voodoo,* filmed entirely in the West Indies, promised to New York moviegoers access to sacred rites usually off limits to white folk.[88]

Opportunities for black Americans to make or participate in independent film were few and far between. In 1920, *Crisis* ran an advertisement calling on readers to buy stock in a new company that intended to make a "Super-Photoplay" called "Toussaint L'Ouverture," with Clarence Muse of the Lafayette Players in the title role.[89] Eight years later, a band of New Englanders, fed up with the way "in which Toussaint has been consistently omitted from histories," announced it would raise $1 million to portray his life in a film of which even the great Louverture himself "would be proud if he could view it."[90] There is no evidence that either film was ever made. Paul Robeson, his statements about O'Neill's realism notwithstanding, had a miserable time in the mid-1930s making films that did not allow him to portray blackness (or at least black men) in the way that he either wanted or intended.[91] Criticized widely for *Sanders of the River,* in which he played an African chief who in grass skirt was the very model of Western fantasies, Robeson justified his efforts as a means to raise funds for a film in which he would play Haitian leader Henri Christophe. If that were successful, one on Menelik II, emperor of Ethiopia, would follow.[92] Neither one came to pass.

The closest Robeson came to portraying either hero was in a British-made film, *Song of Freedom* (1936), directed by J. Elder Wills. Here, Robeson was able finally to depict African and black cultures—and most important, a worldwide black fraternity—more to his satisfaction. Unusually, *Song of Freedom* featured scenes of the slave trade, including the Middle Passage, and of interracial working and living on the docks in England. Robeson played John Zinga, a British dockworker whose transformation into a singing star gives him the opportunity to discover his heritage as the descendant of Queen Zinga of Casanga, an island off the west coast of Africa.[93] Once again, the site for representing black culture was an island, this time closer to the African mainland, rather than the in-between space of Haiti. Onstage in London in the early scenes of *Song of Freedom,* Zinga stars in an opera-in-a-film, "The Black Emperor." It proved a superb reworking of the themes of *The Emperor Jones.* In full regalia unmistakably like that of Brutus Jones, Robeson was able finally to play a man of full stature, one interested in his ancestry and cultural heritage, whose desires were quite distinct from the exploitative ambitions of Brutus Jones. Although Zinga's attitude was akin to Marcus Garvey's neocolonialism, wanting "to bring help to his people" in Africa in the form of medicine and ships ("progress" in Zinga's words), he was ultimately embraced by the natives as one of them, not sharing Brutus Jones's fate of assassination.

Although Robeson was happier with this film, it was still tinged with the white fantasies about black people that had disappointed him about his earlier works.[94] The self-serving witch doctor, in particular, was a shallow rendering of African religion that juxtaposed mysticism against Western "rationalism." The witch doctor was an exoticized creation, a character springing from the primitivist imagination that accounted for the "Negro vogue" on both sides of the Atlantic. Robeson's failures in the expensive medium of film reflected the experience of those in performance genres generally. Every effort by black Americans to connect to Africa and Africans, whether directly or through stepping-stones such as Haiti or "Casanga," was constrained by stereotypes about black people's primitive nature. Those who managed to overcome these strictures found that their plays and operas went unproduced.

Even with all these problems, black Americans' reappraisal of Haiti's history and culture found expression on the 1930s stage—and reached substantial audiences—thanks to federal funding for the arts created as part of Franklin Roosevelt's New Deal, to stimulate the depressed economy. The Works Progress Administration's Federal Theatre Project kept alive the fascination with the Haitian Revolution, even extending the focus on its leaders, making them heroes rather than flawed individuals overtaken by circumstances, as they had appeared in the plays of White, Matheus, Hughes, Hill, and Webb. In 1936, Orson Welles made his debut directing Harlem's Negro Theatre Unit in a version of *Macbeth,* set in Haiti, with costumes and themes designed to remind audiences of *The Emperor Jones.* The play was known locally as "the voodoo *Macbeth.*" On opening night, the eighty-five-piece marching band of a fraternal lodge drew a crowd of 10,000 people onto the streets to follow behind a banner announcing "Macbeth by William Shakespeare." Traffic remained at a standstill for an hour while the crowd enjoyed a streetside performance outside the theatre.[95] Two years later, *Haiti,* rescued by its director from a miserable script about miscegenation and transformed into a celebration of the anticolonial revolution, sold some 20,000 of its 74,000 tickets to black New Yorkers.[96] Those who attended enjoyed the performance, especially when white characters were knocked out by black fists.[97] On the West Coast, posters enticed audiences to experience "The Black Magic of Haiti in the story of the only man Napoleon feared" in a federally funded production of Henri Christophe's life, *Black Empire* (1936).[98] While such plays confirmed old stereotypes about black people's propensity to mysticism and savagery, at the same time they repeatedly conjured up strong black male leaders, played on stage by physically powerful men such as Paul Robeson and Rex Ingram, whose lists of achievement, on and off-stage, were impressive. These performances thereby challenged the assertion that Haitians and other black people were childlike and in need of the care and protection of American power. These were men fit to rule.

Well into the 1930s, white Americans remained transfixed by blacks' performances of song and dance, convinced that what they were seeing was an authentic expression of an age-old culture of a people who were racially inferior to them. An unexpected hit during New York's 1934 stage season demonstrated just how enduring ideas about blackness and primitivism were, even as the white Americans who commented on the play congratulated themselves for shucking off such beliefs. *Kykunkor,* conceived and choreographed by Asadata Dafora, originally from Sierra Leone, revolved around a courting couple. Intending to marry, their plans were thwarted by a curse placed on the bridegroom by a Witch Woman, working on behalf of a jealous rival. A Witch Doctor was summoned to revive him. After much sparring, the doctor saved the day by healing the groom and transferring the spell to the Witch Woman. The final act of joy and celebration, as in earlier plays, featured much dance and music, primarily drumming.[99] *Kykunkor* played to rave reviews in the major and minor white newspapers and magazines, its short season was extended, and the production moved to larger premises.[100]

Though many of the performers were American, white reviewers—and presumably audiences, too, who crammed into small theaters to see Dafora's troupe—believed they had discovered a truly African form. The "thumpings of the tom-toms," wrote one reviewer, "lend such persuasion . . . [that] you feel inclined to lean forward and tap the white man on the shoulder who may be sitting in front of you, and say: 'Dr. Livingstone, I presume.'"[101] Comparisons to *The Emperor Jones,* so feted in the first half of the 1920s, now found O'Neill's play wanting.[102] The opera-play was propelled by "marvelously rhythmic drum beatings, as persistent as those of 'The Emperor Jones,' and much more varied."[103] Tired of American interpretations of Africa, white viewers wanted the "real" thing. Dafora, too, claimed he was the real deal. He was at pains to point out that *Kykunkor* was "based on the true

KYKUNKOR

THE WITCH WOMAN
AFRICAN DANCE DRAMA

White reviewers were beside themselves over the "hypnotic" drumbeats, "barbaric passion," and "authentic frenzy" of Asadata Dafora Horton's "tribal opera." Black attendees also marvelled at the show but attributed its appeal to the hard work its performers had done in rehearsal. (Manuscripts, Archives and Rare Books Division, Schomburg Center for Research in Black Culture, The New York Public Library, Astor, Lenox and Tilden Foundations.)

and original life in Africa"; programs listed the background and origin of each of the African drummers and male performers.[104] The women may have been American born, but the program claimed that "they can trace their lineage back to the tribes from which their forbears came." Moreover, they "received their first training for the stage from Dafora. He had tried using a few dancers from revues, but found they had to unlearn too much of their American-made 'jazz' to be adaptable to the kind of thing he wished to present—authentic African art."[105] Dafora himself had been in the United States for at least five years and was active in the Native African Union, but it was not until his 1934 show that the white press paid him any attention. Authenticity was key to Dafora's success. The program included an endorsement from no less a figure than the curator of the American Museum of Natural History, James P. Chapin. "Never outside of Africa have I ever seen or heard anything so typically Ethiopian," Chapin gushed. Employing a metaphor straight out of the African explorers' manual, he continued: "The drum rhythms and most of the singing rang so true as to carry me back to the dark continent. Asadata Dafora has shown real genius in giving us here so authentic a picture of African native life, especially in dancing."[106]

Where *Kykunkor*'s white reviewers saw untutored genius in the performances, black commentators, quite taken with the display of African culture, nevertheless recognized that it was a performance, honed by much practice. What else could it be? For Leonard Kirstein, writing in the *Nation*, it was "a frenzy of self-hypnosis, diabolical gaiety, anguish, and success which is fiercely dramatic because it is experienced . . . but it is always more of a black sacrament than a good performance."[107] In the opinion of black reviewers, by contrast, the brilliant improvisation was not the gift of racial primitivism but the result of years of hard work.[108] Harlem's *New York Age* praised the players' "masterful artistry."[109] The drummers, in other words, were not "possessed as the action progresses by the very hypnosis of their own playing."[110] Instead, they were improvising, a skill that meant that while any one performance was unique, the performers drew upon a pool of learnt moves and grooves. There was, therefore, no reason that black American dancers and drummers, could not learn and perform similarly. This explains why, when an author in *Opportunity* appraised the Federal Negro Theatre, he wrote that the African Dance Unit "consists of 67 *actors* and *interpreters* of the dance."[111] Likewise when the WPA Federal Theatre Project mounted *Haiti* in 1938, the choir was praised for "interpret[ing] the native Haitian chants with such fidelity." One of the cast, Nancy Hunt, born in Brooklyn in 1915, went on to perform with an African dance group. There she "learned the difficult gyrations of African dancing, and was admitted to the group as a full-fledged African dancer."[112] To be able to dance like an African or drum like an Haitian was not proof positive that all black people were alike, that they contained within them a bit of the jungle. Rather, it was a way of making a living. Where white reviewers continued to see ancient Africa emerging from a wellspring deep within each performer, black Americans had come to see culture as something dynamic, changing, and subject to circumstance.[113]

The most thorough expression on stage of this view of black American culture as dynamic came in a 1932 opera-play-pageant, *Tom-Tom*, by Shirley Graham. Best known for becoming the second Mrs. W.E.B. Du Bois in 1951, at this time Graham was a student at Oberlin College's Conservatory of Music, from which she gained a master's degree in 1935. With a cast of over two hundred and Jules Bledsoe in the leading role, *Tom-Tom* played for two nights at the Cleveland Municipal Stadium, Ohio, and was broadcast over the radio.[114] The plot featured two characters fighting for the allegiance of black people in Harlem, one intending to lead them back to Africa, the other just as determined to remain in the United States. Alongside this main plot, Graham probed the question of what culture had survived enslavement and the Middle Passage—or had been kept alive with dogged determination. She raised the question first by having the same actors play parts in the African, slave-time, and contemporary scenes. No black reviewers stated a desire for more "authentic" performers, straight out of Africa. Rather, the performance "was a musical triumph," garnering the largest crowd of the Cleveland Opera's season.[115]

Even more brilliant than her casting was Graham's aural investigation of diaspora culture. As in *The Emperor Jones, Crisis* noted, the drum held together the entire production.[116] Unlike in O'Neill's show, however, the drumbeat signified more than merely savagery or psychic release. The press release reported:

> Only the percussion instruments of the opera are employed to accompany the unison chants of the opening primitive scenes of the African jungle. Other instruments are added as the opera progresses. In the final scenes of New York the entire orchestra, spirituals and jazz bands are used simultaneously, in various keys. As in the earlier scenes, the tom-tom continues to weave its w[ei]rd spell through to the end.[117]

Graham used the tom-tom, so long taken to represent Africa itself, as not only a precursor to black American life but also in continuing dialogue with present-day black American culture. Culture was a process whose elements changed regularly. There could be no "survival" of African customs, as some anthropologists claimed, because nothing ever stayed the same. The drumbeat may well have continued, but in the United States, people heard it differently.[118]

White audiences' response to *Kykunkor*—it would be fair to call it frenzied—proved that if, as Langston Hughes claimed, white New Yorkers in the 1930s lost interest in Harlem and the supposed primitivism of their black fellow citizens, they had not lost all taste for the jungle.[119] In spite of this enduring fad, black Americans continually tried to find ways to connect to Africa, Africans, and black people elsewhere in the diaspora in ways that did not reproduce the prejudices and assumptions of their white countrymen and, for that matter, of Westerners in general. Their experiences, both present-day and those handed down to them by recitation of memory and by the efforts of the black history movement, gave them something in common with colonized Africans, Haitians, and those under imperial rule elsewhere, too. This was not a simple racial alliance, though their sympathies and affinities took in black people worldwide.

Black Americans took an assumed link between themselves and Africans and forged a transnational alliance whose members turned the idea of national self-determination into something that applied equally to black people as to white. They appropriated Franz Boas's argument, promoted extensively in the black press, that racial evolution was a myth, invented to serve the interests of those who deemed themselves at the top of the ladder of civilization. Regarding all cultures as inherently valuable, they attacked the implicit racial basis of the United States' invasion and occupation of Haiti. Drawing a parallel between their own experiences of racism and those of colonized Haitians—including resistance through the formation of culture—they exposed as farcical American claims that the United States was an isolationist power and an exceptional nation. It was a colonial power like any other. In the past it had engaged in the slave trade and an internal colonialism in the form of slavery. In the present, it had extended its reach to places such as Haiti, beyond national borders.

By using Haiti as a midway point between themselves and Africa, black American artists and activists explored what it meant to be black in America and tried to debunk pervasive ideas about their essentially primitive nature.

As the inheritors of rich traditions of song and dance, they proudly asserted a distinct way of being in the world, one that privileged sound over sight, so marvelous that whole languages could be remediated into a drumbeat. Far from backward nor evidence of primitive consciousness, this was something of which to be proud. Moreover, this assertion of a distinctive black identity was shared by other black communities in the diaspora. The cultures were not identical, but the means of identifying as members of a group were similar, from the United States across various places in the Atlantic, all the way to Africa. If the cultural basis of race—and a diasporic identity—did not completely transcend biology, it was nevertheless an effective basis for transnational self-assertion, collective identity, and political organizing. Becoming African American was not a simple process of claiming just a rich African history. Rather, it also incorporated a feeling of kinship with people all over the diaspora who shared both that history and present-day struggles against colonial rule.

6

Ethiopia Ahoy!

World War II came early for black Americans, when late in 1935 fascist Italy invaded Ethiopia, providing the most decisive event in their transformation into African Americans. At perhaps no other time since the early nineteenth century had black Americans feel such a close kinship with their African "brothers." Ethiopia was beloved because of its special place in black religious traditions of exodus and because it was one of the few remaining independent black nations. In the months leading up to the invasion, Italy repeatedly made clear its intentions to elevate its status among European imperial powers at the expense of the east African monarchy. Black Americans nationwide, and indeed around the diaspora, expressed their unmitigated outrage in any way they could. Once the invasion took place, black newspapers devoted almost every front page to covering the war, filling in what patchy information came out of Ethiopia with optimistic accounts of the brave little nation's struggle against the brutish and better-equipped Italians. Journalists were joined by poets, writers, playwrights, visual artists, and even tap dancers, in expressing their anger with Italy and their allegiance to an imagined black world. So, too, did those black Americans who did not have ready access to avenues of public culture express themselves, in church services, at community meetings, and in hundreds of letters to newspapers and local and national organizations, asking for information as to how to best travel to Ethiopia to join the fight against Mussolini's forces. More directly, they protested the invasion in marches on the streets of cities and towns around the country. After the early months of 1936, it was clear to even the most hopeful of onlookers that Ethiopia had lost its fight.

With the Berlin Olympics drawing near, worldwide attention was zooming in on Hitler's rule in Germany. From 1936, black newspapers and magazines were awash with stories and commentary about German treatment of Jewish people. Likening European anti-Semitism to legal and de facto segregation, violence, and disfranchisement in the United States, black Americans, like so many others, could not anticipate the full implications of Nazi policies. Even after the revelation that thousands and then millions of Jewish people were being murdered en masse, black Americans saw parallels between their own daily experiences of vilification, harassment, and violence and the end point, which the Nazis called the Final Solution. Whether it manifested itself within national boundaries, existing colonial situations, or imperial aggression, racism everywhere seemed to rest on the same structures. Racism was global, and oppressors drew strength from the existence of inequality in other places. Therefore, racism had to be quashed wherever it was found.

The extent of the atrocities in Europe extinguished quickly the racial grounds that black Americans used to ally themselves with Ethiopians and Africans in general. Racism, and especially the Holocaust, made all racial identification suspect. Put another way, racism made it necessary for those who sought justice to cast their vision of an egalitarian future more widely. Thus, the secondary strain in black Americans' identification with Africans, as with Haitians—namely, on the grounds that all were oppressed, not that they were brothers in blood—came to the fore. As the 1930s drew to a close and increasingly during World War II, black Americans came to identify themselves not only with Africans but as part of a worldwide group of colonized people, irrespective of the race of those under the imperial thumb.[1]

Not all antiracist campaigners did away entirely with a sense of allegiance—publicly at least—to the United States. Black Americans were, after all, still American, and most held dear democratic ideals; they were just more than a little weary of the hypocrisy of American political and social institutions that made some Americans more equal than others. The rapid extension of American power overseas—for example, in Haiti—lay bare even further the contradictions between American ideals and reality for people living under U.S. control. Although many black Americans, disgusted with the lack of change in race relations, refused to have anything to do with the war in Europe, others used the fight against fascism in Europe to call for an end of racism at home as well as abroad.

Responses to Mussolini's threats against Ethiopia could not have been more different from that day in early January 1919 when James Weldon Johnson stood on stage at Carnegie Hall and implored his fellow black Americans to think of Africans' plight as their own. Black public life was consumed with outrage at the Italians' audacity, fury at the muted responses of other European nations and the United States, and frustration with an inept League of Nations. The extent of the expression revealed much about the symbiotic expansion of a black American public sphere and a growing culture of black internationalism, which had taken place since 1919. For months from July 1935 on, stories about Ethiopia were on the front page of just about every edition of black newspapers nationwide. Letters, editorials, news pages, foreign sections, and even cartoons focused on Abyssinia's resistance. Not until the eleventh hour did they admit that Italy had the upper hand. Even George Schuyler, a commentator not given to assuming any kind of connection with Africans on the basis of race, declared in his usually satirical column that if black people of the diaspora did not help out, "then Ethiopia will lose her shirt, and we will lose our soul."[2]

In New York, Chicago, and other urban districts, public protests were heated and sometimes violent. Street speakers atop boxes by day or perched on ladders at night made the invasion the centerpiece of dialogues they had with crowds, peppering their accounts with reference to Ethiopia's wonderful history and likening imperialism to domestic racism.[3] Up to 20,000 people staged in Harlem "a mighty demonstration against imperialism and Italian aggression against Ethiopia."[4] That group included antiracist Italians, but on many other occasions anger over foreign affairs made itself felt in belligerence toward the many Italian shopkeepers in the black neighborhood and in calls for their businesses to be boycotted.[5] As the war moved in Italy's favor, such hostility increased, especially after a victory march through Little Italy in downtown Manhattan culminated in the burning of Ethiopia's Emperor Haile Selassie in effigy.[6] Chicago police refused a permit to allow a demonstration against the imminent invasion of Abyssinia, with the Italian forces waiting only until the weather was right before they attacked. Thousands attempted the march in any case, but it was aborted when police arrested hundreds.[7] Heavy-handed policing seemed only more evidence of the parallels between racism in an imperial context and that in the United States. Langston Hughes drew an explicit link in "Air Raid over Harlem," the very title referring to Italy's main method of subduing Ethiopian forces:

The Ethiopian war broke out last night:
BOMBS OVER HARLEM
Cops on every corner
Most of 'em white
COPS IN HARLEM
Guns and billy-clubs
Double duty in Harlem
Walking in pairs
Under every light
Their faces
WHITE
In Harlem
And mixed in with 'em
A black cop or two
For the sake of the vote in Harlem.[8]

Hughes dreamt of a day when workers were united and "a big black giant . . . picks up a cop and lets him fly," sending him to hell. Harlemites could only hope that Ethiopia would live up to the gigantic reputation they had afforded it and do the same to Mussolini.

The pleasure black Americans took in the victories of their sporting heroes intensified when they beat Italians. Joe Louis's victory over Italian boxer Primo Carnera in mid-1935 was, they hoped, a harbinger of Ethiopia's swift victory over Mussolini's men.[9] One editorial cartoon depicted Ethiopians and Italians eagerly watching the two fighters slug it out in the ring, while the chair marked "League of Nations" remained empty. Alongside the section for Ethiopian spectators sat identical men, presumably black Americans.[10] In the ensuing years, Louis would become a surprising object for both white and black Americans' dreams, the former for democracy in general, the latter for a particular kind of campaign against fascism of both the European and the homegrown kind.[11] When Louis beat German Max Baer, thousands of Harlem's residents poured onto the streets, grabbing whatever was available to make noise to celebrate the win.[12] One man climbed onto a taxicab as it crawled slowly through the crowded streets, waving an Ethiopian flag to cheering onlookers.[13] Similar celebrations took place around the country. Louis was not the only sports star transformed into political metaphor. When Ethiopian wrestler Prince Torazze Monango came into town, a New York newspaper printed a photograph of him in his trunks, feet square on the floor, hands on hips, as strong as can be.[14] When he triumphed over Italian Frank Maroni in October 1935, thereby avenging a previous loss, a Harlem newspaper crowed that the "Nubian warrior prince squelched the rough tactics of his Italian opponent to win."[15] With little real news coming out of Abyssinia, and emotionally desperate for it to remain an independent and functioning black nation, black Americans made heroes where they were able.

Black aviators who went to Ethiopia became the focus of much attention. Colonel John Robinson, the Mississippi-born "Brown Condor" of Chicago's South Side, attained his flying credentials by gaining employment as a janitor in the aeronautical school that had rejected his application to study there because he was black. Eventually he was accepted into the program. Robinson slowly acquired Emperor Haile Selassie's trust with his bravery and tenacity, flying many missions in the unarmed planes of the Ethiopian army against the heavily armed Italian warplanes. Arriving back in the United States in 1936, thousands gathered in New York and again in Chicago to greet him.[16] *Chicago Defender* cartoonist "Chase" depicted Robinson's positive impact on young black American men under the heading "Inspiration!"[17] Perhaps it was Robinson's example that inspired the nine men and one woman pictured in a photograph captioned "Harlem Fliers Training for Service in Ethiopia," which appeared in the *New York Times* in July 1935.[18] In any case, Robinson's valor was a welcome remedy to the embarrassment and disgust that followed on the exploits of aviator Hubert Julian. Having wowed Harlem crowds in the 1920s with daring parachute jumps, in 1930 Julian crashed Selassie's brand-new plane, which he was not supposed to be flying, and was expelled from Ethiopia. In 1935, having talked his way back in, Julian resigned his post just one month after the war began in earnest. Black Americans lamented his lack of courage and denounced him as a traitor to the diasporic black nation.[19]

Ethiopia continued to be in the hearts and on the minds of black Americans, particularly in performance. "Ethiopia," a female character representing the best of Africa, was a mainstay of plays and pageants throughout the interwar years, but in 1935 the country's role expanded. On screen, those loyal to the black nation could enjoy *Wings over Ethiopia* (in a double bill

with *Here Comes Cookie* with George Burns and Gracie Allen), a Swiss trav-
elogue featuring scenes of the nation's varied terrain, villages and urban
centers, people, and the royal court. During the war, the film was teamed
with an African dance group for a run at Harlem's Opera House.[20] Ethiopia
moved to center stage even in productions that marshaled familiar stereotypes and caricatures of black people. Haile Selassie's army was given a
dubious showing nationwide in the 1936 edition of George White's annual
revue, *Scandals*.[21] The *Defender* was outraged at the performance of a number,
"Brother Sublime and His Pied Piper of Harlem," that portrayed "Emperor
Haile Selassie as a buffoon and a minstrel clown." A character playing Mussolini declared that the "Italian race" needed a place in the sun and "that's
why darkies were born."[22] It is possible to imagine at a stretch that audiences
may have seen Mussolini's character as the buffoon and in Selassie's more
dignity, but given the huge popularity of a 1931 song, "That's Why Darkies
Were Born," cowritten by one of *Scandals*'s composers, it seems unlikely.[23]

A more pointed critique of Italy's imperial ambitions found its way into a
play, *Warning Drums* (1935), by Lilian Saunders, a white woman living in
St. Louis, Missouri, who sent her script to Walter White at the National Association for the Advancement of Colored People (NAACP), hoping for a
New York production. Its didactic tone was reminiscent of Marcus Garvey's
duologues in his London publication, *Black Man*, and of J. A. Rogers's tone
in his very popular pamphlet, *From "Superman" to Man*. In *Warning Drums*,
Nairobi, also known as Thomas Carteret, an English-educated African man
and "a tall black Negro of magnificent physique and imposing appearance"
explained to a New York journalist, Bryan Forbes, the history of the Afro-
Asiatic Alliance. Forged in the cauldron of the 1919 Pan-African Congress
in Paris, hundreds of "fervid patriots" of the colored races joined together.
"You would hardly believe how easy it was to find recruits," Nairobi told
Forbes. "It was as if the psychological moment had come." Anticipating
the Italian attack on Ethiopia, hundreds of thousands of men amassed
throughout the continent. Turning weakness into strength, the Alliance
made up for its lack of new technology with manpower. Units communi-
cated with one another using drums, which their white enemies thought
mere entertainment, the idle tom-tom thumping of savages. Meanwhile,
each and every group agitated at home for freedom and looked forward to a
day of genuine "civilization," when wars—invariably fought over the black

man's land, Nairobi told his interlocutor—would end. The play's author noted in her 1936 correspondence with White that though circumstances in Ethiopia had changed, the play's message of the need to end racial strife in order to bring about peace remained.[24]

Ethiopia's plight put black Americans' global outlook into fast-forward, and the speed only increased as circumstances worsened in Europe. As fascist powers emerged, black Americans shed any remaining sense that their oppression in the United States was unique. To be exact, it was unique in that they were legally citizens of the place where they lived, as opposed to colonial subjects or conquered peoples (as in Ethiopia). Structurally, however, it seemed that racism's effects were similar everywhere, serving to exclude those thought to be inferior and to reinforce the hierarchy of races at every turn. *Living Newspaper: Ethiopia* (1936), part of a series of New Deal plays financed by the Federal Theatre Project (FTP) that aimed to bring to life current events, reflected this global outlook. With scenes set in the court at Addis Ababa, battlegrounds in Ethiopia, meetings of the League of Nations, London's House of Commons, on the streets in many cities, and even on the deck of a docked boat carrying aviator Hubert Julian back to New York, the show decried the weakness of the League, an international organization, in dealing with what was a worldwide problem. The disparate scenes were held together by a sound that carried the whole way through: the beat of a drum signaling war, rifle shots, and even a gavel wielded by the League's chairman. White and black actors took part, including a troupe of Africans from an opera company stranded in New York without enough cash to get home. It must have been an extraordinary play, at least with a script provocative enough to entice Secretary of State Hull to ban the theater series from portraying directly any ruler or cabinet, fearing, he said, an international incident if such a portrayal were negative.[25] The *Living Newspaper* series director, Elmer Rice, claimed that the ban came only after the FTP head learned that the series' next two productions focused on the Democratic Party's failure both to end unemployment and to stem racist violence in the South. Rice quit in fury, but he nevertheless managed to sneak in a performance of the banned play, in front of print journalists, by calling it a dress rehearsal.[26]

Right around the United States, black Americans pointed out the discrepancy between Europeans' claims to civilization and their imperialist actions. "If Italy goes to war in Africa," a North Carolina religious publication read, "it will be solely a war of conquest, and without a scintilla of moral justification. Surely the Christianity of the twentieth century should voice disapproval of this practice of the ages of barbarism."[27] The *Chicago Defender* took Mussolini to task especially for the numbers of Ethiopians violently killed and suggested, "this is the Roman way of carrying civilization to Ethiopia. A new Cato rules in Ethiopia and like that Cato of old, the new Carthage must be destroyed."[28] Articles, letters, and editorials time and again made snide reference to so-called Western civilization and the purported blessings colonization would bring to Ethiopia as in prior imperial ventures in Africa and elsewhere.[29] Black Americans empathized deeply with Ethiopians and their victimization at the hands of white Italy.

A particularly effective means of conveying black Americans' distrust and scorn of Mussolini's ambitions was in cartooning. With just a sketch and a few words, cartoonists captured the opinions of millions. In "Christianizing Ethiopia!" a woman lay under the sword of a decorated Italian officer, Mussolini, bleeding profusely.[30] "Italy's Name for It" showed an airman wielding a gun labeled "CIVILIZATION" shooting at an Ethiopian school.[31] Just as Italy triumphed in the war and black newspapers finally admitted that all was not going Ethiopia's way in battle, the *New York Amsterdam News* published "Civilization(?) Wins." In this image, a porcine and maniacal Mussolini brandished a champagne bottle in one hand and, in the other, a sword heaving with bloody, miniature Ethiopians.[32] Black Americans were particularly dismayed at the reluctance of the League of Nations to insist on sanctions against Italy, depicting the organization as a sleeping or helpless mother.[33] England and France were similarly held responsible for failing to check Italy's aggression, staying quiet in order to protect the wealth they garnered from their own colonies.[34] In one especially pointed critique of the rationale offered for colonization, "Ethiopia" stood terrified, tied to a stake by a boiling cauldron while the "civilized nations," represented by corpulent men, argued about the helpless nation's fate.[35] Another cartoon deemed the United States to be no better than any of the European powers, as it supplied war materials and stood by idly, doing nothing to stop "Italy's Continued Rape of Ethiopia."[36] The overwhelming sentiment animating these cartoons was that no European nation, nor the United States, had any business trying to civilize anyone else.

Fascist Italy's claim to be bringing civilization to Ethiopia failed to convince black Americans, who seemed to have heard something like that before. ("Civilization (?) Wins." Cartoon by Chase, *New York Amsterdam News*, May 9, 1936. Used with permission.)

Pro-Ethiopian attitudes were limited to neither urban black Americans nor to a black elite. Letters poured into the NAACP headquarters, asking for information about Ethiopia's plight and offering to help. William Little knew several "boys" interested in joining the volunteers he had heard were leaving from New York for Ethiopia.[37] Horace White, of the Mt. Zion Temple in Cleveland, Ohio, claimed to speak for people around the country when he asked executive secretary Walter White for advice about the "legality of American citizens enlisting in the Ethiopian army to fight against Italy when Italy is a friendly nation of ours?"[38] In Okmulgee, Oklahoma, another black man claimed that "100 Negroes of that city had signed to fight for Ethiopia in event of war and that a statewide recruiting movement was under way."[39] Robert Brown, of Greenville, Mississippi, had "a 'good deal of young men

Many critics of the impending invasion of Ethiopia reversed the usual suggestion that Europeans were civilized and Africans barbarian cannibals. ("Awaiting the Verdict of the Civilized Nations." By permission of the Crisis Publishing Co., Inc., the publisher of the magazine of the NAACP; image first published in the October 1935 issue of *The Crisis*.)

[who] want to volunteer' and go and help to fight for that old Mother Land Africa."[40] A black American World War I veteran organized a meeting at the YMCA in Fort Worth, Texas, to protest the imminent invasion. In a draft of a letter he enclosed in his missive to the NAACP, he wrote to Selassie: "My dear emperor: I herewith ask your permission to organize a company of men, by voluntary enlistment, for military duty in behalf of your country. There are a number of local colored men who are ready to spill their blood in behalf of our native land. We are ready at your command, and will request only that your government pay the transportation expense to Ethiopia."[41] Men and youth around the country wanted to help keep Ethiopia free, not just for its sake but also because it was important to them personally.

While men offered their services to fight for Ethiopia, women south of the Mason-Dixon line were more likely to express a desire to emigrate permanently to the free black nation. A digest of letters prepared by the Ethiopian Research Council in Washington, D.C., included this from Henrietta Epps of Baltimore: "'Wishing that I was in Africa now'—as everything is against her." Mrs. Virginia Broome, of Priscilla, Mississippi, expanded upon this sentiment, asking, "we want to go to our Mother Country Africa, and how soon and when will the emigration start. We are on plantation nearly starved to death and nearly naked and barefooted as we can be. Millions of us want to go to Africa and I have 13 children in family and 10 grandchildren (who) want to go to Africa. We are suffering down here and we want to go home."[42] The difference in men's and women's letters is not surprising—men wanted to fight and in doing so prove themselves worthy citizens of the scattered African nation, while women wanted to keep the family together, in better conditions than in the U.S. South during the Depression. Ethiopia was a natural alternative for a black home.

Black men's enthusiasm for battle around the country echoed that in Harlem, where somewhere between 500 and 50,000 residents volunteered to fight.[43] One editorial reported that people were coming into the newspaper's office in scores, seeking information on how to volunteer. "The possibility of losing their citizenship does not deter them," readers were told. "This they would gladly do for the privilege of stopping the destruction of Abyssinia by one of the world's mad dogs—Mussolini. Aroused as never before, colored America present the United States today their first refusal to blindly follow patriotism. To them this is the first direct attack in the series of wars that are certain to follow, and unless checked will engulf the entire civilized world."[44] Rather than American patriotism, they felt an allegiance to Ethiopia, both the sentimental African heart of the international black world and, until now, a shining example of black independence.

As well as organizations designed to assist men in traveling to Abyssinia, several aid organizations sprang up in Harlem and elsewhere. The Research Council in the nation's capital was joined by Friends of Ethiopia (a division of the International Council of Friends of Ethiopia), Ethiopian Pioneers, Pan-African Reconstruction Committee, and many others.[45] Clubs and societies of longer standing turned their attention to the conflict. The Ethiopian Social Club and Ethiopian Seaman's Club organized benefit dinner dances.[46]

Interracial organizations, such as American Aid for Ethiopia, sent supplies—bandages and dressings—prepared mostly by volunteers from Harlem.[47] Such mobilization was, on a smaller scale, just like that of the Ethiopians themselves, as they prepared for Italy's aerial onslaught.

Some societies made education their mission. For example, the Universal Ethiopian Students' Association, composed of local and foreign-born black students, held a mock trial, in which Africa was pitted against the Imperialist Powers "At the Bar of International Justice."[48] The Association also published a booklet, "The Truth about Ethiopia," outlining the history of the conflict with Italy and, following Marcus Garvey, calling for Africans to band together, expel the European powers, and unite as the United States of Africa.[49] In this, they took their lead from Willis N. Huggins, by day a teacher in the New York high school system and long committed to promulgating alternative narratives of black history in public, but also an indefatigable campaigner for Ethiopian freedom. Huggins raised funds for Friends of Ethiopia, lectured frequently, and with John G. Jackson published *An Introduction to African Civilization with Main Currents in the History of Ethiopia,* with its subtitle in large typeface in advertisements.[50] Continuing the tradition of raising consciousness through an awareness of black history, activists hoped to rally ever-increasing numbers of black Americans to the cause.

Black Americans' outrage against Italy was matched by that of black people worldwide. Reading in the papers about Huggins's lectures, Dantès Bellegarde, a Haitian writer and diplomat, wrote to Arthur Schomburg, the bibliophile and scholar in New York, that he had much to offer the cause and would like to be engaged on a lecture tour.[51] Years later, Bellegarde recalled Haiti's valiant efforts at the League of Nations, where its representative allegedly warned those around the table: "'Remember, nations of Europe, that each one of you may be tomorrow the Ethiopia of some other aggressor!'"[52] In Montreal, Canada, a black newspaper publisher opened an unofficial recruiting office and had pledges from 235 people, black and white, that they would fight for Ethiopia should war break out with Italy.[53]

The global response to Ethiopia's plight demonstrated the enduring effects of Garvey's activism. By the time of the invasion, Garvey was settled in London, where his main outlet was an irregularly published magazine, *Black*

Man. His response to Italy's aggression was, unsurprisingly, apoplectic, but for a change, his attitude was typical of black activists worldwide. In Jamaica, Garveyites announced meetings throughout the island to gather together a contingent to join Ethiopia's forces.[54] Gladys Wilson, the *Chicago Defender*'s foreign news correspondent in Jamaica, reminded readers that Ethiopia was their "native home," and if black Americans could join American forces in every war, then they ought to do the same here, for "blood should be thicker than water. . . . Our brothers are in danger."[55] Although pacifists and anticolonialists worldwide opposed Mussolini's stance, it was especially galling for black people to see the one remaining independent black nation assaulted. They expressed their opposition as the brothers and kin of the defeated Africans and as people who had endured similar experiences.

Irrespective of their attachment to Ethiopia as a black nation, many black would-be volunteers found themselves caught up in quite a different war in Spain.[56] They characterized the civil conflict there as part of a worldwide struggle against the forces of fascism, which included racism. Some ninety of the 3,000 Americans who comprised the Abraham Lincoln Brigade were black, all joining the Republican forces in the fight against Francisco Franco and his band of nationalists. Notably, Langston Hughes traveled to the front to report for the Baltimore *Afro-American,* and one black woman, Salaria Kea, served in the American Medical Unit attached to the American outfit.[57] The number of black Americans was not high, but the sentiments of those who served reflected the feelings of many at home. One poet, Jay Hill, put into words the equation many made between the hostilities in Ethiopia and Spain. Inspired by the activities of a son of Ethiopia's prince regent, Ras Imru, who had joined the International Brigade, of which the Americans, too, were part, Hill wrote "An Ethiope in Spain." Published in the NAACP's *Crisis,* its last stanza read:

> At one gate, in silence, fights this Ethiope
>> Goaded by the rape
>> Of motherland, of sisterland—
> Yesterday, a symbol of black majesty,
> Today a victim of civilized barbarity,
> A prince, with no bright jewel in his ear.[58]

Hill's poem encapsulated many of the ways black Americans imagined Africa in the years leading up to fascist Italy's invasion of Ethiopia. It had a regal tradition, it was a glorious motherland to which its scattered children wanted to return, and compared with the so-called civilized world, its people provided a model of how to live, in harmony and peace.

As Italy and Ethiopia went to battle, black Americans likened racism in that colonial setting to racism in the United States and that in turn, in varying degrees, to anti-Semitism in Germany. They debated whether black sportsmen ought to boycott the Berlin Olympic Games and then rejoiced at the success of Jesse Owens and several others on Adolf Hitler's terrain. Hitler and others explained away athletic achievements as evidence of a savage physicality rather than of training and skill, but the athletes' triumphs were evidence of black people's prowess in an arena—international sport—of increasing importance.[59] Able to cross national borders, sports stars were emerging to counter transnational ideas about race, which were pervasive in the West.

International contexts provided black Americans grist for the antiracist mill in the United States. The American government's denunciations of the treatment of Jewish people in Germany rang hollow to those who had experienced Jim Crow segregation, violence, and everyday racism in the United States. Anticipating a technique that was perfected during the Civil Rights campaigns of the 1950s and 1960s, when television made it even more effective, black activists sought to embarrass the United States on the world stage. In response to American accusations of racial prejudice in Europe, one Southern black newspaper article pointed out, "the thoughtful Teutons tell the United States to look after disgraceful affairs in their own confines before attempting to guide the destinies of others." The article's author imagined the following German response: "'We do not lynch each other . . . neither do we tear the clothing off our women and chase them naked through the public streets,' to all of which the United States can answer not one word. The eyes of the entire world, civilized or not, have been turned on America for years, horrified at the cannibalistic rites performed so frequently on helpless Negroes and, more recently, hapless whites. These United States present themselves as an easy target to all foreign countries who have a right to look askance at any criticism leveled at their persecution of unfavored people."[60] The article's sentiments were repeated countless times in black publications nationwide.

While black Americans continued to proclaim their kinship with Africans throughout the war, that imagined family was extended to include victims of racism everywhere. Just as they had reconceived their affinity to black people in Africa and the diaspora along cultural and historical lines, rather than biological ones, so, too, could a similarity of experience determine a nonfamilial kinship to oppressed people in Europe and, for that matter, all over the world. As Germany invaded Poland, the *Chicago Defender* proclaimed that American neutrality did not mean a lack of sympathy. "Black America," it said over and again, sympathized with the Polish people, on the basis of their experiences of "travail and pain . . . the profound spiritual anguish that comes from the denial of manhood rights and civil liberties . . . the terrible physical pain and suffering that comes with mob violence, lynching, Jim-Crowism, segregation, and jobless days with starvation, sickness and death." "These very experiences," it pointed out, revealed "that the enemies of democracy and peace everywhere are the friends of lynching and of the false theories of racism."[61] Antiracist struggles had to be both international and transnational.

For W. E. B. Du Bois, the failure of the powers at the 1919 Paris Peace Conference to include in their program "justice to black folk," in the form of genuine mandates leading to self-government, for which he and other delegates at the adjacent Pan-African Congress had advocated, led to war. It was "the stone which the builders rejected . . . [and] precisely the one whose absence has brought disaster to Europe in the Ethiopian conquest and the German menace."[62] Racial injustice continued into this war, just as in the last. Mussolini was reported not only to be tramping all over the Ethiopians' sovereign rights but to be putting black troops at the head of the Italian lines to do so.[63] Just after Germany invaded Poland, the *New York Amsterdam News* printed a cartoon of colonial troops staggering under the weight of a white warmonger clad in armor. Titled "Black Man's Burden," it played on Rudyard Kipling's famous poem, "The White Man's Burden" (1899), which exhorted the United States to take its place at the big table of the family of nations by carrying out its duty as a colonial power. The cartoon reflected the view of many that, once again, black men would do the fighting for

Just as they had during World War I, colonial troops would bear the greatest burden of the coming war. ("The Black Man's Burden." Cartoon by Chase, *New York Amsterdam News,* September 16, 1939. Used with permission.)

white men's wealth.[64] Countless editorials confirmed the viewpoint expressed in the cartoon, sometimes going beyond identifying those colonized in Africa, India, and elsewhere to include also those "people in Europe who are fighting for their homes, for the right to work in peace and to receive the fruit of their labor; for the right to govern themselves."[65] These were issues with which black people had always been concerned. Only with an end to exploitation of the many for the benefit of the few would genuine peace be achieved.

As quickly as Ethiopia's struggle brought to a climax black Americans' identification with Africans, the slide into World War II and the atrocities of the Holocaust muted it in favor of a more expansive identification with oppressed people everywhere. The "diaspora" itself was an ever-changing product of imperialism, colonialism, the slave trade, and ensuing experiences in different nations and regions. It was further mediated by the social situation—gender and class most notably—of individuals within it.[66] The attempt to fix the diaspora to its origins in Africa, and to "black" people worldwide, had its limits. World War II lay bare what black Americans already knew: biological categories of race were a mystification of bad science. The black nation, then, like being "black" itself, had to mean more than simply African-descended and African-identified. The antiracism that was part and parcel of black identity extended to a well-documented sympathy for Japanese Americans held in detention during the war. So, too, the Afro-Asiatic Alliance of the play *Warning Drums* was emblematic of the triumph at the end of the 1930s of a more broadly conceived transnational identity for black Americans.

Some black Americans allied themselves with those suffering under racism worldwide and at the same time maintained a hope that the American nation could be induced to live up to the ideals enshrined in its founding documents. The most prominent of the wartime strategies aimed at achieving change in the United States was the widespread "Double V" campaign. Spearheaded by the *Pittsburgh Courier* in early 1942, it called for victories against racism abroad and at home. Using a by now familiar approach that would later be central to the freedom struggle, activists invoked the purportedly universal values of the American nation and insisted on their application to all citizens. Editors who supported the campaign came under significant pressure to abandon it, and yet for many black Americans it did not go nearly far enough. Only a revolution could transform the nation that hypocritically called them citizens. They had come to see themselves as the colonial subjects of an increasingly powerful, and malevolent, imperial power.

For many black Americans, the second half of the 1930s and World War II battered their hope that the United States could be reformed. The New Deal, a broad federally funded program to pull Americans out of the pit of economic depression, had only incidental benefits for them. Most of its schemes excluded people of color. So, too, were black Americans excluded from the redefinition of racial categories, which saw most immigrants from Europe become "white." Nowhere was the failure of American democracy more clear than in the response to black Americans' wartime service. Just as in the last world war, black Americans enlisted in the hundreds of thousands, only to be denied the gratitude of the state for their sacrifices. In this instance, the G.I. Bill, another massive injection of funds to create a broad middle class where before there were blue-collar workers, was not extended to black veterans. The long-term effects of these legislative failures are still with us today.

Alongside black volunteers were many black men of enlistment age who were outraged at the expectation that they would train, fight, and perhaps die for a nation that held them in such low esteem. To them, American ideals were without substance. Draft dodgers received immense support from their communities, indicating a widespread disaffection with the United States.[67] If few black Americans were able to emigrate, as Du Bois finally did, renouncing his citizenship and moving to Ghana in 1961 at age 93, many were disillusioned that America could ever be made to live up to the ideals it espoused and for which they went to war in 1917 and 1941. Their allegiance went instead to an imagined global fraternity of those under the thumb.

While Italy's invasion of Ethiopia prompted an outpouring that heralded the apotheosis of black Americans' direct identification with Africa and Africans, it simultaneously brought to the fore an affinity to colonized and oppressed people worldwide. Both of these strains had existed in black politics and culture during the 1920s and 1930s. They would each become more difficult to maintain once relations with the U.S.S.R. broke down and the Cold War began. Nevertheless, black Americans continued to historicize and theorize their experiences with reference to the outside world throughout the long era of the civil rights struggle and into the 1980s, when the name "African American" became commonplace.

Epilogue: What's in a Name?

Black Americans in the interwar years transformed their sense of them-selves from a people whose most defining feature was that they had endured, survived, and resisted American slavery and segregation to a group with connections to people worldwide. For many of these years black Americans directed their attention toward Africans in the past and on black history. By the end of the 1930s, however, black consciousness was now focused firmly on a global black world, defined as broadly as possible. It would be an exag-geration to say that black Americans prior to 1919 had no sense of their con-nections to the outside world. Many, especially in the South, were not so far removed from the last people to arrive from Africa as to have no inherited memory of the place, handed down to them in stories. And how could they not be mindful of Africa, as they were reminded day in and day out that they were a race set apart from America's mainstream? An acute awareness of black Americans' heritage in Africa remained, particularly in folklore and religion. The 1920s and 1930s brought a change in attitudes toward Af-rica. It was no longer simply a place in the past, from which black Ameri-cans had come and developed. Africa was now something living and breath-ing within black identity and at the fore of a newly expanded and dynamic public life.

It is impossible, in fact, to separate the expansion of black public culture from the process of becoming African American. Whether public represen-tations targeted white Americans and hoped to change their attitudes about their black fellow citizens or were intended to rally other black Americans to a particular point of view, they all contributed to the creation of a black modernity that looked outward, not inward. Mobility, along with urbaniza-tion, was key to black modernity, with so many of the inhabitants of northern cities coming from the South and, in eastern metropolises, from the Caribbean as well. Movement was metaphorical as well as real, with an emerging sense that black people's affective connections with people across seas and oceans might well be stronger and more meaningful than their links with other Americans. Debates about the nature of this new identity played out in myriad forums: in print media, including weekly newspapers and monthly magazines; in libraries, history clubs, literary groups, and various societies in all urban centers, which were forging connections to black people worldwide; in political organizations bent on taking black Americans to Africa, on achieving civil rights within the United States, and on class-based revolution; in musicals, folk dramas, comedies, and pageants that were performed on stages from Broadway to Southern churches; in film, made both in the United States and in the United Kingdom; in painting and sculpture that found support in small competitions in all major cities, exhibition spaces in black universities, and increasingly in the broader American public sphere, especially once the Works Progress Administration began to support the work of black visual artists; and in poetry, short stories, novels, and essays, all supported by new New York publishing houses and fostered by competitions run by black political organizations.

Black public culture was suffused with debate about identity, representation, history, and discussion about where black Americans belonged. The concerns of the artists and writers of the Harlem Renaissance, far from being a "vogue" made possible by white patronage that ended with the onset of economic depression, matched those of black Americans across the country.[1] By simply living in a nation where they were told constantly they were not wanted, black Americans were forced just as often to negotiate questions about who they were and where they belonged. Culture and politics were therefore never far apart.

The fervent desire of black Americans to alter most white Americans' perceptions about "the race" was reflected in the urgency with which they addressed the question of what to be called. After decades of battle, on and off, with publishing houses and white editors of newspapers and periodicals, the National Association for the Advancement of Colored People (NAACP) was delighted to announce in 1930, after a year of solid campaigning, that serious headway had been made in convincing many that the word "negro" ought to be printed with a capital *N*.[2] The reasons given both for the change and for refusing to capitalize the word indicate a decided lack of consensus on what the Negro was. Did capitalization recognize a separate race, or was it simply a proper noun for a subgroup of Americans? Was it a reward for achieving "racial self-respect," as the *New York Times* claimed?[3] There were many theories. The Lexington, Kentucky, *Leader* implicitly acknowledged the confusion and avoided taking a position on what "Negro" actually represented, by stating that "if the words Caucasian, and Semite, and African, and Greek, and Roman, and other such racial and national denominations, are capitalized there is every reason for the use of the capital in this instance."[4] Whatever the "Negro" was, the editor seemed to say, it was time to grant this one concession. It was no small act of recognition, either, given the stakes according to the Eatonton, Georgia, *Messenger*. It was a "very bad" idea, wrote the editor, to put into the heads of these "woolly hair[ed]" people that they were anything other than the inferior of whites. To do so would reignite antagonism in the South, where the "two races are getting along together very well."[5] Clearly, there was still progress to be made.

Even more important, the debate over naming centered not on the question of what to be called by others but on what black Americans were to call themselves and how they were to think of themselves. Discussions on this topic, as is the case today, were never resolved conclusively, with some groups preferring one designation over another. In 1919, William Pickens of the NAACP had raised the topic, discarding "colored" as too broad and "Afro-American" as too narrow. Pickens preferred "Negro" as "the most scientific: it designates a race," he argued, "and not a place on the map or an accident of history, but a human stock."[6] It had the advantage, he argued, of including both Africans and black people in the United States, or indeed in any part of the world, even if they had been naturalized in a new country. By the mid-1930s, this attitude was already out of vogue.

By 1934, Willis Huggins and John Jackson suggested that the "chief vexation" over the word "Negro" was that it had "to perform the double function of pointing out color and also that of assuming to signify ethnic or biologic origin." On one point they agreed with Pickens: the word "negress" was an abomination, conjuring "tigress" rather than "princess." All three also stated, optimistically, that words could have whatever power or association that those so named wished to give them. Despite this assertion, choosing the right name was still of paramount importance, and "Negro" would no longer do. Reflecting a now widespread desire to have a name that included something of their origins, Huggins and Jackson pointed out that there was "not . . . a single African people who call themselves *negro* as a tribal name." Just because its use was widespread, they averred, was no reason it ought to continue as the appellation of choice.[7]

Huggins and Jackson were only two of many who wanted Americans to diversify the definitions of who could belong to the nation. Rejecting "Negro," the writers pointed out that, "if not strange, it is at least unique, that American-born Africans become *negroes,* in common parlance, while American born Europeans or Asiatics, remain Italians, Poles, Koreans, or Thibetans."[8] For Huggins and Jackson, the equivalent term, Africans, was not quite accurate. They insisted that black identity was a mix of both inheritance and that which was conditioned by the present day. "Despite the fact that it is too late, indeed impossible, for us to trace our lineage to any particular tribe," they wrote, "yet for all that we remain African, Afro-American, Ethiopian, Ethiopic, or again, if you will Hamitic. Instead of *Afro-American,* Dr. James Weldon Johnson suggests *Aframerican,* a term which is slowly getting wider vogue."[9] Though Huggins and Jackson canvassed many possibilities, some of which echoed the way immigrants remained, say, "Italians," they settled on "Aframerican," a single word that reflected a dual origin. Acknowledging one's origins was no longer un-American; it was the very definition of a modern American.

"Aframerican" was used regularly if not frequently from the mid- to late 1930s. The *New York Amsterdam News* ran a weekly illustrated series depicting "Pages from Negro History," including one captioned "10,000 years ago, the ancestors of the Aframericans lived on the Pacific Islands!"[10] A San Francisco newspaper opened a 1935 editorial about inequality in the job market with the following question: "What are young Aframerican graduates to do?"[11] Writer Claude McKay mused on the experience of African and Aframerican troops on German battlefields.[12] Perhaps most significantly, the satirist George Schuyler took up the term. In 1926, he had used the expression, tongue firmly in cheek, in a debate with poet Langston Hughes, whom Schuyler dubbed the "poet lowrate" for his racialist folk verse. "The Aframerican," Schuyler wrote, "is merely a lampblacked Anglo-Saxon. . . . Aside from his color, which ranges from very dark brown to pink, your American Negro is just plain American."[13] By 1930, he was using "Aframerican" more seriously, and by the time he traveled through the South in 1935, Schuyler was converted. Marveling at finding not one "Negro who did not want to do something to help Ethiopia," not even in the remotest parts of Mississippi, he saw that Africa really was a part of the way black people in the United States thought of themselves.[14] Responding to events in Ethiopia, the chairman of the Pan-African Reconstruction Association had this to say on the issue: "'I like the word African. No more Negroes an' shines an' coons. African!'"[15] The war in east Africa represented a brief moment when the balance in the process of becoming African American tipped most in favor of simply "African."

Yet, neither the name "African" nor "Aframerican" really stuck at this time. "Afro-American," "African-American," and "African American" (without the hyphen) established themselves firmly only in the later decades of the twentieth century, after the years of the black power movement and a revitalized Afrocentrism. Even now, the name "African American" coexists with "black."[16] The strong identification with Ethiopia's plight was expressed in terms of a worldwide black family, and in fact it was "black," rather than "African," that was more frequently adopted into self-naming toward the end of the 1930s and into the 1940s.

World War II, with its cautions against racial identification of any sort, mitigated against a narrowly defined identity as African Americans. For those who believed that the struggle against racism had to be worldwide, "black" was the designation of choice, rather than "African," "Aframerican," or "African American." The term allowed for a burgeoning anticolonialism, by encapsulating a feeling of affinity for oppressed people everywhere. "Black" could be applied, for example, to Aboriginal Australians and subcontinent Indians, both of whom appeared regularly in the pages of black presses of all political persuasions.

The war also put enormous pressure on black Americans to conform, to swear their allegiance to the United States, with the frequent suggestion that to do anything else was tantamount to supporting Hitler. Many did so, writing letters to newspapers in which they declared themselves to be "American" and nothing else. But they were in the minority. If there was one group of people in the United States who had felt consistently the rough side of its majority's beliefs, ideologies, and policies, it was black Americans. Claims that the United States was a nation above all others, the perfectible democracy, and the complete opposite of Nazi Germany, rang hollow in the ears of those subject for generations to enslavement and second-class citizenship. Although many certainly hoped that the United States could be made into a better place, black Americans now traveled through life with at least one eye placed firmly on people and places beyond the nation's borders. The expansion of black public life between the wars enabled a search for roots and for meaningful affiliations to people and places in Africa, in the diaspora, and beyond. The dual identity that resulted, African American, paved the way for the emerging hyphenated identities of so many Americans today.

Notes

Abbreviations

BMDC   Brooklyn Museum Digital Collections: African Art Exhibition of 1923, www.brooklynmuseum.org (accessed 27 Apr. 2007)

GC   L. S. Alexander Gumby Collection of Negroiana, Rare Book and Manuscript Library, Columbia University, New York

MARB   Manuscripts, Archives and Rare Book Division, Schomburg Center for Research in Black Culture, New York Public Library

MSC   Moorland-Spingarn Collection, Howard University, Washington, DC

SC   Schomburg Center for Research in Black Culture, New York Public Library

Introduction

1. Rachel L. Swarns, "'African-American' Becomes a Term for Debate," *New York Times,* 29 Aug. 2004, p. 1.

2. James Sidbury, *Becoming African in America: Race and Nation in the Early Black Atlantic* (Oxford: Oxford University Press, 2007).

3. Robert E. Desrochers Jr., "'Not Fade Away': The Narrative of Venture Smith, an African American in the Early Republic," *Journal of American History* 84, no. 1 (June 1997): 65–66; Sterling Stuckey, *Slave Culture: Nationalist Theory and the Foundations of Black America* (New York: Oxford University Press, 1987), 200–203.

4. W. E. B. Du Bois, *Black Reconstruction in America: An Essay toward a History of the Part Which Black Folk Played in the Attempt to Reconstruct Democracy in America, 1860–1880* (New York: Russell and Russell, 1935), 700–701; David R. Roediger, *The Wages of Whiteness: Race and the Making of the American Working Class,* rev. ed. (London: Verso, 1999).

5. Cornelia Sears, "Africa in the American Mind, 1870–1955: A Study in Mythology, Ideology and the Reconstruction of Race" (PhD diss., University of California, Berkeley, 1997).

6. Enid Schildkrout, "Art as Evidence: A Brief History of the American Museum of Natural History African Collection," in *Art/Artifact: African Art in Anthropology Collections* (New York: Center for African Art, 1988), 153–160; Donna J. Haraway, *Primate Visions: Gender, Race, and Nature in the World of Modern Science* (New York: Routledge, 1989), 26–58.

7. James Weldon Johnson, "Some New Books of Poetry and Their Makers," Editorial, *New York Age*, 7 Sept. 1918, rpt. in *The Selected Writings of James Weldon Johnson*, vol. 1: *The* New York Age *Editorials (1914–1923),* ed. Sondra Kathryn Wilson (New York: Oxford University Press, 1995), 272; James Weldon Johnson, "Introduction," in *The Book of American Negro Poetry* (1922; New York: Harcourt, Brace, 1959), 9; James Weldon Johnson to Clarence Cameron White, 12 Jan. 1935, cited in Jon Michael Spencer, *The New Negroes and Their Music: The Success of the Harlem Renaissance* (Knoxville: University of Tennessee Press, 1997), 103.

8. Kevin K. Gaines, *Uplifting the Race: Black Leadership, Politics, and Culture in the Twentieth Century* (Chapel Hill: University of North Carolina Press, 1996); Evelyn Brooks Higginbotham, *Righteous Discontent: The Women's Movement in the Black Baptist Church, 1880–1920* (Cambridge, MA: Harvard University Press, 1993); Michele Mitchell, *Righteous Propagation: African Americans and the Politics of Racial Destiny after Reconstruction* (Chapel Hill: University of North Carolina Press, 2004).

9. Dickson D. Bruce Jr., "Ancient Africa and the Early Black American Historians, 1883–1915," *American Quarterly* 36, no. 5 (Winter 1984): 684–699; John Ernest, *Liberation Historiography: African American Writers and the Challenge of History* (Chapel Hill: University of North Carolina Press, 2004); Robin D. G. Kelley, "'But a Local Phase of a World Problem': Black History's Global Vision, 1883–1950," *Journal of American History* 86, no. 3 (Dec. 1999): 1051–1055; Wilson Jeremiah Moses, *Afrotopia: The Roots of African American Popular History* (Cambridge: Cambridge University Press, 1998).

10. Lawrence W. Levine, *Black Culture and Black Consciousness: Afro-American Folk Thought from Slavery to Freedom* (Oxford: Oxford University Press, 1977), 3–135.

11. Shane White and Graham White, *Stylin': African American Expressive Culture from Its Beginnings to the Zoot Suit* (Ithaca: Cornell University Press, 1998).

12. Karen Sotiropoulos, *Staging Race: Black Performers in Turn of the Century America* (Cambridge, MA: Harvard University Press, 2006), 123–162.

13. W. E. B. Du Bois, "The Star of Ethiopia," in *The Oxford W. E. B. Du Bois Reader,* ed. Eric J. Sundquist (New York: Oxford University Press, 1996), 305–310; David Krasner, *A Beautiful Pageant: African American Theatre, Drama, and Performance in the Harlem Renaissance, 1910–1927* (New York: Palgrave MacMillan, 2002), 81–96.

14. James T. Campbell, *Songs of Zion: The African Methodist Episcopal Church in the United States and South Africa* (1995; Chapel Hill: University of North Carolina Press, 1998); St. Clair Drake, *The Redemption of Africa and Black Religion* (Chicago: Third World Press, 1970); George M. Frederickson, *Black Liberation: A Comparative History of Black Ideologies in the United States and South Africa* (New York: Oxford University Press, 1995), 57–93; Levine, *Black Culture and Black Consciousness*; Moses, *Afrotopia*; Albert J. Raboteau, *Canaan Land: A Religious History of African Americans* (Oxford: Oxford University Press, 1999); Scott Trafton, *Egypt Land: Race and Nineteenth-Century American Egyptomania* (Durham, NC: Duke University Press, 2004), 62–84, 221–237.

15. Eddie S. Glaude, *Exodus! Religion, Race, and Nation in Early Nineteenth-Century Black America* (Chicago: University of Chicago Press, 2000).

16. On missionaries, see Campbell, *Songs of Zion*; Sylvia M. Jacobs, ed., *Black Americans and the Missionary Movement in Africa* (Westport, CT: Greenwood Press, 1982); Eunjin Park, *"White" Americans in "Black" Africa: Black and White Methodist Missionaries in Liberia, 1820–1875* (New York: Routledge, 2001). On the desire to leave the United States for Africa, see Kenneth C. Barnes, *Journey of Hope: The Back-to-Africa Movement in Arkansas in the Late 1800s* (Chapel Hill: University of North Carolina Press, 2004); Claude A. Clegg, *The Price of Liberty: African Americans and the Making of Liberia* (Chapel Hill: University of North Carolina Press, 2004); Steven Hahn, *A Nation under Our Feet: Black Political Struggles in the Rural South from Slavery to the Great Migration* (Cambridge, MA: Belknap Press/ Harvard University Press, 2004); Clarence E. Hardy, "From Exodus to Exile: Black Pentecostals, Migrating Pilgrims, and Imagined Internationalism," *American Quarterly* 59, no. 3 (Sept. 2007): 737–757; Mitchell, *Righteous Propagation*, 16–50; Wilson Jeremiah Moses, *Liberian Dreams: Back-to-Africa Narratives from the 1850s* (University Park: Pennsylvania State University Press, 1998).

17. "Number and Percent of African Americans in the United States Living in Urban and Rural Communities, 1890–1930," in *In Motion: The African-American Migration Experience,* Digital Library Program, New York Public Library, www .inmotionaame.org (accessed 2 Feb. 2008).

18. Lee D. Baker, *From Savage to Negro: Anthropology and the Construction of Race, 1896–1954* (Berkeley: University of California Press, 1998), 99–126; Mia Bay, *The White Image in the Black Mind: African-American Ideas about White People, 1830–1925* (Oxford: Oxford University Press, 2000), 195–200; Jonathan Scott Holloway, *Confronting the Veil: Abram Harris Jr., E. Franklin Frazier, and Ralph Bunche, 1919–1941* (Chapel Hill: University of North Carolina Press, 2002); George Hutchinson, *The Harlem Renaissance in Black and White* (Cambridge, MA: Belknap Press/Harvard University Press, 1995), 62–77.

19. Flyer, NAACP Papers, part 11, series B, reel 12, frame 617, microfilm reels, British Library.

20. Manfred Berg, "Activists, Leaders and Supporters: On the Role of Whites in the National Association for the Advancement of Colored People," in *Crossing*

Boundaries: The Exclusion and Inclusion of Minorities in Germany and the United States, ed. Larry Eugene Jones (New York: Berghahn Books, 2001), 195.

21. James Weldon Johnson, "Africa in the World Democracy," 6 Jan. 1919, Carnegie Hall, New York, NAACP Papers, part 11, series B, reel 12, frames 876–888, rpt. as "Africa at the Peace Table and the Descendants of Africa in Our American Democracy," in *The Selected Writings of James Weldon Johnson*, vol. 2: *Social, Political, and Literary Essays*, ed. Sondra Kathryn Wilson (New York: Oxford University Press, 1995), 198–206.

22. Ibid., 202.

23. Jonathan Rosenberg, "For Democracy, Not Hypocrisy: World War and Race Relations in the United States, 1914–1919," *International History Review* 21, no. 3 (Sept. 1999): 618.

24. The phrase was the subheading of a special edition of the *Survey Graphic* in March 1925, published in altered form as Alain Locke, ed., *The New Negro* (1925; New York: Atheneum, 1992).

25. Winston James, "The History of Afro-Caribbean Migration to the United States," in *In Motion: The African-American Migration Experience*.

26. Jürgen Habermas, *The Structural Transformation of the Public Sphere: An Inquiry into a Category of Bourgeois Society*, trans. Thomas Burger with Frederick Lawrence (Cambridge, MA: MIT Press, 1989). For discussion of the limits of the public sphere as Habermas would have it, see The Black Public Sphere Collective, ed., *The Black Public Sphere: A Public Culture Book* (Chicago: University of Chicago Press, 1995); Nancy Fraser, "Rethinking the Public Sphere: A Contribution to the Critique of Actually Existing Democracy," in *Habermas and the Public Sphere*, ed. Craig Calhoun (Cambridge, MA: MIT Press, 1992), 109–142.

27. The Black Public Sphere Collective, "Preface," in *The Black Public Sphere*, 1–3.

28. Levine, *Black Culture and Black Consciousness*, 3–135; Robin D. G. Kelley, *Race Rebels: Culture, Politics, and the Black Working Class* (New York: Free Press, 1994), 8–9, 34, 52–53.

29. Brent Hayes Edwards, *The Practice of Diaspora: Literature, Translation, and the Rise of Black Internationalism* (Cambridge, MA: Harvard University Press, 2003); Robin D. G. Kelley and Tiffany Ruby Patterson, "Unfinished Migrations: Reflections on the African Diaspora and the Making of the Modern World," *African Studies Review* 43, no. 1 (Apr. 2000): 11–45; Kenneth W. Warren, "Appeals for (Mis)recognition: Theorizing the Diaspora," in *Cultures of United States Imperialism*, ed. Amy Kaplan and Donald E. Pease (Durham, NC: Duke University Press, 1993), 392–406.

30. Earl Lewis, "To Turn as on a Pivot: Writing African Americans into a History of Overlapping Diasporas," *American Historical Review* 100, no. 3 (June 1995): 765–787.

31. Brent Hayes Edwards, "Langston Hughes and the Futures of Diaspora," *American Literary History* 19, no. 3 (Fall 2007): 689–711.

32. Such politics struggled during the early years of the Cold War. For discussion see: Carol Anderson, *Eyes Off the Prize: The United Nations and the African American Struggle for Human Rights, 1944–1955* (New York: Cambridge University Press, 2003); Mary L. Dudziak, *Cold War Civil Rights: Race and the Image of American Democracy* (Princeton: Princeton University Press, 2000); James H. Meriwether, *Proudly We Can Be Africans: Black Americans and Africa, 1935–1961* (Chapel Hill: University of North Carolina Press, 2002); Brenda Gayle Plummer, *Rising Wind: Black Americans and U.S. Foreign Affairs, 1935–1960* (Chapel Hill: University of North Carolina Press, 1996); Nikhil Pal Singh, *Black Is a Country: Race and the Unfinished Struggle for Democracy* (Cambridge, MA: Harvard University Press, 2004); Penny M. Von Eschen, *Race against Empire: Black Americans and Anticolonialism, 1937–1957* (Ithaca, NY: Cornell University Press, 1997).

33. Mary A. Renda, *Taking Haiti: Military Occupation and the Culture of U.S. Imperialism, 1915–1940* (Chapel Hill: University of North Carolina Press, 2001).

34. Theodore W. Allen, *Invention of the White Race*, 2 vols. (London: Verso, 1994, 1997); Matthew Pratt Guterl, *The Color of Race in America, 1900–1940* (Cambridge, MA: Harvard University Press, 2001); Matthew Frye Jacobson, *Whiteness of a Different Color: European Immigrants and the Alchemy of Race* (Cambridge, MA: Harvard University Press, 1998); Mae M. Ngai, *Impossible Subjects: Illegal Aliens and the Making of Modern America* (Princeton, NJ: Princeton University Press, 2004); David R. Roediger, *Working toward Whiteness: How America's Immigrants Became White: The Strange Journey from Ellis Island to the Suburbs* (New York: Basic Books, 2005); Singh, *Black Is a Country*.

35. Ralph Ellison, *"An American Dilemma:* A Review," in *Shadow and Act* (New York: Vintage Books, 1964), 316. See also Ralph Ellison, "Homage to Duke Ellington on His Birthday," in *Living with Music: Ralph Ellison's Jazz Writings*, ed. Robert G. O'Meally (New York: Modern Library, 2001), 77–86; Eric Lott, "Nation Time," *American Literary History* 7, no. 3 (Autumn 1995): 565–566.

1. Africa the Motherland

1. Marcus Garvey, "The Tragedy of White Injustice," *Negro World* (1927), stanza 67, rpt. in *Marcus Garvey: Life and Lessons*, ed. Robert A. Hill and Barbara Bair (Berkeley: University of California Press, 1987), 138.

2. John Higham, *Strangers in the Land: Patterns of American Nativism, 1860–1925* (1955; New Brunswick, NJ: Rutgers University Press, 2002).

3. Madison Grant, *The Passing of the Great Race, or, The Racial Basis of European History* (1916; York, SC: Liberty Bell Publications, 2006). See also Lothrop Stoddard, *The Rising Tide of Color Against White World-Supremacy* (1920; York, SC: Liberty Bell Publications, 2006).

4. Priscilla Wald, *Constituting Americans: Cultural Anxiety and Narrative Form* (Durham, NC: Duke University Press, 1995).

5. Matthew Frye Jacobson, *Whiteness of a Different Color: European Immigrants and the Alchemy of Race* (Cambridge, MA: Harvard University Press, 1998); Matthew Pratt Guterl, *The Color of Race in America 1900–1940* (Cambridge, MA: Harvard University Press, 2001); Thomas A. Guglielmo, *White on Arrival: Italians, Race, Color, and Power in Chicago, 1890–1945* (New York: Oxford University Press, 2003); Nikhil Pal Singh, *Black Is a Country: Race and the Unfinished Struggle for Democracy* (Cambridge, MA: Harvard University Press, 2004); David R. Roediger, *Working toward Whiteness: How America's Immigrants Became White: The Strange Journey from Ellis Island to the Suburbs* (New York: Basic Books, 2005).

6. Walter Benn Michaels, *Our America: Nativism, Modernism, and Pluralism* (Durham, NC: Duke University Press, 1995), 8.

7. Alys Weinbaum, *Wayward Reproductions: Genealogies of Race and Nation in Transatlantic Modern Thought* (Durham, NC: Duke University Press, 2004), 217–218.

8. Langston Hughes, "Mulatto" (1930), in *Three Negro Plays* (Harmondsworth, UK: Penguin Books, 1969), 56.

9. Hortense J. Spillers, "Mama's Baby, Papa's Maybe: An American Grammar Book," *Diacritics* 17, no. 2 (Summer 1987): 65–81.

10. See Henry McNeal Turner, "The American Negro and His Fatherland," 1895, rpt. in *Classical Black Nationalism: From the American Revolution to Marcus Garvey,* ed. Wilson Jeremiah Moses (New York: New York University Press, 1996), 221–227; George Wilson Brent, "The Ancient Glory of the Hamitic Race," *AME Church Review* 12 (Oct. 1895): 272–275, rpt. in *Social Protest Thought in the African Methodist Episcopal Church, 1862–1939,* ed. Stephen W. Angell and Anthony B. Pinn (Knoxville: University of Tennessee Press, 2000), 148–150; on Martin R. Delany's views, see Paul Gilroy, *The Black Atlantic: Modernity and Double Consciousness* (Cambridge, MA: Harvard University Press, 1993), 23, 25–27. On the masculinity of nineteenth-century religious thought and practice that provided the context for conceiving of Africa as a fatherland, see William H. Becker, "The Black Church: Manhood and Mission," in *African-American Religion: Interpretive Essays in History and Culture,* ed. Timothy E. Fulop and Albert J. Raboteau (New York: Routledge, 1997), 179–199.

11. Lawrence W. Levine, "Marcus Garvey and the Politics of Revitalization," in *Black Leaders of the Twentieth Century,* ed. John Hope Franklin and August Meier (Urbana: University of Illinois Press, 1982), 105–138; Judith Stein, *The World of Marcus Garvey: Race and Class in Modern Society* (Baton Rouge: Louisiana State University Press, 1986); E. David Cronon, *Black Moses: The Story of Marcus Garvey and the Universal Negro Improvement Association* (Madison: University of Wisconsin Press, 1966); Randall K. Burkett, *Garveyism as a Religious Movement: The Institutionalization of a Black Civil Religion* (Metuchen, NJ: Scare-

crow Press and American Theological Library Association, 1978); Wilson Jeremiah Moses, *Black Messiahs and Uncle Toms: Social and Literary Manipulations of a Religious Myth*, 2nd ed. (University Park: Pennsylvania State University Press, 1993), 124–141.

12. John Maynard, "'In the Interests of Our People': The Influence of Garveyism on the Rise of Australian Aboriginal Political Activism," *Aboriginal History* 25 (2005): 12.

13. The story of Garvey's years in the United States has been told many times, most recently in Colin Grant, *Negro with a Hat: The Rise and Fall of Marcus Garvey* (New York: Oxford University Press, 2008).

14. For an assessment of membership, see Cronon, *Black Moses*, 205–207.

15. Grant, *Negro with a Hat*, 276, 279–283, 296–297, 382–387; Ibrahim Sundiata, *Brothers and Strangers: Black Zion, Black Slavery, 1914–1920* (Durham, NC: Duke University Press, 2003), 31–41, 64, 78–79, 108–110; James T. Campbell, *Middle Passages: African American Journeys to Africa, 1787–2005* (New York: Penguin Press, 2006), 235–238.

16. "Negroes Should Link Strength Morally, Financially, Educationally and Physically: Support the Black Star Line and Build a Great Merchant Marine: The Commercial Future of the Continent of Africa Pictured," *Negro World*, 26 Feb. 1921.

17. For more on Garvey's ideas on racial purity, see Paul Gilroy, *Against Race: Imagining Political Culture beyond the Color Line* (Cambridge, MA: Belknap Press/ Harvard University Press, 2000), 231–234; A. James Gregor, *The Search for Neofascism: The Use and Abuse of Social Science* (Cambridge: Cambridge University Press, 2006), 111–136.

18. Garvey, "The Tragedy of White Injustice," 134.

19. Marcus Garvey, "The Black Woman," originally published in *Poetical Meditations of Marcus Garvey* (1927), rpt. in *The Poetical Works of Marcus Garvey*, ed. Tony Martin (Dover, MA: Majority Press, 1983), 44–45. Emphasis mine.

20. Garvey, "The Tragedy of White Injustice," 123.

21. Barbara Bair, "True Women, Real Men: Gender, Ideology, and Social Roles in the Garvey Movement," in *Gendered Domains: Rethinking Public and Private in Women's History*, ed. Dorothy O. Helly and Susan M. Reverby (Ithaca, NY: Cornell University Press, 1992), 154–166; Beryl Satter, "Marcus Garvey, Father Divine and the Gender Politics of Race Difference and Race Neutrality," *American Quarterly* 48, no. 1 (March 1996): 43–76. On the extreme gender fantasies of black nationalism, see E. Frances White, "Africa on My Mind: Gender, Counterdiscourse, and African-American Nationalism" (1990), rpt. in White, *Dark Continent of Our Bodies: Black Feminism and the Politics of Respectability* (Philadelphia: Temple University Press, 2001), 117–150.

22. Martin Summers, *Manliness and Its Discontents: The Black Middle Class and the Transformation of Masculinity, 1900–1930* (Chapel Hill: University of North Carolina Press, 2004), 66–110.

23. Michele Mitchell, *Righteous Propagation: African Americans and the Politics of Racial Destiny after Reconstruction* (Chapel Hill: University of North Carolina Press, 2004), 228; Kate Dossett, *Bridging Race Divides: Black Nationalism, Feminism, and Integration in the United States, 1896–1935* (Gainesville: University Press of Florida, 2008), 151–175.

24. On the United States, see Satter, "Marcus Garvey," 48; Bair, "True Women, Real Men," 157; Erik S. McDuffie, "'[She] devoted twenty minutes condemning all other forms of government but the Soviet': Black Women Radicals in the Garvey Movement and in the Left during the 1920s," in *Diasporic Africa: A Reader,* ed. Michael A. Gomez (New York: New York University Press, 2006), 219–250. On Belize, see Anne MacPherson, "Colonial Matriarchs: Garveyism, Maternalism, and Belize's Black Cross Nurses, 1920–1952," *Gender and History* 15, no. 3 (Nov. 2003): 507–527.

25. Robert A. Hill, "Making Noise: Marcus Garvey, *Dada,* August 1922," in *Picturing Us: African American Identity in Photography,* ed. Deborah Willis (New York: New Press, 1994), 191–194.

26. Marianne Samad, interviewed in the documentary *Look for Me in the Whirlwind,* dir. Stanley Nelson, transcript, American Experience, PBS online, www.pbs.org/wgbh/amex/garvey/ (accessed 19 Feb. 2006).

27. "Negroes: Garvey Again," *Time,* 11 Aug. 1924, www.time.com (accessed 19 Sept. 2007).

28. "Convention Report," New York, 5 Aug. 1924, in *The Marcus Garvey and Universal Negro Improvement Association Papers* [hereafter cited as *Garvey Papers*], vol. 5: *September 1922–August 1924,* ed. Robert A. Hill. (Berkeley: University of California Press, 1986), 665.

29. Ibid., 666.

30. "Negroes: Garvey Again."

31. Robert G. Weisbord, *Ebony Kinship: Africa, Africans, and the Afro-American* (Westport, CT: Greenwood Press, 1973), 56.

32. Ernest E. Mair, "Pink Gods Depict Horrors of White Imperialist Rule in West Africa," *Negro World,* 1922, rpt. in *African Fundamentalism: A Literary and Cultural Anthology of Garvey's Harlem Renaissance,* ed. Tony Martin (1983; Dover, MA: Majority Press, 1991), 271–273.

33. Ralph Casimir to George Tobias, 24 Aug. 1920, J. R. Ralph Casimir Papers, box 1, folder 1, MARB.

34. William Ferris, "Watchman What of the Night?" *Spokesman,* Mar. 1925, p. 5, cited in Hill, "Making Noise," 194.

35. Arthur P. Davis, "Growing up in the New Negro Renaissance: 1920–1935," *Negro American Literature Forum* 2, no. 3, Protest and Propaganda Literature (Autumn 1968): 59.

36. *Baltimore Afro-American,* 20 July 1923, cited in Judith Stein, "The Ideology and Practice of Garveyism," in *Garvey: His Work and Impact,* ed. Rupert

Lewis and Patrick Bryan (Trenton, NJ: Africa World Press, 1991), 204. See also Mary Gambrell Rolinson, "The Universal Negro Improvement Association in Georgia: Southern Strongholds of Garveyism," in *Georgia in Black and White: Explorations in the Race Relations of a Southern State, 1865–1950,* ed. John C. Inscoe (Athens: University of Georgia Press, 1994), 202–224, esp. 217–219; Mary Gambrell Rolinson, "The Garvey Movement in the Rural South, 1920–1927" (PhD diss., Georgia State University, 2002), 45–54, 89; Barbara Bair, "Garveyism and Contested Political Terrain in 1920s Virginia," in *Afro-Virginian History and Culture,* ed. John Saillant (New York: Garland Publishing, 1999), 227–249; on Arkansas UNIA followers who wanted to leave for Africa on the Black Star Line, see Esther B. Nelson, *Leaving on the Black Star Line: The Story of African American Families in the Marcus Garvey Movement* (Carmel, IN: Cork Hill Press, 2004).

37. Michelle Ann Stephens, *Black Empire: The Masculine Global Imaginary of Caribbean Intellectuals in the United States, 1914–1962* (Durham: Duke University Press, 2005), 109–110.

38. Stein, *The World of Marcus Garvey,* 61–88, 255–256; Wilson Jeremiah Moses, *Creative Conflict in African American Thought: Frederick Douglass, Alexander Crummell, Booker T. Washington, W. E. B. Du Bois, and Marcus Garvey* (Cambridge: Cambridge University Press, 2004), 248–249, 251; Levine, "Marcus Garvey and the Politics of Revitalization," 126–127; Cronon, *Black Moses,* 60–61.

39. For example, Edwin Patrick Kilroe, deputy attorney general of New York from 1916 to 1923, believed in June 1919 that "the 'Black Star' was only a phantom fleet": Draft of a *World* news report [New York, 22 June 1919], in *Garvey Papers,* 1:440.

40. Marcus Garvey's Farewell Speech [New York, 22 Feb. 1921], *Garvey Papers,* 3:232.

41. Garvey, "The Tragedy of White Injustice," 134.

42. "Garvey Buys Ships to Take Negroes to Africa; 3,000 Pay 50 Cents Each to View It at Pier," *New York Times,* 18 Aug. 1924, 1.

43. "Christening 'Booker T. Washington,' Garvey's Latest Ocean Liner, as It Leaves Moorings for Maiden Trip," *Pittsburgh Courier,* 31 Jan. 1925, 2; "Black Cross Liner off on Maiden Trip," *New York Times,* 19 Jan. 1925, 18.

44. Shirley Graham, "Tom-Tom," in *The Roots of African American Drama: An Anthology of Early Plays, 1858–1938,* ed. Leo Hamalian and James V. Hatch (Detroit, MI: Wayne State University Press, 1991), 283.

45. Konrad Bercovici, "The Black Blocks of Manhattan," *Harper's Monthly Magazine,* Oct. 1924, 620.

46. For an example of a stock certificate, see *Garvey Papers,* 5:574.

47. See, for example, "Application for Transportation to Liberia," *Garvey Papers,* 5:576.

48. S.B. Smith, cited in Mary G. Rolinson, *Grassroots Garveyism: The Universal Negro Improvement Association in the Rural South, 1920–1927* (Chapel Hill: University of North Carolina Press, 2007), 154.

49. For example, see "Garvey 'Rides' Here," *New York Amsterdam News,* 3 Sept. 1930, 3; "Withstands Flames," *New York Amsterdam News,* 14 Feb. 1934, 3; "Spirit of Garvey Still Lives in Harlem," *Chicago Defender,* 7 May 1938, 10.

50. For example, see telegram from J.A. Craigen, Jacksonville, Florida, to Marcus Garvey, Federal Prison, Atlanta, Georgia, 20 Sept. 1927, Laura Adorkor Kofey Research Collection, box 1, folder 11, MARB; "Hon. J.A. Craigen Gives Facts Nailing," *Negro World,* 7 Apr. 1928, 2.

51. William A. Shack, "Ethiopia and Afro-Americans: Some Historical Notes, 1920–1970," *Phylon* 35, no. 2 (2nd quart., 1974): 146–148.

52. Robert G. Weisbord, "Black America and the Italian-Ethiopian Crisis: An Episode in Pan-Negroism," *Historian* 34, no. 2 (Feb. 1972): 233–234; Jacob S. Dorman, "The Black Israelites of Harlem and the Professors of Oriental and African Mystic Science in the 1920's" (PhD diss., University of California, Los Angeles, 2004), 286–303.

53. Arden Bryan and C.B. Cumberbatch to Secretary-General of the League of Nations, 18 Sept. 1933, Records of the Institute of the Black World, part 3, MARB.

54. "National Grapevine," *Chicago Defender,* 17 Oct. 1942, 15; "Cult Head Denies Link to Jap Spy," *Chicago Defender,* 13 Feb. 1943, 9; "Pot Calls the Skillet Non-White," *Chicago Defender,* 1 July 1944, 13.

55. A. Philip Randolph, "The Only Way to Redeem Africa," *Messenger* 6, no. 11 (Nov. 1922): 524.

56. Wallace Thurman and William Jourdan Rapp, "Jeremiah, the Magnificent" (1930?) mss., Act I, p. 1, microfilm, SC.

57. *Negro World,* 8 Oct. 1921, rpt. in *Harlem on My Mind: Cultural Capital of Black America, 1900–1968,* ed. Allon Schoener (1968; New York: New Press, 1995), 55.

58. For the anthem, see Speech during 1920 convention, quoted in the documentary *Marcus Garvey: Look for Me in the Whirlwind.* For the flag in New York, see "Article in the *New York Globe:* 2 August 1921," in *Garvey Papers,* 3:588–589; for the UNIA flag used overseas, see Speech by Marcus Garvey [Liberty Hall, New York, 20 July 1921], in *Garvey Papers,* 3:541–542. For the passports, see Marcus Garvey's Farewell Speech [New York, 22 Feb. 1921], in *Garvey Papers,* 3:232.

59. "Speeches by Marcus Garvey and Charles H. Duvall [*Liberty Hall,* 2 Aug. 1921]," *Garvey Papers,* 3:605.

60. John Henrik Clarke, "Africa—Ethiopia—Etc." n.d. (before late 1935), Clarke Papers, box 40, folder 1, MARB. These words were reprinted in a booklet as Universal Ethiopian Students' Association, *The Truth about Ethiopia: A Nation Blocked from the Sea* (New York: UESA, 1936), 11.

61. W. E. B. Du Bois, "The Black Star Line," *Crisis* 24, no. 5 (Sept. 1922): 210–214; W. E. B. Du Bois, "The U.N.I.A.," *Crisis* 25, no. 3 (Jan. 1923): 120–122.

62. Editorial cartoons in the *Chicago Defender:* "America's Greatest Laugh Maker," 7 Oct. 1922, 12; "It Won't Budge," 17 May 1924, 12; "Then the Bottom Fell out," 16 Sept. 1922, 12; "He'll Make an Impression if His Head Holds out," 18 Nov. 1922, 12.

63. Thurman and Rapp, "Jeremiah, the Magnificent"; Percy Werway, "Sweet Chariot—at Chestnut," *Philadelphia News,* 7 Oct. 1930, Fredi Washington Papers, reel 2, SC; *The Black King,* dir. Bud Pollard (1932).

64. Amy Jacques Garvey in Lerone Bennett Jr., "The Ghost of Marcus Garvey: Interviews with the Crusader's Two Wives," *Ebony* (Mar. 1960): 53–61, 59–60.

65. Sigmund Freud, *Civilization and Its Discontents,* trans. Joan Riviere (London: Hogarth Press, 1930), 89.

66. Benjamin Brawley, *A Social History of the Negro, Being a History of the Negro Problem in the United States, including a History and Study of the Republic of Liberia* (New York: Macmillan, 1921), 19–20.

67. W. E. B. Du Bois, *Darkwater: Voices from within the Veil* (London: Constable, 1920), 74.

68. Dorothy C. Guinn, "Out of the Dark: A Pageant" (1924) in *Plays and Pageants from the Life of the Negro,* ed. Willis Richardson (1930; Great Neck, NY: Core Collection Books, 1979), 307.

69. Ibid., 312.

70. "A Proposed Exhibition and Pageant Illustrating the Part Which the American Negro Has Played in the Making of America," NAACP Papers, part 11, series A, reel 1, frames 378–380, microfilm reels, British Library.

71. Frances Gunner, "The Light of the Women: A Ceremonial for the Use of Negro Groups," in *Plays and Pageants,* 335.

72. Du Bois, *Darkwater,* 166.

73. Martin de Vere Stuart, "Sonnet to Africa," *Negro World,* 21 June 1924, 7.

74. "The World Gone Mad—Force Only Argument to Correct Human Ills," *Negro World,* 19 May 1923, 1.

75. Lewis Alexander, "Africa" (1924), rpt. in *Caroling Dusk: An Anthology of Verse by Black Poets of the Twenties,* ed. Countée Cullen (1927; New York: Citadel Press, 1993), 123.

76. Arthur A. Schomburg, "African Exploration," in *Negro: Anthology Made by Nancy Cunard 1931–1933* (London: Wishart, 1934), 604.

77. Anne McClintock, *Imperial Leather: Race, Gender, and Sexuality in the Colonial Contest* (New York: Routledge, 1995), 24.

78. W. E. B. Du Bois, *The Souls of Black Folk* (1903; New York: Penguin, 1989), 5.

79. William Pickens to Marcus Garvey (draft), July 1922, NAACP Papers, part 11, series A, reel 35, frames 781–782.

80. "Garvey Denounced at Negro Meting," *New York Times,* 7 Aug. 1922, 7.

81. See Jonathan Hansen, *The Lost Promise of Patriotism: Debating American Identity, 1890–1920* (Chicago: University of Chicago Press, 2003).

82. M.O. Fesler to Walter White, 28 March 1938, White to Fesler, 30 Mar. 1938, NAACP Papers, part 11, series A, reel 15, frames 105, 107–108.

83. J.A. Rogers, "From 'Superman' to Man," *New York Amsterdam News,* 7 Nov. 1923, 12.

84. James Weldon Johnson, *Along This Way: The Autobiography of James Weldon Johnson* (1933; New York: Penguin Books, 1990), 290. Published as "The Poet's Corner: Negro National Anthem," *New York Amsterdam News,* 11 July 1923, 12.

85. Author's statement, "Phillis Wheatley: A Pageant," program, Booker T. Washington Junior High School, 26 and 27 May 1933, in Mary Church Terrell Papers, box 102–6, folder 165, MSC.

86. Katharine Capshaw Smith, "Constructing a Shared History: Black History for Children during the Harlem Renaissance," *Children's Literature* 27 (Annual 1999): 53.

87. "The Balance," NAACP Papers, part 11, series A, reel 32, frames 3, 5–6, 8–10, 12, 15–16 18–21.

88. "President Sees New Play: Zangwill's 'The Melting Pot' Produced in Washington," *New York Times,* 6 Oct. 1908, 9.

89. James Weldon Johnson, "Africa in the 'World Democracy," 6 Jan. 1919, Carnegie Hall, New York, NAACP Papers, part 11, series B, reel 12, frames 876–888, rpt. as "Africa at the Peace Table and the Descendants of Africa in Our American Democracy," in *The Selected Writings of James Weldon Johnson,* vol. 2: *Social, Political, and Literary Essays,* ed. Sondra Kathryn Wilson (New York: Oxford University Press, 1995), 201; James Weldon Johnson, "African Colonization Schemes," *New York Age,* 12 Aug. 1922, rpt. in *The Selected Writings of James Weldon Johnson,* vol. 1: *The* New York Age *Editorials (1914–1923),* ed. Sondra Kathryn Wilson (New York: Oxford University Press, 1995), 132.

90. Letter from Mrs. Maria Isaac Milam, *Negro World.* 24 Feb. 1923, 7.

91. Michele Paige McElya, "Monumental Citizenship: Reading the National Mammy Memorial Controversy of the Early Twentieth Century" (PhD diss., New York University, 2003); Micki McElya, "Commemorating the Color Line: The National Mammy Monument Controversy in the 1920s," in *Monuments to the Lost Cause: Women, Art, and the Landscapes of Southern Memory,* ed. Cynthia Mills and Pamela H. Simpson (Knoxville: University of Tennessee, 2003), 203–218; Joan Marie Johnson, "'Ye Gave Them a Stone': African American Women's Clubs, the Frederick Douglass Home, and the Black Mammy Monument," *Journal of Women's History* 17, no. 1 (2005): 62–86. For context of the United Daughters of the Confederacy's efforts at history making, see W. Fitzhugh Brundage, "No Deed but Memory," in *Where These Memories Grow: History, Memory, and Southern Identity,* ed.

Brundage (Chapel Hill: University of North Carolina Press, 2000), 1–28; David W. Blight, *Race and Reunion: The Civil War in American Memory* (Cambridge, MA: Belknap Press/Harvard University Press, 2000), 286–289, 459–460n.57; and Joan Marie Johnson, "'Drill into Us . . . the Rebel Tradition': The Contest over Southern Identity in Black and White Women's Clubs, South Carolina, 1898–1930," *Journal of Southern History* 66, no. 3 (Aug. 2000): 525–562.

92. "Sculptors in Tilt over Mammy Statue," *New York Amsterdam News,* 4 July 1923, 7.

93. "EXTRA: 'Mammy' Statue Bill Passed," *New York Amsterdam News,* 7 Mar. 1923, 1.

94. "Colored Editor Favors Monument," *New York Amsterdam News,* 14 Mar. 1923, 12.

95. "Negro Tenant Farmer Shot to Kill and Should Have a Monument," *Negro World,* 19 Jan. 1924, 2.

96. Chandler Owen, "Black Mammies," *Messenger* 5, no. 4 (Apr. 1923): 670.

97. On the creation of a mythical mammy figure in "Old South" mythology, see Jesse W. Pankhurst, "The Role of the Black Mammy in the Plantation Household," *Journal of Negro History* 23, no. 3 (July 1938): 349–369; Deborah Gray White, *Ar'n't I A Woman: Female Slaves in the Plantation South* (New York: Norton, 1985), 47–48, 58, 61; Cheryl Thurber, "The Development of the Mammy Image and Mythology," in *Southern Women: Histories and Identities,* ed. Virginia Bernhard, Betty Brandon, Elizabeth Fox-Genovese, and Theda Perdue (Columbia: University of Missouri Press, 1992), 87–108.

98. "Black Mammies," *New York Amsterdam News,* 21 Mar. 1923, 12.

99. "Since Statues Seem to Be All the Rage, Suppose We Erect One: A White Daddy," *Chicago Defender,* 21 Apr. 1923, in McElya, "Commemorating the Color Line," 213–214.

100. Owen, "Black Mammies," 670.

101. Gunner, "The Light of the Women," 337.

102. Virginia P. Jackson, "Africa," *Crisis* 17, no. 4 (Feb. 1919): 166.

103. Du Bois, *Darkwater,* 50.

104. Ibid., 166.

105. "Liberia Needs a Pilot," *New York Age,* 4 Feb. 1933, 4.

106. "America's Responsibility," *New York Age,* 25 Feb. 1933, 4.

107. George S. Schuyler, "Uncle Sam's Black Step-Child" (1933), in *Rac[e]ing to the Right: Selected Essays of George S. Schuyler,* ed. Jeffrey B. Leak (Knoxville: University of Tennessee Press, 2001), 19.

108. "Rampant Imperialism," *Norfolk Journal and Guide,* 8 Oct. 1932, NAACP Papers, part 11, series B, reel 14, frame 181.

109. Archibald H. Grimké, "Her Thirteen Black Soldiers," *Messenger* (Sept. 1919), rpt. in The Messenger *Reader: Stories, Poetry, and Essays from* The Messenger *Magazine,* ed. Sondra Kathryn Wilson (New York: Modern Library, 2000), 6–8.

110. Anne Stavney, "'Mothers of Tomorrow': The New Negro Renaissance and the Politics of Maternal Representation," *African American Review* 32, no. 4 (Winter 1998): 536–537; Langston Hughes, "Christ in Alabama," in *The Collected Poems of Langston Hughes,* ed. Arnold Rampersad and David Roessel (New York: Vintage Books, 1994), 143.

111. Du Bois, *Darkwater,* 172.

112. On Du Bois's use of "the body of Pan-Africa," see Eric J. Sundquist, *To Wake the Nations: Race in the Making of American Literature* (Cambridge, MA: Belknap Press/Harvard University Press, 1993), 584.

113. Darlene Clark Hine, "Rape and the Inner Lives of Black Women in the Middle West: Preliminary Thoughts on a Culture of Dissemblance," *Signs,* 14, no. 4 (Summer 1989): 912–920; Danielle L. McGuire, "'It Was Like All of Us Had Been Raped': Sexual Violence, Community Mobilization, and the African American Freedom Struggle," *Journal of American History* 91, no. 3 (Dec. 2004): 906–931.

114. Rolinson, *Grassroots Garveyism,* 135–141; Mitchell, *Righteous Propagation,* 218–240.

115. Mitchell, *Righteous Propagation,* 221.

116. Cited in Satter, "Marcus Garvey, Father Divine," 48.

117. "The New Negro Woman," *Messenger* 5, no. 7 (July 1923): 757.

118. See, for instance, Anne Moody, *Coming of Age in Mississippi* (New York: Dial Press, 1968); Angela Davis, *Angela Davis: An Autobiography* (1974; New York: International Publishers, 1988). Also see Michelle M. Wright, *Becoming Black: Creating Identity in the African Diaspora* (Durham: Duke University Press, 2004), 124–182.

119. A. Philip Randolph, quoted by Henry Louis Gates Jr., "The Trope of a New Negro and the Reconstruction of the Image of the Black," *Representations* no. 24 (Autumn 1988): 147.

120. R. Savon Pious, no title, *Opportunity* 9, no. 11 (Nov. 1931): cover.

121. These works are far too numerous to list. The best-known novel on the topic is Nella Larsen, *Quicksand* in *Quicksand and Passing,* ed. Deborah E. McDowell (New Brunswick, NJ: Rutgers University Press, 1986).

122. For example, see Alain Locke, "The Saving Grace of Realism: Retrospective Review of the Negro Literature of 1933," *Opportunity* 12, no. 1 (Jan. 1934): 8–11, 30, rpt. in *The Critics and the Harlem Renaissance,* ed. Cary D. Wintz (New York: Garland, 1996), 272–277; Wallace Thurman, "High, Low, Past, and Present: Review of *The Walls of Jericho, Quicksand,* and *Adventures of an African Slaver,*" *Harlem: A Forum of Negro Life* 1 (Nov. 1928): 32, rpt. in *The Collected Writings of Wallace Thurman: A Harlem Renaissance Reader,* ed. Amritjit Singh and Daniel M. Scott III (New Brunswick, NJ: Rutgers University Press, 2003), 218–221. In 1937, Sterling Brown commented disparagingly that Fauset "records a class in order to praise a race"; cited in Cheryl A. Wall, *Women of the Harlem Renaissance* (Bloomington: Indiana University Press, 1995), 212n.7.

123. Jessie Fauset, "Nostalgia," *Crisis* 22 (1921): 157.

124. Cf. Brent Hayes Edwards, who has interpreted Fauset's essay as sentimental and limited in its interpretation of black internationalism: *The Practice of Diaspora: Literature, Translation, and the Rise of Black Internationalism* (Cambridge, MA: Harvard University Press, 2003), 141–143.

2. Discovering a Usable African Past

1. Howard Carter and A.C. Mace, *The Tomb of Tut-ankh-Amen: Discovered by the Late Earl of Carnarvon and Howard Carter,* vol. 1 (London: Cassell & Company, 1923), 96.

2. "Foot Notes to African History (by the Hamitic League): Inevitable Africa," *New York Amsterdam News,* 4 July 1923, 12.

3. For recent debate on the race of ancient Egyptians, see Martin Bernal, *Black Athena: The Afroasiatic Roots of Classical Civilization,* 2 vols. (London: Free Association Books, 1987, 1991); Mary Lefkowitz, *Not out of Africa: How Afrocentrism Became an Excuse to Teach Myth as History* (New York: Basic Books, 1996); Mary R. Lefkowitz and Guy MacLean Rogers, eds., Black Athena *Revisited* (Chapel Hill: University of North Carolina Press, 1996); Jacques Berlinerblau, *Heresy in the University: The* Black Athena *Controversy and the Responsibilities of American Intellectuals* (New Brunswick, NJ: Rutgers University Press, 1999). For an incisive summary of these debates, see Wilson Jeremiah Moses, *Afrotopia: The Roots of African American Popular History* (Cambridge: Cambridge University Press, 1998), 1–17.

4. Historians have called this "contributionist" or "vindicationist" history: Orlando Patterson, "Rethinking Black History," *Harvard Educational Review* 41, no. 3 (Aug. 1971): 297–315; St. Clair Drake, *Black Folk Here and There: An Essay in History and Anthropology,* vol. 1 (Los Angeles: Center for Afro-American Studies, University of California, Los Angeles, 1987). For discussion of the two concepts, see Moses, *Afrotopia,* 23, 85.

5. John Bodnar, *Remaking America: Public Memory, Commemoration, and Patriotism in the Twentieth Century* (Princeton, NJ: Princeton University Press, 1992); Michael G. Kammen, *Mystic Chords of Memory: The Transformation of Tradition in American Culture* (New York: Knopf, 1991).

6. Van Wyck Brooks first used the phrase in a 1915 essay, "America's Coming of Age," but it is best known from his "On Creating a Usable Past," *Dial* 64 (11 Apr. 1918): 337–341.

7. On early historians, see Dickson D. Bruce Jr., "Ancient Africa and the Early Black American Historians, 1883–1915," *American Quarterly* 36, no. 5 (Winter 1984): 684–699; Moses, *Afrotopia;* Robin D.G. Kelley, "'But a Local Phase of a World Problem': Black History's Global Vision, 1883–1950," *Journal of American History* 86, no. 3 (Dec. 1999): 1051–1055; John Ernest, *Liberation Historiography: African American Writers and the Challenge of History* (Chapel Hill: University of North Carolina Press, 2004).

8. David W. Blight, *Race and Reunion: The Civil War in American Memory* (Cambridge, MA: Belknap Press/Harvard University Press, 2002); W. Fitzhugh Brundage, *The Southern Past: A Clash of Race and Memory* (Cambridge, MA: Belknap Press/Harvard University Press, 2005).

9. Michelle Ann Stephens, *Black Empire: The Masculine Global Imaginary of Caribbean Intellectuals in the United States, 1914–1962* (Durham, NC: Duke University Press, 2005).

10. Georg Wilhelm Friedrich Hegel, *The Philosophy of History*, trans. J. Sibree (New York: Dover Publications, 1956), 91–99, esp. 86, 99; Nikhil Pal Singh, *Black Is a Country: Race and the Unfinished Struggle for Democracy* (Cambridge, MA: Harvard University Press, 2004), 75–76.

11. Cited in "The Creative Art of Negroes," *Opportunity* 1, no. 8 (Aug. 1923): 240.

12. Cornelia Sears, "Africa in the American Mind, 1870–1955: A Study in Mythology, Ideology and the Reconstruction of Race" (PhD diss., University of California, Berkeley, 1997), 297–302; Karla F.C. Holloway, *Passed On: African American Mourning Stories, a memorial* (Durham, NC: Duke University Press, 2002), 100–102.

13. Sears, "Africa in the American Mind," 303–307.

14. Moses, *Afrotopia*, 238.

15. Photo of "Colossal Bust of an Egyptian King, 1450 B.C. No. 1608 Berlin Museum," *Crisis* 34, no. 2 (Apr. 1927): 40.

16. "King Tut a Negro," *Negro World*, 21 Apr. 1923, 6.

17. "The Resurrection of Tut-Ankh-Amen," *Negro World*, 3 Mar. 1923, 4.

18. "The Mysterious Egyptians," *Crisis* 30, no. 5 (Sept. 1925): 230–231 and photo on p. 242.

19. "The Real 'Land of the Free,'" *Crisis* 24, no. 6 (Oct. 1922): 274. In 1914, incensed by Theodore Roosevelt's pronunciations on race relations in Brazil, Du Bois wrote "Brazil," *Crisis* 7 (Apr. 1914): 286–287. For discussion, see David Levering Lewis, *W. E. B. Du Bois: Biography of a Race* (New York: Holt, 1993), 479.

20. Carter G. Woodson, *The Negro in Our History* (1922), cited in Kelley, "'But a Local Phase of a World Problem,'" 1061. For accounts of the application of Boas's theories, see Lee D. Baker, *From Savage to Negro: Anthropology and the Construction of Race, 1896–1954* (Berkeley: University of California Press, 1998), 99–126; Mia Bay, *The White Image in the Black Mind: African-American Ideas about White People, 1830–1925* (Oxford: Oxford University Press, 2000), 195–200; George Hutchinson, *The Harlem Renaissance in Black and White* (Cambridge, MA: Belknap Press/Harvard University Press, 1995), 62–77.

21. "Elks March in Downpour of Rain," *New York Amsterdam News*, 24 Aug. 1927, 4.

22. "All Colored Harlem at Walker Wedding," *New York Times*, 25 Nov. 1923, 18; A'Lelia Bundles, *On Her Own Ground: The Life and Times of Madam C. J. Walker* (New York: Scribner, 2001), 284.

23. The items are in a private collection.

24. J. A. Rogers, "From 'Superman' to Man: A Story Which Blasts the Idea of White Supremacy," *New York Amsterdam News,* 22 Aug. 1923, 12.

25. James Weldon Johnson, "The Larger Success," commencement address, Hampton Institute, Virginia, June 1923, and *Southern Workman* 52 (1923): 427–436, both rpt. in *The Selected Writings of James Weldon Johnson,* vol. 2: *Social, Political, and Literary Essays,* ed. Sondra Kathryn Wilson (New York: Oxford University Press, 1995), 55.

26. "White Civilization in Death Throes," *New York Amsterdam News,* 21 Feb. 1923, 3.

27. James Weldon Johnson, "Africa at the Peace Table and the Descendants of Africa in Our American Democracy," speech given at NAACP annual meeting, Carnegie Hall, New York, 6 Jan. 1919, rpt. in *Selected Writings,* 2: 198–206, 202. Johnson made the same statements nearly word for word in "The Larger Success," 55–56.

28. Carter Godwin Woodson, *The Mis-Education of the Negro* (1933; Trenton, NJ: Africa World Press, 1993), 191–192.

29. Johnson, "Africa at the Peace Table," 202.

30. Jacqueline Francis, "Modern Art, 'Racial Art': The Work of Malvin Gray Johnson and the Challenges of Painting, 1928–1934" (PhD diss., Emory University, 2000), 129–148.

31. Jacqueline Francis, "Making History: Malvin Gray Johnson and Earle W. Richardson's Studies for *Negro Achievement,*" in *The Social and the Real: Political Art of the 1930s in the Western Hemisphere,* ed. Alejandro Anreus, Diana L. Linden, and Jonathan Weinberg (University Park: Pennsylvania State University Press, 2006), 135–153. The panels are housed in the Art and Artifacts Division, SC.

32. Johnson, "The Larger Success," 55.

33. Robert E. Eleazer, *America's Tenth Man: A Brief Survey of the Negro's Past in American History,* Commission on Interracial Cooperation, Atlanta, GA, Apr. 1931, NAACP Papers, part 11, series B, reel 4, frames 299–308, Microfilm reels, British Library.

34. Johnson, "The Larger Success," 55.

35. Leo Wiener, *Africa and the Discovery of America,* 3 vols. (Philadelphia: Innes and Sons, 1920–1922).

36. Madeline G. Allison, comp., "The Horizon," *Crisis* 22, no. 4 (Feb. 1922): 171.

37. April Schultz, "'The Pride of the Race Had Been Touched': The 1925 Norse-American Immigration Centennial and Ethnic Identity," *Journal American History* 77, no. 4 (Mar. 1991): 1289.

38. "Negroes Came before Columbus," *New York Amsterdam News,* 12 Nov. 1930, 14.

39. "Color No Handicap," *New York Age,* 17 May 1933.

40. J. A. Rogers, "The Negro in European History," *Opportunity* (June 1930), rpt. in *The* Opportunity *Reader: Stories, Poetry, and Essays from the Urban League's*

Opportunity Magazine, ed. Sondra Kathryn Wilson (New York: Modern Library, 1999), 503.

41. George S. Schuyler, "The Negro Honors His Past," NAACP Papers, part 11, series B, reel 35, frames 324–329.

42. "Is Africa to Be Avenged?" *New York Amsterdam News,* 7 Feb. 1923, 12.

43. William J. Maxwell, *New Negro, Old Left: African-American Writing and Communism between the Wars* (New York: Columbia University Press, 1999), 29.

44. Lionel M. Yard, "George Weston: Organizer of UNIA Branches, Oral Historian of the Garvey Movement, Black Nationalist," June 1975, pp. 12–13 in George A. and Maudelle Weston Papers, box 1, folder 3, MARB.

45. Woodson, *The Mis-Education of the Negro,* 20. See also pp. 136, 137.

46. Marcus Garvey, "African Fundamentalism: Speeches by Marcus Garvey" in *Marcus Garvey: Life and Lessons,* ed. Robert A. Hill and Barbara Bair (Berkeley: University of California Press, 1987), 10.

47. Rev. Reverdy C. Ransom Jr., "Ancient Civilization of the Negro," *New York Amsterdam News,* 14 Jan. 1925, A16.

48. "Negroes Came before Columbus."

49. See, for example, John E. Bruce, "King Tut Again," *Negro World,* 28 Apr. 1923, 4; Ransom, "Ancient Civilization of the Negro"; James Weldon Johnson, "Native African Races and Culture" (1927), rpt. in *Selected Writings,* 2:255; W. E. B. Du Bois, *Black Folk Then and Now: An Essay in the History and Sociology of the Negro Race* (1939; New York: Octagon Books, 1970), 17–18, 22–26, 38. See Moses, *Afrotopia,* 23–24, 91–92.

50. Rogers, "From 'Superman' to Man." Rogers wrote elsewhere of "Ancient Egypt, where the population, according to Herodotus and Aristotle, was black": J. A. Rogers, *100 Amazing Facts about the Negro, with Complete Proof: A Short Cut to the World History of the Negro,* 19th rev. ed. (New York: Published by the author, 1934), 10.

51. "Foot Notes to African History."

52. Frantz Fanon, *The Wretched of the Earth* (1961), trans. Constance Farrington (New York: Grove Press, 1963), 210.

53. Ibid., 211.

54. Cedric J. Robinson, *Black Marxism: The Making of the Black Radical Tradition* (1983; Chapel Hill: University of North Carolina Press, 2000), 81.

55. Leon F. Litwack, *Been in the Storm So Long: The Aftermath of Slavery* (1979; New York: Random House, 1980), 102.

56. For example, see Marcus Garvey, "A Dialogue: What's the Difference?" *The Blackman* 1, no. 7 (June 1935): 12; Marcus Garvey, "African Fundamentalism," *Negro World,* 6 June 1925, rpt. in *Marcus Garvey: Life and Lessons,* 4.

57. Marcus Garvey, "The British West Indies in the Mirror of Civilization—History Making by Colonial Negroes," *African Times and Orient Review of London,* Oct. 1913, 158–60, rpt. in William Ferris, "The Spectacular Career of Garvey," *New York Amsterdam News,* 11 Feb. 1925, 9.

58. "Negroes: Garvey Again," *Time*, 11 Aug. 1924, www.time.com (accessed 19 Sept. 2007).

59. Marcus Garvey, "The Negro Race," *The Blackman* 1, no. 5 (May–June 1934): 16. See also Marcus Garvey, "The Negro as Colonizer! Colonization Is Good," *The Blackman* 1, no. 4 (Mar.–Apr. 1934): 16.

60. E. C. Douglas, "Black Man and Africa," *New York Age*, 8 Nov. 1919.

61. John Haughton, "Our Right in Africa," *New York Age*, 1 Feb. 1919.

62. W. E. B. Du Bois, *The World and Africa: An Inquiry into the Part Which Africa Has Played in World History* (1947; New York: International Publishers, 1965), 10; "Ban on Negro Congress," *New York Times*, 2 Feb. 1919, 4.

63. Bundles, *On Her Own Ground*, 136.

64. "Resolutions Votées Par Le Congres Pan-Africain [19, 20, 21 Feb. 1919, Paris] pour la protection des indigènes d'Afrique et des peuples d'origine Africaine," NAACP Papers, part 11, series B, reel 18, frames 15–16.

65. Glenda Sluga, *The Nation, Psychology and International Politics, 1870–1919* (Basingstoke, UK: Palgrave Macmillan, 2006).

66. "Colonizing Africa," *Messenger* 2, no. 9 (Oct. 1920): 113.

67. Cyril V. Briggs, "Dr. Du Bois Misrepresents Negrodom," *Crusader* 1, no. 9 (May 1919): 1.

68. "The New Philosophy of the New Negro," *Messenger* 2, no. 11 (Dec. 1919): 5.

69. William N. Colson, "Phases of Du Bois," review of *Darkwater*, *Messenger* 2, no. 4–5 (Apr.–May 1920): 11.

70. Wilson Moses has identified two main strands of thought in black history at the time. One was a "utopianism of the past," and other rested on a model of "unstoppable progress toward a racially enlightened and egalitarian society in the future": Moses, *Afrotopia*, 238.

71. Colson, "Phases of Du Bois," 10–11.

72. A. Philip Randolph, "The Only Way to Redeem Africa" [part 3], *Messenger* 5, no. 1 (Jan. 1923): 569; and "The Only Way to Redeem Africa" [part 4], *Messenger* 5, no. 2 (Feb. 1923): 614.

73. Elie Garcia, UNIA Commissioner to Liberia, to Marcus Garvey and the UNIA, August 1920 untitled report, esp. part 2, in *The Marcus Garvey and Universal Negro Improvement Association Papers*, vol. 2, ed. Robert A. Hill (Berkeley: University of California Press, 1983), 666–673; Theodore G. Vincent, *Black Power and the Garvey Movement* (Berkeley, CA: Ramparts Press, 1971), 111, 180–181.

74. Theodore Kornweibel, *Seeing Red: Federal Campaigns against Black Militancy, 1919–1925* (Bloomington: Indiana University Press, 1998), 100–131.

75. "Drum Propaganda Stirs up Africans," *New York Times*, 7 Apr. 1923, 5.

76. James T. Campbell, *Songs of Zion: The African Methodist Episcopal Church in the United States and South Africa* (Chapel Hill: University of North Carolina Press, 1998), 300–305. See also Adebowale Adefuye, "Marcus Garvey and Nigeria," in *Garvey: His Work and Impact*, ed. Rupert Lewis and Patrick Bryan (Trenton, NJ: Africa World Press, 1991), 189–198; Tony Emmett, "Popular Resistance in

Namibia, 1920–1925" in *Resistance and Ideology in Settler Societies*, ed. Tom Lodge (Johannesburg: Ravan Press, 1986), 6–48; Robert A. Hill and Gregory A. Pirio, "'Africa for the Africans': The Garvey Movement in South Africa, 1920–1940," in *The Politics of Race, Class, and Nationalism in Twentieth-Century South Africa*, ed. Shula Marks and Stanley Trapido (London: Longman, 1987), 209–253; Arnold Hughes, "Africa and the Garvey Movement in the Interwar Years," in *Garvey: Africa, Europe, the Americas*, ed. Rupert Lewis and Maureen Warner-Lewis (Trenton, NJ: Africa World Press, 1986), 99–120; Rupert Lewis, *Marcus Garvey: Anti-Colonial Champion* (Trenton, NJ: Africa World Press, 1988), 153–168; R. L. Okonkwo, "The Garvey Movement in British West Africa," *Journal of African History* 21, no. 1 (1980): 105–117; G. O. Olusanya, "Garvey and Nigeria," in *Garvey: Africa, Europe, the Americas*, 121–134; Robert Trent Vinson, "'Sea Kaffirs': 'American Negroes' and the Gospel of Garveyism in Early Twentieth-century Cape Town," *Journal of African History* 47, no. 2 (July 2006): 281–292.

77. Singh, *Black Is a Country*, 48.

78. Carter G. Woodson, "Fifty Years of Negro Citizenship as Qualified by the United States Supreme Court," *Journal of Negro History* 6, no. 1 (Jan. 1921): 1. Kelley notes that the essay "was reprinted and widely circulated three years later as a small booklet": "'But a Local Phase of a World Problem,'" 1049.

79. W. E. B. Du Bois, "The Souls of Whitefolk," in *Darkwater: Voices within the Veil* (New York: Harcourt, Brace and Howe, 1920), 49, cited in Nikhil Pal Singh, "Culture/Wars: Recoding Empire in an Age of Democracy," *American Quarterly* 50, no. 3 (1998): 483–484.

80. Arthur A. Schomburg, "The Negro Digs up His Past," in *The New Negro*, ed. Alain Locke (1925; New York: Atheneum, 1992), 232.

81. "Dramatization of Negro History by Mabel Travis Wood," *New York Amsterdam News*, 4 July 1923, 12.

82. "High Points of Achievement," *New York Age*, 9 Jan. 1926.

83. W. E. B. Du Bois, "The Black Man Brings His Gifts," *Survey Graphic* 6, no. 6 (Mar. 1925): 655–657, 710. Du Bois's earlier pageant, *The Star of Ethiopia* (1913), was originally titled "The Jewel of Ethiopia: The People of Peoples and Their Gifts to Men." See David Krasner, *A Beautiful Pageant: African American Theatre, Drama, and Performance in the Harlem Renaissance, 1910–1927* (New York: Palgrave Macmillan, 2002), 87.

84. As well as Du Bois, W. A. Domingo, Jessie Fauset, and Montgomery Gregory wrote articles about gift giving. See Barbara Foley, *Spectres of 1919: Class and Nation in the Making of the New Negro* (Urbana: University of Illinois Press, 2003), 226–227, 229.

85. Schuyler, "The Negro Honors His Past."

86. "America's Making: A Festival and Exhibit of Three Centuries of Immigrant Contributions to Our National Life," NAACP Papers, part 11, series A, reel 1, frame 381.

87. "'America's Making' in Pageant Tonight," *New York Times,* 29 Oct. 1921, 12.

88. "A Proposed Exhibition and Pageant Illustrating the Part Which the American Negro Has Played in the Making of America," 3pp., NAACP Papers, part 11, series A, reel 1, frames 375–380.

89. James Weldon Johnson, "Preface" to *The Book of American Negro Poetry* (1922) and *Along This Way: The Autobiography of James Weldon Johnson* (1933), cited in Brent Hayes Edwards, *The Practice of Diaspora: Literature, Translation, and the Rise of Black Internationalism* (Cambridge, MA: Harvard University Press, 2003), 45.

90. Pero Gaglo Dagbovie, "Black Women, Carter G. Woodson, and the Association for the Study of Negro Life and History, 1915–1950," *Journal of African American History* 88, no. 1 (Winter 2003): 21–41.

91. Frances Gunner, "The Light of the Women," in *Plays and Pageants from the Life of the Negro,* ed. Willis Richardson (1930; Great Neck, NY: Core Collection Books, 1979), 333–342.

92. Willis Richardson, "Introduction," in *Plays and Pageants,* xlvi.

93. Paul Gilroy, *The Black Atlantic: Modernity and Double Consciousness* (Cambridge, MA: Harvard University Press, 1993), 190. Gilroy draws on Molefi Kete Asante, *Afrocentricity,* rev. ed. (Trenton, NJ: Africa World Press, 1989), 106–107.

94. Rogers, "The Negro in European History," 502.

95. "Human Race Began in Africa," *New York Amsterdam News,* 25 Feb. 1925, 16.

96. Singh, *Black Is a Country,* 31–32, 36–38.

3. Institutionalizing Africa, Past and Present

1. Nell Irvin Painter, "Soul Murder and Slavery: Toward a Fully Loaded Cost Accounting," in *Southern History across the Color Line* (Chapel Hill: University of North Carolina Press, 2002), 15–39; Orlando Patterson, *Slavery and Social Death: A Comparative Study* (Cambridge, MA: Harvard University Press, 1992). See also Alex Bontemps, *The Punished Self: Surviving Slavery in the Colonial South* (Ithaca, NY: Cornell University Press, 2001); Saidiya V. Hartman, *Scenes of Subjection: Terror, Slavery, and Self-Making in Nineteenth-Century America* (Oxford: Oxford University Press, 1997).

2. Steven Hahn, *A Nation under Our Feet: Black Political Struggles in the Rural South from Slavery to the Great Migration* (Cambridge, MA: Belknap Press/ Harvard University Press, 2004).

3. Quoted in Ellen Fitzpatrick, *History's Memory: Writing America's Past, 1880–1980* (Cambridge, MA: Harvard University Press, 2002), 49.

4. August Meier and Elliott Rudwick, *Black History and the Historical Profession, 1915–1980* (Urbana: University of Illinois Press, 1986), 73–101.

5. Peter Novick, *That Noble Dream: The "Objectivity Question" and the American Historical Profession* (Cambridge: Cambridge University Press, 1988), 229–231.

6. Digital archives of the *American Historical Review* and *Mississippi Valley Historical Review* at www.jstor.org (accessed 15 Feb. 2007).

7. David Levering Lewis, *W. E. B. Du Bois: The Fight for Equality and the American Century, 1919–1963* (New York: Holt, 2000), 483, 365.

8. W. Fitzhugh Brundage, *The Southern Past: A Clash of Race and Memory* (Cambridge, MA: Belknap Press/Harvard University Press, 2005), 155–157.

9. Elinor Des Verney Sinnette, "Arthur Alfonso Schomburg (1874–1938), Black Bibliophile and Collector," in *Black Bibliophiles and Collectors: Preservers of Black History,* ed. W. Paul Coates and Thomas C. Battle (Washington, DC: Howard University Press, 1990), 35–45.

10. Arthur A. Schomburg, "Racial Integrity: A Plea for the Establishment of a Chair of Negro History in Our Schools and Colleges, etc." Paper presented at a meeting of the Negro Society for Historical Research, July 1913, 6–7, cited in Adalaine Holton, "Decolonizing History: Arthur Schomburg's Afrodiasporic Archive," *Journal of African American History* 92, no. 2 (Spring 2007): 221.

11. George Steiner, "Our Homeland, the Text," in *No Passion Spent: Essays 1978–1996* (London: Faber and Faber, 1996), 304–327.

12. Avril Johnson Madison and Dorothy Porter Wesley, "Dorothy Burnett Porter Wesley: Enterprising Steward of Black Culture," *Public Historian* 17, no. 1 (Winter 1995): 15–40.

13. Aubrey Bowser, "A Negro Documentarian," *New York Amsterdam News,* 13 Aug. 1930; L. S. Alexander Gumby, "The Gumby Scrapbook Collection of Negroana," *Columbia Library World* 5 (1951): 1–8; "L. S. Alexander Gumby Is Dead," *New York Times,* 18 Mar. 1961, 23; Richard Bruce Nugent, "On Alexander Gumby," in *Gay Rebel of the Harlem Renaissance: Selections from the Work of Richard Bruce Nugent,* ed. Thomas H. Wirth (Durham, NC: Duke University Press, 2002), 223–226. On the Art Students' Club exhibitions, see GC, vol. 36.

14. John Henrik Clarke, "Portrait of a Liberation Scholar," John Henrik Clarke Virtual Museum, Virtual Museums of the Masters, www.nbufront.org (accessed 14 Feb. 2007).

15. John Henrik Clarke, "The Influence of Arthur A. Schomburg on My Concept of Africana Studies," *Phylon* 49, no. 1–2 (Spring–Summer 1992): 4–9.

16. "John Henrik Clarke's Autobiographical Obituary," posted by News Service (27 July 1998) at www.mumia.org/wwwboard/messages/1346.html (accessed 23 Apr. 2003).

17. Brundage, *The Southern Past,* 146–147.

18. "Circle of Knowledge," Minutes of meetings, 4pp., Miscellaneous American Letters and Papers, box 2, MARB.

19. Toomer cited in Elizabeth McHenry, *Forgotten Readers: Recovering the Lost History of African American Literary Societies* (Durham, NC: Duke University Press, 2002), 258.

20. Jean Toomer, "The Negro Emergent" (unpub. 1924), in *Jean Toomer: Selected Essays and Literary Criticism,* ed. Robert B. Jones (Knoxville: University of Tennessee Press, 1996), 48.

21. McHenry, *Forgotten Readers*, 259.

22. Clarke, "Portrait of a Liberation Scholar."

23. "John Henrik Clarke's Autobiographical Obituary."

24. Clarke, "The Influence of Arthur A. Schomburg," 7. Clarke also remembered seeing Nkrumah at meetings of the Blyden Society, which was also devoted to the study of African history: John Henrik Clarke, "Kwame Nkrumah: His Years in America," *Black Scholar* 6, no. 2 (Oct. 1974): 11. Nkrumah himself never mentioned his involvement with these groups; see Marika Sherwood, *Kwame Nkrumah: The Years Abroad 1935–1947* (Legon, Ghana: Freedom Publications, 1996), 40–42; Kevin K. Gaines, *American Africans in Ghana: Black Expatriates and the Civil Rights Era* (Chapel Hill: University of North Carolina Press, 2006), 42–43.

25. "Negro Educator Is Found Drowned," *New York Times,* 19 July 1941, 28.

26. Ralph L. Crowder, "Willis Nathaniel Huggins (1886–1941): Historian, Activist, and Community Mentor," *Afro-Americans in New York Life and History* 30, no. 2 (July 2006): 130.

27. UESA Membership Application Form, John Henrik Clarke Papers, box 39, folder 1, MARB.

28. Letter from the UESA to Professor Willis Huggins, 12 June 1932, Clarke Papers, box 39, folder 2.

29. Ibid.

30. Report to *Negro World* and *New York Amsterdam News,* 5 June 1932, Clarke Papers, box 39, folder 1.

31. Samuel Williams, Pres., Buffalo Liberian Research Society, to UESA, 3 July 1934; Edward G. Martin, Pres., Dumas Literary Club, to UESA [ca. May 1931]; Chas. Moultey [?], Istmo-African Bureau, to UESA, 29 Sept. 1931; Egbert Wallace, Secretary, The Ethiopian Social Club, to UESC, 12 Apr. 1932; all four of the preceding can be found in the Clarke Papers, box 39, folder 4. T. C. Murray, Pres., African Patriotic Students Club to UESA, 6 May 1931; Alfred R. Green, Los Angeles Liberian Research Society, to UESA, 13 Oct. 1934; Louis Maponyane, National Organizer, The Liberian-American League, Chicago, to UESA, 19 July 1934; Cape Palmas Club to UESA [n.d.]; The Committee, Yoruba Literary and Debating Club to UESA, 20 Nov. 1934; the preceding five are located in the Clarke Papers, box 39, folder 6.

32. Arthur P. Davis, "Growing up in the New Negro Renaissance: 1920–1935," *Negro American Literature Forum* 2, no. 3, Protest and Propaganda Literature (Autumn 1968): 54.

33. John Henrik Clarke, "Portrait of a Liberation Scholar."

34. William Pickens, "Hubert H. Harrison: Philosopher of Harlem," *New York Amsterdam News*, 7 Feb. 1923, rpt. in *Speech and Power: The African-American Essay and Its Cultural Content from Polemics to Pulpit*, ed. Gerald Early, vol. 1 (Hopewell, NJ: Ecco Press, 1992), 41–43.

35. Davis, "Growing up in the New Negro Renaissance," 58; Irma Watkins-Owens, *Blood Relations: Caribbean Immigrants and the Harlem Community, 1900–1930* (Bloomington: Indiana University Press, 1996), 95–98.

36. G. James Fleming, notes from an interview with David Levering Lewis, June 1976, Voices of the Harlem Renaissance, box 1, folder 1, MARB.

37. The Black Public Sphere Collective, "Preface," in *The Black Public Sphere: A Public Culture Book,* ed. The Black Public Sphere Collective (Chicago: University of Chicago Press, 1995), 2–3. See also Jürgen Habermas, *The Structural Transformation of the Public Sphere: An Inquiry into a Category of Bourgeois Society* (1962), trans. Thomas Burger with Frederick Lawrence (Cambridge, MA: MIT Press, 1989), 31–43.

38. Barbara Ransby, *Ella Baker and the Black Freedom Movement: A Radical Democratic Vision* (Chapel Hill: University of North Carolina Press, 2003), 69.

39. Jacob S. Dorman, "The Black Israelites of Harlem and the Professors of Oriental and African Mystic Science in the 1920's" (PhD diss., University of California, Los Angeles, 2004), 177–187.

40. Advertisement, *New York Amsterdam News,* 11 Apr. 1923.

41. "Milestones," *Time,* 8 Aug. 1938, www.time.com (accessed 19 Sept. 2007); Richard Bruce Nugent, "On Harlem," in *Gay Rebel of the Harlem Renaissance,* 155.

42. "Harlem's 'Hitler' Jailed for Speech," *New York Times,* 20 Jan. 1935, N1.

43. See Winston C. McDowell, "Keeping Them 'In the Same Boat Together'? Sufi Abdul Hamid, African Americans, Jews, and the Harlem Jobs Boycotts," in *African Americans and Jews in the Twentieth Century: Studies in Convergence and Conflict,* ed. V. P. Franklin, Nancy L. Grant, Harold M. Kletnick, and Genna Rae McNeil (Columbia: University of Missouri Press, 1998), 225.

44. McKay, "Harlem Glory," mss., p. 95, Claude McKay letters and manuscripts 1915–1952, part 4, MARB. According to McKay's biographer, the manuscript was written in the late 1930s: Wayne F. Cooper, *Claude McKay: Rebel Sojourner in the Harlem Renaissance, A Biography* (New York: Schocken Books, 1987), 347–348.

45. Rev. Father J. C. O'Flaherty, "An Exclusive Interview with Paul Robeson," *West African Review* (Aug. 1936): 12–13, rpt. in *Paul Robeson Speaks: Writings, Speeches, Interviews, 1918–1974,* ed. Philip S. Foner (London: Quartet Books, 1978), 114. For a full discussion of this idea, see Clare Corbould, "Streets, Sounds and Identity in Interwar Harlem," *Journal of Social History* 40, no. 4 (Summer 2007): 859–894.

46. Wallace Thurman, *Negro Life in New York's Harlem: A Lively Picture of a Popular and Interesting Section* (Girard, KS: Haldeman-Julius Publications, 1934), 9–10.

47. Maya Angelou, *I Know Why the Caged Bird Sings* (1969; London: Virago Press, 1984), 4, 6.

48. Marcus Garvey, "A Dialogue: What's the Difference?" *The Blackman* 1, no. 7 (June 1935): 10–12.

49. E. C. Williams, "*Unsung Heroes* by Elizabeth Ross Haynes," *Journal of Negro History* 7, no. 2 (Apr. 1922): 224.

50. Jessie Fauset, "No End of Books," *Crisis* 23, no. 5 (Mar. 1922): 209.

51. "The Negro in Our History," *New York Amsterdam News,* 21 Mar. 1923, 12.

52. Paul Robeson, "I Want to Be African" (1934), rpt. in *Paul Robeson Speaks,* 89.

53. Violet J. Harris, "African American Children's Literature: The First One Hundred Years," *Journal of Negro Education* 59, no. 4 (Autumn 1990): 547.

54. Lillie Buffum Chance Wyman, "'The Bravest of the Brave': A True Story" (1920), rpt. in *The Best of the Brownies' Book,* ed. Dianne Johnson-Feelings (New York: Oxford University Press, 1996), 83–85.

55. Lewis, *W. E. B. Du Bois,* 33; Harris, "African American Children's Literature," 546.

56. Sarah Talbert Keelan, "Olive Plaatje" (Dec. 1921), rpt. in *The Best of the Brownies' Book,* 107–108.

57. Carry S. Bond, "A Fairy Story," *Crisis,* spec. issue: *Children's Number* 18, no. 6 (Oct. 1919): 290–291.

58. Inez M. Burke, "Two Races: A Pageant," in *Plays and Pageants from the Life of the Negro,* ed. Willis Richardson (1930; Great Neck, NY: Core Collection Books, 1979), 297.

59. Michelle Rief, "Thinking Locally, Acting Globally: The International Agenda of African American Clubwomen, 1880–1940," *Journal of African American History* 89, no. 3 (Summer 2004): 216.

60. Margaret Murray Washington, untitled notes, 10 Nov. 1924, rpt. in Eleanor Hinton Hoytt, "International Council of Women of the Darker Races: Historical Notes," *Sage* 3, no. 2 (Fall 1986): 54–55; Robert B. Eleazer, *America's Tenth Man: A Brief Survey of the Negro's Past in American History,* Commission on Interracial Cooperation, Atlanta, GA, April 1931, NAACP Papers, part 11, series B, reel 4, frames 299–308, microfilm reels, British Library; Marc Gallicchio, *The African American Encounter with Japan and China: Black Internationalism in Asia, 1895–1945* (Chapel Hill: University of North Carolina Press, 2000), 41, 219n.39; Brundage, *The Southern Past,* 148–149.

61. Evelyn Brooks Barrett, "Nannie Burroughs and the Education of Black Women," in *The Afro-American Woman: Struggles and Images,* ed. Sharon Harley and Rosalyn Terborg-Penn (1978; Baltimore: Black Classic Press, 1997), 103.

62. "Want Negro History Study Included in School Curriculum," *New York Age,* 7 Feb. 1925.

63. Cited in Adam Fairclough, *A Class of Their Own: Black Teachers in the Segregated South* (Cambridge, MA: Belknap Press/Harvard University Press, 2007), 287; Brundage, *The Southern Past,* 140, 144–145.

64. Brundage, *The Southern Past,* 139; Leon F. Litwack, *Been in the Storm So Long: The Aftermath of Slavery* (1979; New York: Vintage Books, 1980), 472–476; Leon F. Litwack, *Trouble in Mind: Black Southerners in the Age of Jim Crow* (1998; New York: Vintage Books, 1999), 52–113; Hahn, *A Nation under Our Feet,* 97–99, 276–280; Heather Andrea Williams, *Self-Taught: African American Education in Slavery and Freedom* (Chapel Hill: University of North Carolina Press, 2005).

65. Brundage, *The Southern Past,* 143; Fairclough, *A Class of Their Own,* 263, 297.

66. Brundage, *The Southern Past,* 149–152; Fairclough, *A Class of Their Own,* 223–224.

67. "Notes," *Journal of Negro History* 13, no. 1 (Jan. 1928): 110.

68. C. G. Woodson, "The Celebration of Negro History Week, 1927," *Journal of Negro History* 12, no. 2 (Apr. 1927): 108–109.

69. "Negro History Week—the Ninth Year," *Journal of Negro History* 19, no. 2 (Apr. 1934): 115, 116.

70. "Negro History Week—the Fourth Year," *Journal of Negro History* 14, no. 2 (Apr. 1929): 112.

71. Richardson, ed., *Plays and Pageants;* and Willis Richardson and May Miller, eds., *Negro History in Thirteen Plays* (Washington, DC: Associated Publishers, 1935).

72. Carter G. Woodson, "Introduction," in *Negro History in Thirteen Plays,* iv.

73. Brundage, *The Southern Past,* 167.

74. On inquiries, see C. G. Woodson, "Negro History Week," *Journal of Negro History* 11, no. 2 (Apr. 1926): 241; on the press, see C. G. Woodson, "Negro History Week—the Third Year," *Journal of Negro History* 13, no. 2 (Apr. 1928): 121–124; and "Negro History Week—the Fourth Year," 110–111.

75. Woodson, "Negro History Week," 238.

76. John Hope Franklin, Gerald Horne, Harold W. Cruse, Allen B. Ballard, and Reavis L. Mitchell Jr., "Black History Month: Serious Truth Telling or a Triumph in Tokenism?" *Journal of Blacks in Higher Education* 18 (Winter 1997–1998): 91.

77. Randolph Edmonds, "The High Court of Historia," in *The Land of Cotton and Other Plays* (Washington, DC: Associated Publishers, 1942), 229–267.

78. Fairclough, *A Class of Their Own,* 249, 319–321.

79. Mildred M. Williams et al., *The Jeanes Story: A Chapter in the History of American Education, 1908–1968* (Atlanta, GA: Southern Education Foundation, 1979), 5.

80. "Negro History Week—the Fourth Year," 113. For a contemporary review that discussed the significance of Woodson's book, see Alain Locke, "The Negro in Our History," *Journal of Negro History* 12, no. 1 (Jan. 1927): 99–101.

81. See, for example, "Negro History Week—the Fifth Year," *Journal of Negro History* 16, no. 2 (Apr. 1931): 128.

82. The preface was retained in later editions, see Carter G. Woodson, *The Negro in Our History*, 7th ed. (Washington, DC: Associated Publishers, 1941), 1.

83. Maghan Keita, *Race and the Writing of History: Riddling the Sphinx* (New York: Oxford University Press, 2000), 67.

84. "Notes," *Journal of Negro History* 13, no. 1 (Jan. 1928): 109.

85. "Report of the New York Public Library for 1921," *Bulletin of the New York Public Library* 27 (Apr. 1923): 427, cited in Sarah A. Anderson, "'The Place to Go': The 135th Street Branch Library and the Harlem Renaissance," *Library Quarterly* 73, no. 4 (Oct. 2003): 389.

86. Anderson, "'The Place to Go,'" 394.

87. Nancy Tolson, "Making Books Available: The Role of Early Libraries, Librarians, and Booksellers in the Promotion of African American Children's Literature," *African American Review* 32, no. 1, *Children's and Young-Adult Literature Issue* (Spring 1998): 11–12.

88. On the UNIA, see Barbara Bair, "Garveyism and Contested Political Terrain in 1920s Virginia," in *Afro-Virginian History and Culture,* ed. John Saillant (New York: Garland, 1999), 229.

89. Assistant Director of Branches to Louis Campbell, Secretary, Gary Branch, NAACP, 25 Oct. 1921, NAACP Papers, part 12, series C, reel 8, frames 466–469.

90. David Glassberg, *American Historical Pageantry: The Uses of Tradition in the Early Twentieth Century* (Chapel Hill: University of North Carolina Press, 1990).

91. Ibid., 285. See also Michael G. Kammen, *Mystic Chords of Memory: The Transformation of Tradition in American Culture* (New York: Knopf, 1991), 278–281, 425.

92. Wilson J. Moses, "Literary Myth and Ethnic Assimilation: Israel Zangwill and Sutton Griggs," *New Hungarian Quarterly* 21, no. 80 (Winter 1980): 134; Joe Kraus, "How the Melting Pot Stirred America: The Reception of Zangwill's Play and Theater's Role in the American Assimilation Experience," *Melus* 24, no. 3 (Fall 1999): 13–14.

93. Glassberg, *American Historical Pageantry,* 254–255.

94. "Music and Drama," *Chicago Defender,* 30 Apr. 1927, 11.

95. "Dramatization of Negro History by Mabel Travis Wood," *New York Amsterdam News,* 4 July 1923, 12.

96. Carter Godwin Woodson, *The Mis-Education of the Negro* (1933; Trenton, NJ: Africa World Press, 1993), 96.

97. Clarke, "The Influence of Arthur A. Schomburg," 7; Sigmund Freud, "Mourning and Melancholia" (1917), in *On Metapsychology, the Theory of Psychoanalysis: Beyond the Pleasure Principle, The Ego and the Id, and Other Works,* ed.

James Strachey and Angela Richards (Harmondsworth, England: Penguin Books, 1984), 251–268.

98. For discussion of these concepts, see Dominick LaCapra, "Revisiting the Historians' Debate: Mourning and Genocide," *History and Memory* 9, no. 1/2 (Fall 1997): 80–112; Dominick LaCapra, *Writing History, Writing Trauma* (Baltimore: Johns Hopkins University Press, 2000).

99. For example, see "Negro Music and Pageant," *Christian Science Monitor,* 8 Dec. 1920, 3; "200 Negroes Act Pageant," *New York Times,* 23 Nov. 1921, 13; "Washington Likes Show 'Open Door,'" *Chicago Defender,* 24 Mar. 1923, 1; "Negroes to Present Big Pageant Here," *Atlanta Constitution,* 9 Mar. 1924, C3; "'The Open Door,' Negro Pageant, Shown Saturday," *Atlanta Constitution,* 16 Mar. 1924, 14.

100. "'Open Door' Pageant to Be Given in Newark," *New York Age,* 21 Jan. 1922.

101. Program for "The 'Open Door' Pageant-Drama," Atlanta University, Saturday, 15 Mar. 1924, Clarence Cameron White Papers, box 209-14, folder 2, MSC.

102. Dorothy C. Guinn, "Out of the Dark: A Pageant," in *Plays and Pageants,* 313.

103. Brundage, *The Southern Past,* 171.

104. "Pageant of Negro History Presented at Mother Zion," *New York Age,* 5 May 1934.

105. Mary Church Terrell, "Historical Pageant-Play Based on the Life of Phyllis Wheatley," Mary Church Terrell Papers, box 102-6, folder 159, MSC.

106. Kelley, "'But a Local Phase of a World Problem,'" 1058.

107. Ula Yvette Taylor, *The Veiled Garvey: The Life and Times of Amy Jacques Garvey* (Chapel Hill: University of North Carolina Press, 2002), 77. On circulation of the contents of black newspapers in the South, including the rural South, see Mary Gambrell Rolinson, "The Garvey Movement in the Rural South, 1920–1927" (PhD diss., Georgia State University, 2002), 80–82, 101–102, 107–108, 117, 130–131.

108. "Proceedings of the Annual Meeting of the Association for the Study of Negro Life and History Held in Washington, D.C., from October 29 to November 1, 1933," *Journal of Negro History* 19, no. 1 (Jan. 1934): 12. The proceedings were reprinted in "Current Events of Importance in Negro Education," *Journal of Negro Education* 3, no. 2 (Apr. 1934): 310.

109. Interview with Olivia Pearl Stokes, 25 Sept. 1979, in *The Black Women Oral History Project,* vol. 9, ed. Ruth Edmonds Hill (Westport, CT: Meckler, 1991), 127–128.

110. Letter from Hagar to editor, *Negro World,* 17 Apr. 1920, rpt. in *African Fundamentalism: A Literary and Cultural Anthology of Garvey's Harlem Renaissance,* ed. Tony Martin (Dover, MA: Majority Press, 1991), 10.

111. Deborah Wolfe interviewed by Marcia Greenlee, 6 Nov. 1979, in *The Black Women Oral History Project,* vol. 10, 391.

112. Alva Hudson, "Reading Achievements, Interests, and Habits of Negro Women," *Journal of Negro Education* 1, no. 3/4 (Oct. 1932): 367–373.

113. Jessie Redmon Fauset, *Comedy, American Style* (1933; New York: AMS Press, 1969), 39.

114. Ibid., 89.

115. Fairclough, *A Class of Their Own*, 302; Brundage, *The Southern Past*, 142; James D. Anderson, *The Education of Blacks in the South, 1860–1935* (Chapel Hill: University of North Carolina Press, 1988), 110–147.

116. Fairclough, *A Class of Their Own*, 298.

117. Ibid., 265–306.

118. Ibid., 272.

119. Ibid., 245–251, 303–306.

120. Tolson, "Making Books Available," 11.

121. Louis Shores, "Library Service and the Negro," *Journal of Negro Education* 1, no. 3/4 (Oct. 1932): 374–380.

122. Dorothy G. Williams, "Adult Education in Public Libraries and Museums," *Journal of Negro Education* 14, no. 3, Adult Education for Negroes in the United States (Summer 1945): 323.

123. Final draft of proposal, n.d. [probably 1931], Locke Papers, box 164-163, folder 18, MSC. Other proposal drafts in box 164-163, folder 19. Also see Locke's correspondence with Mordecai Johnson, President, Howard University, 9 June and 6 Dec. 1928, box 164-41, folder 1.

124. Woodson to Locke, 1 Oct. 1927, Locke Papers, box 164-95, folder 4. See also Woodson, *The Mis-Education of the Negro,* 132–138.

125. Woodson to Locke, 1 Oct. 1927, Locke Papers, box 164-95, folder 4; "Notes," *Journal of Negro History* 13, no. 1 (Jan. 1928): 115–119.

126. "Negro History Week—the Fourth Year," 114; "Annual Report of the Director," *Journal of Negro History* 13, no. 4 (Oct. 1928): 410–411; "Annual Report of the Director," *Journal of Negro History* 14, no. 4 (Oct. 1929): 366–367; "Notes," *Journal of Negro History* 14, no. 4 (Oct. 1929): 537–538.

127. Willis N. Huggins and John G. Jackson, *A Guide to Studies in African History: Directive Lists for Schools and Clubs* (New York: Federation of History Clubs, 1934), 20.

128. For example, see [Anon,] *"The Gift of Black Folk* by W.E. Burghardt Du Bois," *Journal of Negro History* 9, no. 4 (Oct. 1924): 572–573; C. G. Woodson, "Black Folk Then and Now," *Journal of Negro History* 24, no. 4 (Oct. 1939): 460–463.

129. Henry Noble Sherwood, *"The Negro in Our History* by Carter G. Woodson," *Mississippi Valley Historical Review* 14, no. 3 (Dec. 1927): 421.

130. Arthur A. Schomburg, "The Negro Digs up His Past," in *The New Negro,* ed. Alain Locke (1925; New York: Atheneum, 1992), 236.

131. Zora Neale Hurston, *Dust Tracks on a Road: An Autobiography* (1942; London: Virago Press, 1986), 202.

132. See George Shepperson, "The Afro-American Contribution to African Studies," *Journal of American Studies* 8, no. 3 (1974): 294–297.

133. "Columbia Group Sponsors African Program," *New York Age,* 14 Apr. 1934.

134. Letters from James L. Brown, President, UESA to Editor, *Pittsburgh Courier,* 9 Aug. 1931 and n.d. (but approx. one week later), Clarke Papers, box 39, folder 3.

135. On debate between Schuyler and Du Bois over Liberia, see James T. Campbell, *Middle Passages: African American Journeys to Africa, 1787–2005* (New York: Penguin Press, 2006), 226–267.

136. Letter from unsigned, UESA to Istmo African Pioneering Club, Ancon, Canal Zone, 24 Apr. 1932, Clarke Papers, box 39, folder 2.

137. Circular letter from Louis Austin, Chairman, UESA, n.d., Clarke Papers, box 39, folder 3.

138. Universal Ethiopian Students' Association, *The Truth about Ethiopia: A Nation Blocked from the Sea* (New York: UESA, 1936).

139. See Robert W. Connell, "Why Is Classical Theory Classical?," *American Journal of Sociology* 102, no. 6 (May 1997): 1511–1557.

140. Kelley, "'But a Local Phase of a World Problem.'"

141. Dorothy Ross, *The Origins of American Social Science* (Cambridge: Cambridge University Press, 1991).

142. Ralph J. Bunche, "French Administration in Togoland and Dahomey" (PhD diss., Harvard University, 1934), 48.

143. Cited in Patrick J. Gilpin and Marybeth Gasman, *Charles S. Johnson: Leadership beyond the Veil in the Age of Jim Crow* (Albany: State University of New York Press, 2003), 94.

144. Edgar T. Thompson, "Sociology and Sociological Research in the South" (1945), cited in Gilpin and Gasman, *Charles S. Johnson,* 99–100; Rupert B. Vance and Katharine Jocher, "Howard W. Odum," *Social Forces* 33, no. 3 (Mar. 1955): 203–217.

145. Jonathan Scott Holloway, *Confronting the Veil: Abram Harris Jr., E. Franklin Frazier, and Ralph Bunche, 1919–1941* (Chapel Hill: University of North Carolina Press, 2002), 88–90, 115–120.

146. "Proceedings of the Annual Meeting of the Association for the Study of Negro Life and History Held in Washington, D.C., from October 29 to November 1, 1933," *Journal of Negro History* 19, no. 1 (Jan. 1934): 13.

147. "Editorial Comment: Why a Journal of Negro Education," *Journal of Negro Education* 1, no. 1 (Apr. 1932): 2, 3.

148. "Current Events of Importance in Negro Education," *Journal of Negro Education* 3, no. 2 (Apr. 1934): 310.

149. August Meier and John H. Bracey Jr., "The NAACP as a Reform Movement, 1909–1965: 'To Reach the Conscience of America,'" *Journal of Southern History* 59, no. 1 (Feb. 1993): 18; Simon Topping, "'Supporting Our Friends and Defeating Our Enemies': Militancy and Nonpartisanship in the NAACP, 1936–1948," *Journal of African American History* 89, no. 1 (Winter 2004): 19.

150. Mia Bay, *The White Image in the Black Mind: African-American Ideas about White People, 1830–1925* (New York: Oxford University Press, 2000), 216–217.

151. Robert E. Park, "The Conflict and Fusion of Cultures with Special Reference to the Negro," *Journal of Negro History* 4, no. 2 (Apr. 1919): 116.

152. Lee D. Baker, *From Savage to Negro: Anthropology and the Construction of Race, 1896–1954* (Berkeley: University of California Press, 1998), 177.

153. Clarence E. Walker, "Black Reconstruction in America: W. E. B. Du Bois's Challenge to 'The Dark and Bloody Ground of Reconstruction Historiography,'" in *Deromanticizing Black History: Critical Essays and Reappraisals* (Knoxville: University of Tennessee Press, 1991), 73–86; Anthony Bogues, *Black Heretics, Black Prophets: Radical Political Intellectuals* (New York: Routledge, 2003), 69–93.

154. David W. Blight, "W. E. B. Du Bois and the Struggle for American Historical Memory," in *History and Memory in African-American Culture,* ed. Geneviève Fabre and Robert O'Meally (New York: Oxford University Press, 1994), 45–71.

155. Nancy Cunard, ed., *Negro: Anthology Made by Nancy Cunard 1931–1933* (London: Wishart, 1934).

156. Lewis, *W. E. B. Du Bois,* 453.

157. Pamphlet for the "Encyclopaedia of the Negro," Locke Papers, box 164-26, folder 9.

158. Gunnar Myrdal, *An American Dilemma: The Negro Problem and Modern Democracy* (New York: Harper and Brothers, 1944), 205.

159. Carol Anderson, *Eyes Off the Prize: The United Nations and the African American Struggle for Human Rights, 1944–1955* (New York: Cambridge University Press, 2003); Mary L. Dudziak, *Cold War Civil Rights: Race and the Image of American Democracy* (Princeton: Princeton University Press, 2000); James H. Meriwether, *Proudly We Can Be Africans: Black Americans and Africa, 1935–1961* (Chapel Hill: University of North Carolina Press, 2002); Brenda Gayle Plummer, *Rising Wind: Black Americans and U.S. Foreign Affairs, 1935–1960* (Chapel Hill: University of North Carolina Press, 1996); Nikhil Pal Singh, *Black Is a Country: Race and the Unfinished Struggle for Democracy* (Cambridge, MA: Harvard University Press, 2004); Penny M. Von Eschen, *Race against Empire: Black Americans and Anticolonialism, 1937–1957* (Ithaca, NY: Cornell University Press, 1997).

160. Franklin et al., "Black History Month," 88.

4. The Artistic Capital of Africa

1. Alain Locke, "The Message of the Negro Poets," *Carolina Magazine* 58, no. 7 (May 1928): 14.

2. The phrase was the subheading of a special edition of the *Survey Graphic* in March 1925, published in altered form as Alain Locke, ed., *The New Negro* (1925; New York: Atheneum, 1992).

3. Henry Louis Gates Jr., "The Trope of a New Negro and the Reconstruction of the Image of the Black," *Representations* no. 24 (Autumn 1988): 129–155.

4. Ibid., 136–141.

5. Kevin K. Gaines, *Uplifting the Race: Black Leadership, Politics, and Culture in the Twentieth Century* (Chapel Hill: University of North Carolina Press, 1996); Evelyn Brooks Higginbotham, *Righteous Discontent: The Women's Movement in the Black Baptist Church, 1880–1920* (Cambridge, MA: Harvard University Press, 1993); W. E. B. Du Bois, "The Talented Tenth," in *The Negro Problem: A Series of Articles by Representative American Negroes of To-Day*, contributions by Booker T. Washington, W. E. B. Du Bois, Paul Laurence Dunbar, Charles W. Chesnutt, and others (New York: James Pott, 1903), 31–75.

6. Langston Hughes, "The Negro Artist and the Racial Mountain," *The Nation*, 23 June 1926, rpt. *The Collected Works of Langston Hughes*, vol. 9, ed. Christopher C. De Santis (Columbia: University of Missouri Press, 2002), 36.

7. W. E. B. Du Bois, "Two Novels," *Crisis* 35, no. 6 (June 1928): 202.

8. Countée Cullen, "Heritage," in *The New Negro*, ed. Locke, 250–253. The others were Gwendolyn Bennett, "Heritage," *Opportunity* (Dec. 1923), rpt. in *The* Opportunity *Reader: Stories, Poetry, and Essays from the Urban League's* Opportunity *Magazine*, ed. Sondra Kathryn Wilson (New York: Modern Library, 1999), 3; Mae V. Cowdery, "Heritage" (1936), rpt. in *Shadowed Dreams: Women's Poetry of the Harlem Renaissance*, ed. Maureen Honey (New Brunswick, NJ: Rutgers University Press, 1989), 119; Dorothy Kruger, "Heritage," *Crisis* 35, no. 11 (Nov. 1928): 372; Claude McKay, "Heritage" (1922), rpt. in *Selected Poems of Claude McKay*, ed. Joan R. Sherman (Mineola, NY: Dover Publications, 1999), 36–37.

9. Jonathan M. Hansen, *The Lost Promise of Patriotism: Debating American Identity, 1890–1920* (Chicago: University of Chicago Press, 2003).

10. James T. Campbell, *Middle Passages: African American Journeys to Africa, 1787–2005* (New York: Penguin Press, 2006), xxiv.

11. Julia May Boddewyn, "Selected Chronology of Exhibitions, Auctions, and Magazine Reproductions, 1910–1957," in *Picasso and American Art*, ed. Michael FitzGerald (New York: Whitney Museum of American Art; New Haven, CT: Yale University Press, 2006), 328–377.

12. Lee D. Baker, *From Savage to Negro: Anthropology and the Construction of Race, 1896–1954* (Berkeley: University of California Press, 1998), 99–126.

13. Robert E. Park, "The Conflict and Fusion of Cultures with Special Reference to the Negro," *Journal of Negro History* 4, no. 2 (Apr. 1919): 116.

14. Ibid., 118.

15. Mae M. Ngai, *Impossible Subjects: Illegal Aliens and the Making of Modern America* (Princeton, NJ: Princeton University Press, 2004), 167–224; Donna R. Gabaccia, "Policy, Politics, and the Remaking of Immigration History," *American Quarterly* 57, no. 2 (June 2005): 533–540.

16. W.E.B. Du Bois, "Criteria of Negro Art," *Crisis* 32, no. 6 (Oct. 1926): 290–297.

17. Stewart Culin, "Preface," in *Primitive Negro Art: Chiefly from the Belgian Congo, with Illustrations and Notes by Stewart Culin* (Brooklyn, NY: Brooklyn Museum, Department of Ethnology, 1923), 2, BMDC.

18. Ibid., 1.

19. For example, see Margaret Bruening, "Large Exhibit of African Negro Art at Modern Museum," *New York Post*, 23 Mar. 1935, 22; Royal Cortissoz, "French Decorations and African Curios," *New York Herald Tribune,* 24 Mar. 1935, 10; Helen Appleton Read, "The Museum of Modern Art Glances Back at African Sculpture—Gallery Notes," *Brooklyn Daily Eagle,* 24 Mar. 1935, C5; "Man's Need of Art from the Beginning," *Christian Science Monitor,* 7 May 1923, 18.

20. For example, see "Primitive Negro Art" catalog, BMDC.

21. See photographs of exhibition at BMDC.

22. "Primitive Negro Art," 19, 18, BMDC.

23. Photographs of exhibition, BMDC.

24. Grace V. Kelly, "Negroes to Buy Art of Africa for City: Will Have Cleveland Painter Spend $1,000 in Native Villages for Work of Craftsmen," *Plain Dealer,* 15 Dec. 1927, NAACP Papers, part 12, series C, reel 22, frame 816, microfilms reels, British Library.

25. For a sustained discussion of the influence of these categories on exhibitions and museums, see Steven Conn, *Museums and American Intellectual Life, 1876–1926* (Chicago: University of Chicago Press, 1998), 75–113.

26. Christa Clarke, "Defining African Art: *Primitive Negro Sculpture* and the Aesthetic Philosophy of Albert Barnes," *African Arts* 36, no. 1 (Spring 2003): 40–51, 92–93.

27. Ibid., 44–47.

28. Paul Guillaume and Thomas Munro, *Primitive Negro Sculpture* (New York: Harcourt, Brace, 1926), 1.

29. Alain Locke to editor of the *Nation,* 16 Mar. 1927, 290.

30. Melville J. Herskovits, "Race, Cultural Groups, Social Differentiation," *Social Forces* 5, no. 2 (Dec. 1926): 295.

31. Clarke, "Defining African Art," 46.

32. Hal Foster, "The 'Primitive' Unconscious of Modern Art, or White Skin Black Masks," in *Recodings: Art, Spectacle, Cultural Politics* (Port Townsend, WA: Bay Press, 1985), 180–208; James Clifford, "Histories of the Tribal and the Modern," in *Race-ing Art History: Critical Readings in Race and Art History,* ed. Kymberly N. Pinder (New York: Routledge, 2002), 217–231.

33. "African Art," *Negro World,* 6 Oct. 1923, 6; "African Negro Art," *New York Amsterdam News,* 18 Apr. 1923, 5; "Congo Art Proves High Culture: Examples from Central Africa at Brooklyn Museum Show That Africans Had Developed High Culture," *New York Amsterdam News,* 30 May 1923, 9.

34. "Primitive Negro Sculpture on View in B'klyn Art Museum," *New York Amsterdam News,* 16 May 1923, 12.

35. See correspondence file, BMDC.

36. Letters between Stewart Culin and Louise Latimer between 4 and 25 June 1924, correspondence file, BMDC.

37. For correspondence on all of these points, see Circular Letter from Alain Locke, Locke Papers, box 164–68, folder 21, MSC; and "Organizations—Harlem Museum of African Art Blondiau Catalog," Locke Papers, box 164–179, folder 27.

38. Circular letter about Harlem Art Museum, by Locke, Secretary of the Committee, Locke Papers, box 164–68, folder 21.

39. Brochure/Catalog, 8 Feb. 1929, Locke Papers, box 164–89, folder 26.

40. Edith Isaacs to Alain Locke, 30 May, 1928, Locke Papers, box 164–89, folder 26; Circular letter about Harlem Art Museum, by Locke, Secretary of the Committee, Locke Papers, box 164–68, folder 21.

41. "African Art Works Given to Tuskegee," *Chicago Defender,* 23 Apr. 1927, A1.

42. James Weldon Johnson, "Race Prejudice and the Negro Artist," *Harper's Monthly Magazine* 157 (1928): 769–776.

43. "The Theatre Arts Exhibit of African Art," press release, 15 Jan. 1927, Locke Papers, box 164–179, folder 24.

44. Editorial, "More about African Art," *Opportunity* 5, no. 5 (May 1927): 126.

45. See hundreds of clippings, scrapbook #19, 1935 Museum Exhibition #39, African Negro Art, PI MF 5, Archives, Museum of Modern Art, New York.

46. Lisa Meyerowitz, "The Negro in Art Week: Defining the 'New Negro' through Art Exhibition," *African American Review* 31, no. 1 (Spring 1997): 77.

47. Ibid., 78–79.

48. Thomas E. Jones to Alain Locke, 11 June 1928, Locke Papers, box 164–42, folder 1.

49. "Items in Brief," *New York Times,* 12 May 1935, X7; *Bulletin of the Museum of Modern Art* 2, no. 6–7 (Mar.–Apr. 1935), cited in Virginia-Lee Webb, *Perfect Documents: Walker Evans and African Art, 1935* (New York: Metropolitan Museum of Art, 2000), 22.

50. Walter White, "The Road to Africa," *The Nation,* 26 June 1929, 770–771.

51. For example, see "More Morand," *Time,* 3 June 1929, 44; "Tales of the Negro in Paul Morand's 'Black Magic,'" *New York Times,* 28 Apr. 1929, 63; Paul Souday, "Paul Morand Writes about the Negroes," *New York Times,* 29 July 1928, BR5.

52. White, "The Road to Africa"; Aubrey Bowser, "Harlem Isn't Africa," review of Paul Morand's *Black Magic, New York Amsterdam News,* 12 June 1929, 20; "Just Like the Rest of Them," *New York Amsterdam News,* 3 Dec. 1930, 20; W. E. B. Du Bois, "The Negro in Literature," *Crisis* 36, no. 11 (Nov. 1929): 376. The French

reception was similarly divided into two camps, see Brett A. Berliner, *Ambivalent Desire: The Exotic Black Other in Jazz-Age France* (Amherst: University of Massachusetts Press, 2002), 230–232; see also Brent Hayes Edwards, *The Practice of Diaspora: Literature, Translation, and the Rise of Black Internationalism* (Cambridge, MA: Harvard University Press, 2003), 163–171.

53. Walter White, draft of review of Paul Morand, *Black Magic,* and André Gide, *Travels in the Congo,* NAACP Papers, part 11, series B, reel 35, frames 567–570.

54. David Levering Lewis, *W. E. B. Du Bois: The Fight for Equality and the American Century, 1919–1963* (New York: Holt, 2000), 43; Jessie Fauset, "Impressions of the Second Pan-African Congress," *Crisis* 23, no. 1 (Nov. 1921): 12–18.

55. Bowser, "Harlem Isn't Africa."

56. Editorial, "More about African Art," *Opportunity* 5, no. 5 (May 1927): 126.

57. Locke, circular letter or text for a brochure, n.d. [probably 1928 or 1929], Locke Papers, box 164–179, folder 23.

58. Alain Locke, "African Art Necessary to Negro Culture: Congo Region Produces Fine Craftsmen," *Negro World,* 19 Feb. 1927, 7.

59. Amy Helene Kirschke, *Aaron Douglas: Art, Race, and the Harlem Renaissance* (Jackson: University Press of Mississippi, 1995), 29.

60. Aaron Douglas, notes from interview with David Levering Lewis, 24 July 1974, "Voices of the Harlem Renaissance," box 1, folder 1, MARB.

61. Benjamin Brawley, *The Negro Genius: A New Appraisal of the Achievement of the American Negro in Literature and the Fine Arts* (New York: Dodd, Mead, 1937), 324.

62. Romare Bearden and Harry Henderson, *A History of African-American Artists: From 1792 to the Present* (New York: Pantheon Books, 1993), 201.

63. Ibid., 204.

64. Ibid., 213.

65. Ibid., 390–391.

66. Cited in Catherine Bernard, "Preface," in *The Life and Art of Loïs Mailou Jones,* ed. Tritobia Hayes Benjamin (New York: Pomegranate Artbooks, 1994), x.

67. Albert A. Smith to Arthur A Schomburg, Apr. 1932, Arthur A. Schomburg Papers, reel 5, SC.

68. Aaron Douglas to Alta Sawyer (ca. 1924–1926), Aaron Douglas Papers, letter #29, box 2, folder 3, MARB.

69. Douglas to Sawyer (ca. 1924–1926), Aaron Douglas Papers, letter #13, box 1, folder 2.

70. Interview in the *San Francisco Chronicle,* 6 Oct. 1935, cited in Bearden and Henderson, *A History of African-American Artists,* 221.

71. Lowery Stokes Sims, "The Structure of Narrative: Form and Content in Jacob Lawrence's Builders Paintings, 1946–1998," in *Over the Line: The Art and Life of Jacob Lawrence,* ed. Peter T. Nesbett and Michelle DuBois (Seattle: University of

Washington Press in association with Jacob and Gwendolyn Lawrence Foundation, 2000), 201–203.

72. Ibid., 202.

73. Michel Feith, "The Syncopated African: Constructions of Origins in the Harlem Renaissance (Literature, Music, Visual Arts)," in *Temples for Tomorrow: Looking Back at the Harlem Renaissance,* ed. Geneviève Fabre and Michel Feith (Bloomington: Indiana University Press, 2001), 61–62.

74. Mary Ann Calo, "African American Art and Critical Discourse between World Wars," *American Quarterly* 51, no. 3 (Sept. 1999): 598.

75. John J. Smith, "Liberty," *Negro World,* 12 May 1923, 6.

76. Alain Locke, "African Art Necessary to Negro Culture: Congo Region Produces Fine Craftsmen," *Negro World,* 19 Feb. 1927, 7.

77. Alain Locke, *Negro Art: Past and Present* (Washington, DC: Associates in Negro Folk Education, 1936), 2–4.

78. Ibid., 70.

79. Alain Locke, "The Legacy of the Ancestral Arts," in *The New Negro,* 254; and Alain Locke, *The Negro and His Music* (Port Washington, NY: Kennikat Press, 1936), 139.

80. Wallace Thurman, "High, Low, Past, and Present: Review of *The Walls of Jericho, Quicksand,* and *Adventures of an African Slaver,*" *Harlem: A Forum of Negro Life,* Nov. 1928, rpt. in *The Collected Writings of Wallace Thurman: A Harlem Renaissance Reader,* ed. Amritjit Singh and Daniel M. Scott III (New Brunswick, NJ: Rutgers University Press, 2003), 221.

81. "Our Book Shelf," *Opportunity* 6, no. 10 (Oct. 1928): 308–309.

82. Jean Toomer, "Negro Psychology in *The Emperor Jones*" (1921), in *Jean Toomer: Selected Essays and Literary Criticism,* ed. Robert B. Jones (Knoxville: University of Tennessee Press, 1996), 6.

83. Jean Toomer, *Cane* (1923; New York: Norton, 1988), 23.

84. Paul Allen Anderson, *Deep River: Music and Memory in Harlem Renaissance Thought* (Durham, NC: Duke University Press, 2001), 69.

85. Toomer, *Cane,* 12.

86. Matthew Pratt Guterl, *The Color of Race in America, 1900–1940* (Cambridge, MA: Harvard University Press, 2001), 176–183; Cynthia Earl Kerman and Richard Eldridge, *The Lives of Jean Toomer: A Hunger for Wholeness* (Baton Rouge: Louisiana State University, 1987), 344; George B. Hutchinson, "Jean Toomer and the 'New Negroes' of Washington," *American Literature* 63, no. 4 (Dec. 1991): 683–692.

87. Toomer to Ernestine Rose, as transcribed by Rose in her own letter to Alain Locke, n.d., Locke Papers, box 164–90, folder 12.

88. George Hutchinson, *In Search of Nella Larsen: A Biography of the Color Line* (Cambridge, MA: Belknap Press/Harvard University Press, 2007).

89. Earl Lewis and Heidi Ardizzone, *Love on Trial: An American Scandal in Black and White* (New York: Norton, 2001).

90. Langston Hughes, "American Interest in African Culture," 4 pp., June 1962, in Glenn C. Carrington Papers, box 145-18, folder 16, MSC. For fuller accounts of Hughes's engagement with Africa, see Campbell, *Middle Passages,* 188–225; Arnold Rampersad, *The Life of Langston Hughes,* vol. 1: *1902–1941: I, Too, Sing America* (New York: Oxford University Press, 1986), 73–81; Kenneth W. Warren, "Appeals for (Mis)recognition: Theorizing the Diaspora," in *Cultures of United States Imperialism,* ed. Amy Kaplan and Donald E. Pease (Durham, NC: Duke University Press, 1993), 392–406.

91. Langston Hughes, "The Negro Speaks of Rivers" (1921), in *The Collected Poems of Langston Hughes,* ed. Arnold Rampersad and David Roessel (New York: Vintage Books, 1994), 23.

92. Stephen Kern, *The Culture of Time and Space, 1880–1918* (Cambridge, MA: Harvard University Press, 1983), 64.

93. Langston Hughes to Carrie M. Clark, 3 July 1923, in Rampersad, *The Life of Langston Hughes,* 1:73–74.

94. Langston Hughes, *The Big Sea: An Autobiography* (1940; New York: Thunder's Mouth Press, 1986), 325.

95. Melville J. Herskovits, "The Negro's Americanism," in *The New Negro,* ed. Locke, 353–360; Melville J. Herskovits, "Acculturation and the American Negro," *Southwestern Political and Social Science Quarterly* 8, no. 3 (Dec. 1927): 211–225, rpt. as a pamphlet of the same name, 14 pp., quotation from pp. 5–6, Melville and Frances Herskovits Papers, box 41, MARB; Melville J. Herskovits, *The American Negro: A Study in Racial Crossing* (New York: Alfred A. Knopf, 1928).

96. Melville J. Herskovits, *The Myth of the Negro Past* (New York: Harper and Brothers, 1941); see also Meville J. and Frances S. Herskovits, "What Has Africa Given America?," *New Republic,* 4 Sept. 1935; Jerry Gershenhorn, *Melville J. Herskovits and the Racial Politics of Knowledge* (Lincoln: University of Nebraska Press, 2004), 107.

5. Haiti, a Stepping-Stone to Africa

1. Herbert Aptheker, *American Negro Slave Revolts* (1943; New York: International Publishers, 1974), 15, 43–44, 96–101, 249; Elizabeth Rauh Bethel, "Images of Hayti: The Construction of an Afro-American *Lieu De Mémoire,*" *Callaloo* 15, no. 3 (Summer 1992): 827–841; Alfred N. Hunt, *Haiti's Influence on Antebellum America: Slumbering Volcano in the Caribbean* (Baton Rouge: Louisiana State University Press, 1988); Eric Sundquist, *To Wake the Nations: Race in the Making of American Literature* (Cambridge, MA: Belknap Press, 1993), 31–36.

2. Chris Dixon, *African America and Haiti: Emigration and Black Nationalism in the Nineteenth Century* (Westport, CT: Greenwood Press, 2000), 177–216; Laurie Maffly-Kipp, "The Serpentine Trail: Haitian Missions and the Construction of African-American Religious Identity," in *The Foreign Missionary Enterprise at*

Home: Explorations in North American Cultural History, ed. Daniel H. Bays and Grant Wacker (Tuscaloosa: University of Alabama Press, 2003), 29–43.

3. Hans Schmidt, *The United States Occupation of Haiti, 1915–1934* (1971; New Brunswick, NJ: Rutgers University Press, 1995), 42–63.

4. Rayford Whittingham Logan, *Haiti and the Dominican Republic* (New York: Oxford University Press, 1968); Brenda Gayle Plummer, *Haiti and the Great Powers, 1902–1915* (Baton Rouge: Louisiana State University Press, 1988).

5. Mary A. Renda, *Taking Haiti: Military Occupation and the Culture of U.S. Imperialism, 1915–1940* (Chapel Hill: University of North Carolina Press, 2001).

6. Ibid., 220–221; Kristin Hoganson, *Consumers' Imperium: The Global Production of American Domesticity, 1865–1920* (Chapel Hill: University of North Carolina Press, 2007).

7. Pauline E. Hopkins, "Toussaint L'Overture," *Colored American Magazine* 2 (Nov. 1900): 9–24.

8. Alain Locke, "The Magic Island," *Opportunity* 7, no. 6 (June 1929): 190.

9. Lansing cited in Logan, *Haiti and the Dominican Republic,* 126.

10. Paul Morand, *New York,* trans. Hamish Miles (New York: Holt, 1930), 269–270.

11. John Houston Craige, *Black Bagdad: The Arabian Nights Adventures of a Marine Captain in Haiti* (New York: Minton, Balch, 1933), and *Cannibal Cousins* (New York: Minton, Balch, 1934); Blair Niles, *Black Haiti: A Biography of Africa's Eldest Daughter* (New York: Grosset & Dunlap, 1926); William Seabrook, *The Magic Island* (New York: Harcourt, Brace, 1929); Edna Taft, *A Puritan in Voodoo-Land* (Philadelphia: Penn, 1938); John W. Vandercook, *Black Majesty* (New York: Harper Brothers, 1928); Faustin Wirkus, *The White King of La Gonave* (Garden City, NY: Doubleday, Doran, 1931), and "When I Was King" (1932), NAACP Papers, part 11, series B, reel 36, frames 392–399, microfilm reels, British Library. On white Americans' accounts of Haiti, see Laënnec Hurbon, "American Fantasy and Haitian Vodou," in *Sacred Arts of Haitian Vodou,* ed. Donald J. Cosentino (Los Angeles: UCLA Fowler Museum, 1995), 181–197; and Renda, *Taking Haiti,* 229–260.

12. References to Harlem as "Little Africa" include "Along Rainbow Row: Heart of Little Africa a Lively Place on a Summer Night," *New York Times,* 15 Aug. 1921, E18; "Whole City Radiant on Glorious Easter," *New York Times,* 17 Apr. 1922, 3; "Negro Swarms See Remains of Body," *New York Times,* 2 Sept. 1922, 20; "In the Negro Cabarets: Nightly Attractions in Harlem's 'Little Africa,'" *New York Times,* 5 Sept. 1922, 36; "Scion of a Zulu Chief Admits Stealing Gin," *New York Times,* 4 May 1923, 20; "Colored Citizens Prosperous Here," *New York Times,* 11 Aug. 1929, N5; The following three clippings, "'Champion Daredevil' Parachutes to Tenement," "Strange Crimes of Little Africa," "When Rural Negro Reaches Crucible," are rpt. in *Harlem on My Mind: Cultural Capital of Black America, 1900–1968,* ed. Allon Schoener (1968; New York: New Press, 1995), 60–61, 67–68,

70–71. Reference to Harlem as a "negro colony" can be found in "Garvey Denounced at Negro Meeting," *New York Times*, 7 Aug. 1922, 7.

13. See Barbara Bair, "Remapping the Black/White Body: Sexuality, Nationalism, and Biracial Antimiscegenation Activism in 1920s Virginia," in *Sex, Love, Race: Crossing Boundaries in North America*, ed. Martha Hodes (New York: New York University Press, 1999), 401; Wilson Jeremiah Moses, *Black Messiahs and Uncle Toms: Social and Literary Manipulations of a Religious Myth*, rev. ed. (University Park: Pennsylvania State University Press, 1993), 165–170.

14. Ronald Radano, "Hot Fantasies: American Modernism and the Idea of Black Rhythm," in *Music and the Racial Imagination*, ed. Ronald Radano and Philip V. Bohlman (Chicago: University of Chicago Press, 2000), 459–480.

15. Sigmund Freud, "Totem and Taboo: Some Points of Agreement between the Mental Lives of Savages and Neurotics" (1913, first published in English in 1918), in *The Origins of Religion:* Totem and Taboo, Moses and Monotheism *and Other Works*, ed. Albert Dickson, trans. James Strachey (Harmondsworth, England: Penguin Books, 1985), 43–224. See Marianna Torgovnick, *Gone Primitive: Savage Intellects, Modern Lives* (Chicago: University of Chicago Press, 1990), 8; Nathan Irvin Huggins, *Harlem Renaissance* (New York: Oxford University Press, 1971), 89–93; Jeffrey C. Stewart, "Paul Robeson and the Problem of Modernism," in *Rhapsodies in Black: Art of the Harlem Renaissance*, ed. Richard J. Powell and David A. Bailey (Berkeley: University of California Press, 1997), 96–97; Robert Walser, "Deep Jazz: Notes on Interiority, Race, and Criticism," in *Inventing the Psychological: Toward a Cultural History of Emotional Life in America*, ed. Joel Pfister and Nancy Schnog (New Haven, CT: Yale University Press, 1997), 271–296.

16. Carl Jung, *Memories, Dreams, Reflections* (first published as *Erinnerungen, Träume, Gedanken*, in 1962), excerpted in *Encountering Jung: Jung on Evil*, ed. Murray Stein (Princeton, NJ: Princeton University Press, 1995), 103.

17. Eugene O'Neill, "The Emperor Jones," in *The Emperor Jones* (1922; London: Jonathan Cape, 1969), 145.

18. This myth appeared in May Miller's play *Christophe's Daughters* (1935), rpt. in *Black Female Playwrights: An Anthology of Plays before 1950*, ed. Kathy A. Perkins (Bloomington: Indiana University Press, 1989), 174; and Clarence Cameron White's music lesson plans, Lesson XVI (on Jamaica) in "Lessons & Examinations," Clarence Cameron White Papers, reel 4, SC. On O'Neill's mixing up of the revolutionary figures, see VèVè A. Clark, "Haiti's Tragic Overture: (Mis)Representations of the Haitian Revolution in World Drama (1796–1975)," in *Representing the French Revolution: Literature, Historiography, and Art*, ed. James A. W. Heffernan (Hanover, NH: University Press of New England, 1992), 248.

19. Alexander Woollcott, "Second Thoughts on First Nights: The New O'Neill Play," *New York Times*, 7 Nov. 1920, 88.

20. O'Neill, "The Emperor Jones," 151.

21. Ibid., 152.

22. Jean Toomer, "Negro Psychology in *The Emperor Jones*" (1921), in *Jean Toomer: Selected Essays and Literary Criticism,* ed. Robert B. Jones (Knoxville: University of Tennessee Press, 1996), 6.

23. Interview with William Lundell (Oct. 1933), cited by Martin Bauml Duberman, *Paul Robeson* (London: Pan Books, 1989), 622.

24. Robert Blauner, "Internal Colonialism and Ghetto Revolt," *Social Problems* 16, no. 4 (Spring 1969): 393–408. Also see Bob Blauner, *Racial Oppression in America* (New York: Harper and Row, 1972), esp. 1–123; Stokely Carmichael and Charles V. Hamilton, *Black Power: The Politics of Liberation in America* (New York: Random House, 1967), esp. 2–32; Eldridge Cleaver, "The Land Question and Black Liberation," in *Eldridge Cleaver: Post-Prison Writings and Speeches,* ed. Robert Scheer (New York: Random House, 1969), 57–72.

25. Hubert Harrison, "The Emperor Jones," *Negro World,* 4 June 1921, rpt. in *A Hubert Harrison Reader,* ed. Jeffrey B. Perry (Middletown, CT: Wesleyan University Press, 2001), 378–383, quotation on 381.

26. Cf. Renda, *Taking Haiti,* 207; Hazel V. Carby, *Race Men* (Cambridge, MA: Harvard University Press, 1998), 78.

27. J. Cogdell, "Truth in Art in America," *Messenger* 5, no. 3 (Mar. 1923): 635; Renda, *Taking Haiti,* 209–212.

28. Mrs. William A. Corbin, "Emperor Jones on the Pacific Coast," in *Negro World,* 3 Mar. 1923, 10.

29. Haines J. Washington, "Death of the Emperor Jones," *New York World,* 9 May 1930, 11.

30. "'Pudden Jones,' Farce Comedy, at Lafayette," *Negro World,* 23 May 1925, 6; "'Pudden Jones' Scores as Delightful Little Farce," *New York Amsterdam News,* 13 May 1925, 6.

31. Langston Hughes, *The Big Sea* (1940; New York: Thunder's Mouth Press, 1986), 258. A *Negro World* reviewer reported that at the Harlem premiere of the 1933 film version, those in the audience did not like the film at all; see Tony Martin, *Literary Garveyism: Garvey, Black Arts, and the Harlem Renaissance* (Dover, MA: Majority Press, 1983), 118.

32. James Weldon Johnson, "Self-Determining Haiti," I–IV, *Nation,* 28 Aug.– 25 Sep. 1920.

33. Johnson, *Along This Way: The Autobiography of James Weldon Johnson* (1933; New York: Penguin Books, 1990), 360; Henry Lewis Suggs, "The Response of the African American Press to the United States Occupation of Haiti, 1915–1934," *Journal of Negro History* 73, no. 1/4 (Winter–Autumn, 1988): 36–37; Brenda Gayle Plummer, "The Afro-American Response to the Occupation of Haiti, 1915–1934," *Phylon* 43, no. 2 (Summer 1982): 134–136.

34. "Howard Players Appear in Their Own Plays," *Chicago Defender,* 3 June 1922, 5.

35. Helen Webb Harris, "Genifrede" (1922), in *Negro History in Thirteen Plays*, ed. Willis Richardson (Washington, DC: Associated Publishers, 1935), 221, 223. (The play was published under Webb's married name.)

36. See, for instance, plays in the following collections: Kathy A. Perkins, ed., *Black Female Playwrights: An Anthology of Plays before 1950* (Bloomington: Indiana University Press, 1989); Jennifer Burton, ed., *Zora Neale Hurston, Eulalie Spence, Marita Bonner, and Others: The Prize Plays and Other One-Acts Published in Periodicals* (New York: G. K. Hall, 1996); and Kathy A. Perkins and Judith L. Stephens, eds., *Strange Fruit: Plays on Lynching by American Women* (Bloomington: Indiana University Press, 1998).

37. Moses, *Black Messiahs and Uncle Toms.*

38. See "Hon. Wm. Sherrill Names Greatest Men of the Negro Race," *Negro World,* 10 Mar. 1923, 2; Vere E. Johns, "Evidence from Jamaica Shows Marcus Garvey Racially Dead," *New York Age,* 10 Sept. 1932, 7; "Garvey Planning African Empire: Black Queen Aids Garvey Plan Empire," *Evening Graphic,* 25 Nov. 1927, GC, vol. 32.

39. Arnold Rampersad, *The Life of Langston Hughes,* vol. 1, *1902–1941: I, Too, Sing America* (New York: Oxford University Press, 1986), 165–166; Tammy L. Kernodle, "Arias, Communists, and Conspiracies: The History of Still's 'Troubled Island,'" *Musical Quarterly* 83, no. 4 (Winter 1999): 488; 1963 revised version in the MARB.

40. Langston Hughes, "Emperor of Haiti," in *Black Drama in America: An Anthology,* ed. Darwin T. Turner, 2nd ed. (Washington, DC: Howard University Press, 1994), 31.

41. Ibid., 34–35.

42. Ibid., 40.

43. Ibid., 56–57.

44. Gail Bederman, *Manliness and Civilization: A Cultural History of Gender and Race in the United States, 1880–1917* (Chicago: University of Chicago Press, 1995).

45. Clarence Cameron White, "A Musical Pilgrimage to Haiti, the Island of Beauty, Mystery and Rhythm," *Etude,* July 1929, 505, NAACP Papers, part 11, series B, reel 9, frames 816–817; John F. Matheus, "Precis methodique d'histoire d'Haiti; Black Democracy" (book reviews), *Journal of Negro History* 21, no. 4 (Oct. 1936): 433.

46. Clarence Cameron White and John F. Matheus, *Tambour,* Clarence Cameron White papers, reel 10, SC. *Tambour* was produced in 1929 by the Allied Arts Players, Boston, dir. Maud Cuney-Hare; see Bernard L. Peterson Jr., *Early Black Playwrights and Dramatic Writers: A Biographical Directory and Catalog of Plays, Films, and Broadcasting Scripts* (Westport, CT: Greenwood Press, 1990), 132.

47. White and Matheus, *Tambour.*

48. Diary of Melville J. Herskovits, 5 Mar. 1931, Melville and Frances Herskovits Papers, box 9, folder 41, MARB.

49. Clarence Cameron White, "Lesson III: The Tom-Tom Language of the Africans." White's information came from an an article by Mme. Grall, "The Tom-Tom Language of the Africans," *La Revue du Monde Noir,* Apr. 1932, which was later reprinted in Maud Cuney-Hare, *Negro Musicians and Their Music* (Washington, DC: Associated Press, 1936), 398.

50. White, "Lesson III."

51. White, "Lesson XI."

52. Clarence Cameron White and John Frederick Matheus, *Ouanga* (1932), no publication details, p. 4, Clarence Cameron White Papers, reel 4, SC.

53. Ibid., 3. *Ouanga* was performed in concert form in 1932 and as a full opera for the first time in 1949. See Peterson, *Early Black American Playwrights and Dramatic Writers,* 263.

54. Michael Largey, *Vodou Nation: Haitian Art Music and Cultural Nationalism* (Chicago: University of Chicago Press, 2006), 164.

55. Leslie Pinckney Hill, *Toussaint L'Ouverture: A Dramatic History* (Boston: Christopher Publishing House, 1928), 8.

56. See Sidney Mintz and Michel-Rolph Trouillot, "The Social History of Haitian Vodou," in *Sacred Arts of Haitian Vodou,* ed. Donald J. Cosentino (Los Angeles: UCLA Fowler Museum, 1995), 123–147. Cf. Robert Farris Thompson, "From the Isle Beneath the Sea: Haiti's Africanizing Vodou Art," in the same volume, 91–119. On the relationship between culture and politics generally, see Lawrence W. Levine, *Black Culture and Black Consciousness: Afro-American Folk Thought from Slavery to Freedom* (Oxford: Oxford University Press, 1977). Zora Neale Hurston mimicked the adaptability of voodoo culture in her inscrutable ethnographic account, *Tell My Horse* (1938); see Daphne Lamothe, *Inventing the New Negro: Narrative, Culture, and Ethnography* (Philadelphia: University of Pennsylvania Press, 2008), 141–159.

57. Lawrence W. Levine, *Highbrow/Lowbrow: The Emergence of Cultural Hierarchy in America* (Cambridge, MA: Harvard University Press, 1988).

58. Hill, *Toussaint L'Ouverture,* 7.

59. James Weldon Johnson, no title, no date, NAACP Papers, part 11, series B, reel 8, frames 452–456; see also Johnson, *Along This Way,* 360.

60. Hill, *Toussaint L'Ouverture,* 7. Hill also wrote a pageant, *Jethro* (1931), which argued that the concept of representative government was developed by an Ethiopian, see Peterson, *Early Black American Playwrights and Dramatic Writers,* 104.

61. Hill, *Toussaint L'Ouverture,* 7.

62. Langston Hughes, "The Em-Fuehrer Jones" (1938), in *Lost Plays of the Harlem Renaissance, 1920–1940,* ed. James V. Hatch and Leo Hamalian (Detroit, MI: Wayne State University Press, 1996), 358–361.

63. Largey, *Vodou Nation,* 12; Schmidt, *The United States Occupation of Haiti,* 150–151.

64. Dantès Bellegarde to Arthur A. Schomburg, 11 Mar. 1932, Schomburg Papers, reel 1, SC. A copy of the speech is on reel 5. A press release containing a description of some of the exhibited items is at NAACP Papers, part 11, series B, reel 10, frame 23. In 1934, President Stenio Vincent visited the library; see Arthur A Schomburg to Stenio Vincent, 3 May 1934, Schomburg Papers, reel 8. By 1938, the library held 700 titles on Haiti; see letter from Schomburg to Rene J. Rosemond, 19 May 1938, Schomburg Papers, reel 8.

65. "No. 17. Fighting for Negro Freedom in Foreign Lands," NAACP Papers, part 11, series A, reel 30, frames 532–538; a series of letters from James Weldon Johnson to Moorfield Storey between Sep. 1920 and May 1921, NAACP Papers, part 1, reel 17, frames 312, 313, 329, 330, 337, 352; Leon D. Pamphile, *Haitians and African Americans: A Heritage of Tragedy and Hope* (Gainesville: University Press of Florida, 2001), 117–118; Plummer, "The Afro-American Response," 133; Renda, *Taking Haiti,* 191. Other organizations included the American-Haitian Benevolent Club and the Save Haiti Committee; see, respectively, Plummer, "The Afro-American Response," 135, and "Save Haiti," NAACP Papers, part 11, series B, reel 9, frame 746.

66. Clarence Cameron White Collection, Photographs and Prints, box 2, SC.

67. See Clarence Cameron White, "Introduction," in Cuney-Hare, *Negro Musicians and Their Music,* xii.

68. White, Lesson XIII.

69. Cuney-Hare, *Negro Musicians and Their Music,* 1.

70. Clarence Cameron White, Lesson XV.

71. J.A. Rogers, "Jazz at Home," in *The New Negro,* ed. Alain Locke (1925; New York: Atheneum, 1992), 220.

72. Alain Locke, *The Negro and His Music* (Port Washington, NY: Kennikat Press, 1936), 72.

73. Clarence Cameron White, Lesson XV.

74. William Grant Still, "An Afro-American Composer's Viewpoint" (1933), rpt. in *William Grant Still and the Fusion of Cultures in American Music,* ed. Robert Haas (Los Angeles: Black Sparrow Press, 1975), 112.

75. Locke, *The Negro and His Music,* 139.

76. Ibid., 130–131.

77. Ibid., 138.

78. Sidney J. Lemelle and Robin D. G. Kelley, "Introduction: Imagining Home: Pan-Africanism Revisited," in *Imagining Home: Class, Culture and Nationalism in the African Diaspora,* ed. Lemelle and Kelley (London: Verso, 1994), 9.

79. Walter Benn Michaels, *Our America: Nativism, Modernism, and Pluralism* (Durham, NC: Duke University Press, 1995), 127.

80. Carla Kaplan, "On Modernism and Race," *Modernism/Modernity* 4, no. 1 (Jan. 1997): 157–169.

81. See Errol G. Hill and James V. Hatch, *A History of African American Theatre* (Cambridge: Cambridge University Press, 2003), 244–249.

82. Clarence Cameron White, unpublished autobiography, typescript, p. 39, Clarence Cameron White Papers, box 209-8, folder 2, MSC.

83. Kernodle, "Arias, Communists, and Conspiracies," 487.

84. Matheus to White, 15 Nov. 1931, reel 1; letters between White and Ona B. Talbot, 4 Nov. 1932, reel 1, and 5 Feb. 1934, reel 2; letter from Talbot to Paul Robeson (4 Nov. 1932), reel 1; all in the White Papers, SC. On the Paris production, see Mary Church Terrell, "Local Composer Wins Medal for Best American Opera," *Washington Evening Star*, 28 May 1933, 6.

85. Sheila Tully Boyle and Andrew Bunie, *Paul Robeson: The Years of Promise and Achievement* (Amherst: University of Massachusetts Press, 2001), 327, 339.

86. For example, *White Zombie*, dir. Victor Halperin, 1932; see Renda, *Taking Haiti*, 226–227. *Ouanga* (1935), set on "Paradise Island" in the West Indies, was filmed initially on Haiti but moved to Jamaica; see Bryan Senn, *Drums of Terror: Voodoo in the Cinema* (Baltimore: Midnight Marquee Press, 1998), 38–40.

87. "Coast Codgings," *Chicago Defender*, 12 May 1934, 9.

88. "Film 'Voodoo' Now Running on Broadway," *Chicago Defender*, 8 Apr. 1933, 5.

89. "Toussaint L'Ouverture," *Crisis* 20, no. 6 (Oct. 1920): 297.

90. "Life of Toussaint to Be Told in $1,000,000 Film," *Chicago Defender*, 28 Apr. 1928, 2.

91. Of particular note is the film *Sanders of the River*, dir. Zoltan Korda, 1935; see "Robeson Film Called Propaganda Justifying British Imperialism," *Afro-American*, week of 6 July 1935, GC, vol. 112; Duberman, *Paul Robeson*, 179–180. Some have been skeptical of Robeson's claim that he was duped into thinking the film more progressive than it turned out to be; see Boyle and Bunie, *Paul Robeson*, 323–327; Stewart, "Paul Robeson and the Problem of Modernism," 97–99. In any case, as Robeson told an interviewer in 1935, if a black actor wanted to work, he had to take roles "with which he is not ideologically in agreement." Cited in Carby, *Race Men*, 79.

92. "Robeson to Play King Christophe in British Production, He Reveals," *New York Amsterdam News*, 5 Oct. 1935, 1; "Paul Robeson in Moscow," *Chicago Defender*, 22 Aug. 1936, 24.

93. *Song of Freedom*, dir. J. Elder Wills, 1936.

94. On Robeson's feelings, see Duberman, *Paul Robeson*, 204.

95. "Crowds Jam Streets as 'Macbeth' Opens," *New York Times*, 15 Apr. 1936, 25.

96. "Lafayette Incident Rebuke to Cultural Pride of Community," Press Releases of Department of Information, Record Group 69, National Archives, quoted in Rena Fraden, *Blueprints for a Black Federal Theatre, 1935–1939* (Cambridge: Cambridge University Press, 1994), 156.

97. Renda, *Taking Haiti*, 286–287.

98. John O'Connor and Lorraine Brown, eds., *"Free, Adult, Uncensored":* *The Living History of the Federal Theatre Project* (London: Eyre Methuen, 1980), 120.

99. For a fuller account of the plot and staging, see Maureen Needham, "*Kykunkor, or the Witch Woman:* An African Opera in America, 1934," in *Dancing Many Drums: Excavations in African American Dance,* ed. Thomas DeFrantz (Madison: University of Wisconsin Pres, 2002), 233–266.

100. For short and long programs, see Asadata Dafora (Horton) Papers, box 1, folders 6 and 7, MARB.

101. John Mason Brown, "Two on the Aisle: Africa Comes to Manhattan—The Unusual Dancers and Drummers Now Performing at the Unity Theatre," *New York Post,* 19 May 1934, Dafora Papers, box 1, folder 8.

102. "African Opera 50 Stories off the Ground," *Daily News,* 24 May 1934, Dafora Papers, box 1, folder 8; Brown, "Two on the Aisle."

103. "African Opera 50 Stories off the Ground".

104. Advertisement for "A Night in Africa," a revue Dafora staged in 1933, featuring a sketch from *Kykunkor,* Dafora Papers, box 1, folder 6; programs, Dafora Papers, box 1, folders 6 and 7.

105. Program for *Kykunkor,* Dafora Papers, box 1, folder 7.

106. Ibid.

107. Kirstein, cited in John O. Perpener III, *African-American Concert Dance: The Harlem Renaissance and Beyond* (Urbana: University of Illinois Press, 2001), 113.

108. On the improvisational aspects of West African dance, see Perpener, *African-American Concert Dance,* 112. Jacqui Malone argues the most prized ability in African American dance is to look "cool" by making what is controlled appear effortless; see Malone, *Steppin' on the Blues: The Visible Rhythms of African American Dance* (Urbana: University of Illinois Press, 1996), 33–34.

109. "Native African Sketch Given at Saratoga Club," *New York Age,* 31 Mar. 1934. See also Stabooni, "Mother Africa," *New York Age,* 28 June 1933.

110. John Martin, "The Dance: African Lore," *New York Times,* 13 May 1934, X6.

111. J. F. McDougald, "The Federal Government and the Negro Theatre," *Opportunity* 14, no. 5 (May 1936): 135. Emphasis mine.

112. "Nancy Hunt Rose from School Glee Club to Broadway Fame," NAACP Papers, part 10, reel 8, frames 173–175.

113. For a discussion of anthropology and black American dance, see Julia L. Foulkes, *Modern Bodies: Dance and American Modernism from Martha Graham to Alvin Ailey* (Chapel Hill: University of North Carolina Press, 2002), 51–78.

114. "Radio Dial Flashes," *Washington Post,* 26 June 1932, A2.

115. "Cleveland Sees Bledsoe Star in 'Aida,'" *Chicago Defender,* 16 July 1932, 3.

116. *Crisis* 39, no. 8 (Aug. 1932): 258, cited in Gerald Horne, *Race Woman: The Lives of Shirley Graham Du Bois* (New York: New York University Press, 2000), 60.

117. "Premiere of Tom-Tom, First All-Negro Opera, Interests White Singers," Press Release, Stadium Opera, Laurence Productions, NAACP Papers, part 11, series A, reel 31, frames 740–742. See also "From Africa to Harlem," *New York Times*, 26 June 1932, XX5.

118. Shirley Graham, "Tom-Tom," in *The Roots of African American Drama: An Anthology of Early Plays, 1858–1938,* ed. Leo Hamalian and James V. Hatch (Detroit, MI: Wayne State University Press, 1991), 238–286.

119. Hughes, *The Big Sea*, 334–335.

6. Ethiopia Ahoy!

1. James H. Meriwether, *Proudly We Can Be Africans: Black Americans and Africa, 1935–1961* (Chapel Hill: University of North Carolina Press, 2002); Brenda Gayle Plummer, *Rising Wind: Black Americans and U.S. Foreign Affairs, 1935–1960* (Chapel Hill: University of North Carolina Press, 1996); Penny M. Von Eschen, *Race against Empire: Black Americans and Anticolonialism, 1937–1957* (Ithaca, NY: Cornell University Press, 1997).

2. George Schuyler, "Views and Reviews," *Pittsburg Courier*, 7 Mar. 1936, cited in Robert A. Hill, "Introduction," in George S. Schuyler, *Ethiopian Stories* (Boston: Northeastern University Press, 1994), 23.

3. William R. Scott, *The Sons of Sheba's Race: African-Americans and the Italo-Ethiopian War, 1935–1941* (Bloomington: Indiana University Press, 1993), 136; Ira De A. Reid, *The Negro Immigrant: His Background, Characteristics and Social Adjustment, 1899–1937* (New York: Columbia University Press, 1939), 159.

4. "Shoulder to Shoulder," *New York Amsterdam News*, 10 Aug. 1935, 10.

5. Edward Dillon, "Harlem Drive upon Italians Stirs Disorder," 4 Oct. 1935, newspaper clipping, GC, vol. 40.

6. "Selassie Hanged in Effigy Here," *New York Times*, 6 May 1936, 18; "Mob of 400 Battles the Police in Harlem; Italian Stores Raided, Man Shot in Crowd," *New York Times*, 19 May 1936, 6.

7. "Deny Permit for Parade of Ethiopian Sympathizers," *Chicago Daily Tribune*, 25 Aug. 1935, 2; "300 Arrested in Chicago in Protest against War," *New York Times*, 1 Sept. 1935, 1; "Police Halt Big Protest Meeting Here," *Chicago Defender*, 7 Sept. 1935, 2.

8. Langston Hughes, "Air Raid over Harlem," in *The Collected Poems of Langston Hughes,* ed. Arnold Rampersad and David Roessel (New York: Vintage Books, 1994), 185–188.

9. Scott, *The Sons of Sheba's Race,* 106, 137.

10. "Ethiopia Shall Stretch Forth—," editorial cartoon, *Chicago Defender*, 25 May 1935, 16.

11. Wilson Jeremiah Moses, *Black Messiahs and Uncle Toms: Social and Literary Manipulations of a Religious Myth,* rev. ed. (University Park: Pennsylvania State University Press, 1993), 156–160.

12. Richard Wright, "High Tide in Harlem: Joe Louis as a Symbol of Freedom," *New Masses*, 5 July 1938, rpt. in *Speech and Power: The African-American Essay and Its Cultural Content from Polemics to Pulpit*, ed. Gerald Early, vol. 1 (Hopewell, NJ: Ecco Press, 1992), 153–157.

13. "Harlem Hilarious over Louis: 200,000 Negroes Celebrate Victory of Bomber in Wild Night of Joy," newspaper clipping, GC, vol. 41.

14. "The Ethiopian Prince," *New York Amsterdam News*, 26 Oct. 1936, 13.

15. "Ethiop Grappler Defeats Italian," *New York Amsterdam News*, 16 Nov. 1935, 16.

16. Scott, *The Sons of Sheba's Race*, 69–80.

17. "Inspiration!" *New York Amsterdam News*, 23 May 1936, 12.

18. "Harlem Fliers Training for Service in Ethiopia," *New York Times*, 25 July 1935, 20.

19. Scott, *The Sons of Sheba's Race*, 81–95.

20. "Nancy Hunt Rose from School Glee Club to Broadway Fame," NAACP Papers, part 10, reel 8, frames 173–175, microfilm reels, British Library.

21. "The 'Selassie' Dancers Play Boston House," *Chicago Defender*, 23 May 1936, 11; "New 'Scandals' Comely, Comic, and Bountiful," *Chicago Daily Tribune*, 29 June 1936, 13; "Trio Tip Top in Taps," *Chicago Defender*, 23 Jan. 1937, 10.

22. "Calls 1936 'Scandals' Burlesque on Race," *Chicago Defender*, 11 Jan. 1936, 9.

23. "'Scandals' Author," *Chicago Daily Tribune*, 6 Sept. 1936, D4.

24. Lilian Saunders to Walter White, 18 Apr. 1936, and "Warning Drums: One Way to Peace," NAACP Papers, part 11, series A, reel 35, frames 578–595.

25. "WPA Drama Stirs Strife," *New York Times*, 22 Mar. 1936, E10; Arthur Arent, "'Ethiopia': The First 'Living Newspaper,'" intro. by Dan Isaac, *Educational Theatre Journal* 20, no. 1 (Mar. 1968): 15–31.

26. "A Statement by Elmer Rice: Given to the Press at the January 24 Showing of *Ethiopia*," in *New Theatre and Film, 1934 to 1937: An Anthology*, ed. Herbert Kline (San Diego: Harcourt Brace Jovanovich, 1985), 102–103.

27. "From the Press of the Nation," *Crisis* 42, no. 8 (Aug. 1935): 243.

28. "Graziani the International Butcher," *Chicago Defender*, 13 Mar. 1937, 18.

29. For example, see George Padmore, "The Missionary Racket in Africa," *Crisis* 42, no. 7 (July 1935): 198, 214; "Civilization Is Taken to Ethiopia," *Crisis* 42, no. 11 (Nov. 1935): 337.

30. "Christianizing Ethiopia!," editorial cartoon, *Chicago Defender*, 30 May 1936, 16.

31. "Italy's Name for It," editorial cartoon, *New York Amsterdam News*, 2 Nov. 1935, 8.

32. "Civilization (?) Wins," editorial cartoon, *New York Amsterdam News*, 9 May 1936, 12.

33. "While Mother Sleeps," editorial cartoon, *New York Amsterdam News,* 20 July 1935, 12; "The Helpless Mother," editorial cartoon, *New York Amsterdam News,* 25 Apr. 1936, 12.

34. "The Deserter," *New York Amsterdam News,* 27 June 1936, 12; "Using His Head," *New York Amsterdam News,* 16 Nov. 1935, 8.

35. "Awaiting the Verdict of the Civilized Nations," *Crisis* 42, no. 10 (Oct. 1935): 306.

36. "Fiddlin' While Ethiopia Burns," editorial cartoon, *Chicago Defender,* 2 Nov. 1935, 16.

37. William Little to Gentlemen at NAACP, 26 July 1935, NAACP Papers, part 11, series A, reel 30, frame 772.

38. Horace White, Mt. Zion Temple, Cleveland, Ohio, to Walter White, 8 Aug. 1935, NAACP Papers, part 11, series A, reel 30, frame 793.

39. "Negroes Willing to Fight: Proffer Their Services to Emperor of Ethiopia," newspaper clipping, NAACP Papers, part 11, series A, reel 30, frame 807.

40. From a digest of letters received by the Ethiopian Research Council, Washington, DC, NAACP Papers, part 11, series A, reel 30, frames 796–798.

41. "Negroes Willing to Fight"; "Texas Group May Enlist," *New York Times,* 14 July 1935, 3.

42. Digest of letters received by the Ethiopian Research Council, Washington, DC.

43. "500 Harlemites Volunteer for Abyssinian Campaign as Community Is Stirred," clipping, UNIA Papers, New York Division, box 15, SC; Robin D. G. Kelley, *Race Rebels: Culture, Politics, and the Black Working Class* (New York: Free Press, 1994), 129–130.

44. "50,000 Volunteers for Abyssinia Warn World 'Africa for the Africans,'" *New York News,* clipping, UNIA Papers, New York Division, box 15. For a fuller account of the activities and attitudes of people in Harlem, see Scott, *Sons of Sheba's Race,* 101–120.

45. "Funds Sought Here to Aid Ethiopians," *New York Times,* 6 Oct. 1935, 29; George S. Schuyler, "Views and Reviews," *Courier,* 23 Nov. 1935, cited in Robert A. Hill, "Introduction," 19; "Harlem Mobilization Planned," *Los Angeles Times,* 21 July 1935, A5.

46. UNIA, Records of the Central Division (New York), e54, e55, SC.

47. "Supplies for Ethiopians," *New York Times,* 17 Nov. 1938, 17.

48. UNIA, Records of the Central Division (New York), e56.

49. Universal Ethiopian Students' Association (UESA), *The Truth about Ethiopia: A Nation Blocked from the Sea* (New York: UESA, 1936).

50. *Chicago Defender,* 24 July 1937, 2.

51. Dantès Bellegarde to Arthur Schomburg, 2 Oct. 1935, Arthur A. Schomburg Papers, reel 2, SC.

52. Dantès Bellegarde, "Haiti's Voice at the Peace Table," trans. Sydney A. Clark, *Opportunity* 21, no. 4 (Oct. 1943): 154–155, 197.

53. "Canadians Would Aid Ethiopia," *New York Times,* 25 July 1935, 10.

54. Rupert Lewis, *Marcus Garvey: Anti-Colonial Champion* (Trenton, NJ: Africa World Press, 1988), 168–175.

55. Gladys L. Wilson, "Significance of Black Man in War Told," *Chicago Defender,* 10 Aug. 1935, 12.

56. Danny Duncan Collum, ed., and Victor A. Berch, chief researcher, *African Americans in the Spanish Civil War: This Ain't Ethiopia, but It'll Do* (New York: G.K. Hall, 1992).

57. Langston Hughes, *I Wonder as I Wander: An Autobiographical Journey* (1956; New York: Hill and Wang, 1993), 321–400; The Negro Committee to Aid Spain, *A Negro Nurse in Republican Spain* (1938), rpt. in Collum, ed., *African Americans in the Spanish Civil War,* 123–134.

58. Jay N. Hill, "An Ethiope in Spain," *Crisis* 44, no. 7 (July 1937): 202.

59. Barbara J. Keys, *Globalizing Sport: National Rivalry and International Community in the 1930s* (Cambridge, MA: Harvard University Press, 2006).

60. "From the Press of the Nation," *Crisis* 42, no. 10 (Oct. 1935): 307.

61. "Peace and Democracy in the New World," *Chicago Defender,* 16 Sept. 1939, 14.

62. W. E. B. Du Bois, *Black Folk Then & Now: An Essay into the History and Sociology of the Black Race* (1939; New York: Octagon Books, 1970), 338.

63. "From the Press of the Nation," *Crisis* 43, no. 3 (Mar. 1936): 83.

64. "'The Black Man's Burden,'" editorial cartoon, *New York Amsterdam News,* 16 Sept. 1939, 6.

65. "Our Stake in the European War," *Chicago Defender,* 23 Sept. 1939, 14.

66. James Clifford, "Diasporas," *Cultural Anthropology* 9, no. 3 (1994): 302–338; Robin D.G. Kelley and Tiffany Ruby Patterson, "Unfinished Migrations: Reflections on the African Diaspora and the Making of the Modern World," *African Studies Review* 43, no. 1 (Apr. 2000): 11–45; Earl Lewis, "To Turn as on a Pivot: Writing African Americans into a History of Overlapping Diasporas," *American Historical Review* 100, no. 3 (June 1995): 765–787.

67. Lee Finkle, "The Conservative Aims of Militant Rhetoric: Black Protest during World War II," *Journal of American History* 60, no. 3 (Dec. 1973): 707–710.

Epilogue: What's in a Name?

1. David Levering Lewis, *When Harlem Was in Vogue* (1979; New York: Penguin Books, 1997).

2. "Capital 'N' Negro Widens," *New York Times,* 9 Mar. 1930, 21; Donald L. Grant and Mildred Bricker Grant, "Some Notes on the Capital 'N,'" *Phylon* 36, no. 4 (4th quart., 1975): 435–443.

3. "'Negro' with a Capital 'N,'" *New York Times,* 7 Mar. 1930, 20.

4. "The Negro," *Leader* [Lexington, KY], 30 Mar. 1930, in NAACP Papers, part 11, series B, reel 4, frame 29, microfilm reels, British Library.

5. "Negro with a Capital N," *Messenger* [Eatonton, GA], 20 Mar. 1930, in NAACP Papers, part 11, series A, reel 13, frame 582.

6. William Pickens, "Naming the Race," *New York Age,* 6 Dec. 1919.

7. Willis N. Huggins and John G. Jackson, *A Guide to Studies in African History: Directive Lists for Schools and Clubs* (New York: Federation of History Clubs, 1934), 32.

8. Ibid.

9. Huggins and Jackson, *A Guide to Studies in African History,* 32.

10. "Pages from Negro History," *New York Amsterdam News Magazine,* 1 June 1935, 6A.

11. "Editorial of the Month: Graduated—for What?" *Crisis* 42, no. 7 (July 1935): 211.

12. Claude McKay, "Once More the Germans Face Black Troops," *Opportunity* 17, no. 11 (Nov. 1939): 324–328.

13. George S. Schuyler, "The Negro-Art Hokum," rpt. in *The Portable Harlem Renaissance Reader,* ed. David Levering Lewis (New York: Viking, 1994), 97.

14. George S. Schuyler, "Open Letter No. 7," 13 Jan. 1930, NAACP Papers, part 1, reel 23, frame 135; George S. Schuyler, "Views and Reviews," *Courier,* 23 Nov. 1935, cited in Robert A. Hill, "Introduction," in George S. Schuyler, *Ethiopian Stories* (Boston: Northeastern University Press, 1994), 19.

15. "Harlemites Rally to Ethiopia's Aid," *New York Times,* 15 July 1935, 7.

16. The term continues to be much debated. See, for example, K. A. Dilday, "Go Back to Black," *New York Times,* 27 Feb. 2008, A25; "Letters: The Words We Use to Talk about Race," *New York Times,* 3 Mar. 2008, A20.

Index